Connecting Through Talk

Connecting Through Talk

Nurturing Children's Development With Language

by

David K. Dickinson, Ed.D.
Peabody College
Vanderbilt University
Nashville, Tennessee

and

Ann B. Morse, M.Ed.
Nashville, Tennessee

·P A U L·H·
BROOKES
PUBLISHING C⁰ ®

Baltimore • London • Sydney

Paul H. Brookes Publishing Co.
Post Office Box 10624
Baltimore, Maryland 21285-0624
USA

www.brookespublishing.com

Typeset by BMWW, Baltimore, Maryland.
Manufactured in the United States of America by
Sheridan Books, Inc., Chelsea, Michigan.

The individuals described in this book are composites or real people whose situations are masked as needed and are based on the authors' experiences. Real names and identifying details are used by permission.

Cover photo © iStockphoto.com. Cover photo of David K. Dickinson by E. Anne Rayner/Vanderbilt University. Cover photo of Ann B. Morse by Marie C. Dillion. The photographs in this book are used courtesy of Ann B. Morse and the following organizations:
Program profile opening photos for Play and Learning Strategies (PALS), Video Interaction Project (VIP), Home Instruction for Parents of Preschool Youngsters (HIPPY), Imagination Library, Family Reading Partnership, Photo courtesy of Ann B. Morse.
Program profile opening photo for 30 Million Words ©iStockphoto/(monybusinessimages).
Program profile opening photo for Save the Children courtesy of C.J. Clark. © 2015 Save the Children. All rights reserved.
Program profile opening photo for Reach Out and Read courtesy of Reach Out and Read National Center.
Program profile opening photo for Bookstart courtesy of Yørgen Koopmanschap. © BoekStart. All rights reserved.
Program profile opening photos for Israel's Book Distribution Programs courtesy of Maya Haykin © Sifriyat Pijama, and Alaa Zaatre © 2016 Maktabat al-Fanoos. All rights reserved.
Program profile opening photo for the Emerging Programs courtesy of Melissa Baralt.
Figure 2.1 adapted from "The human brain – Illustration" © iStockphoto/(blueringmedia).

The videotaped vignettes were provided by the individuals who are depicted and are used with their permission.

Library of Congress Cataloging-in-Publication Data

Names: Dickinson, David K., author. | Morse, Ann B., author.
Title: Connecting through talk: nurturing children's development with language / by David K. Dickinson, Ed.D., Peabody College of Education, Vanderbilt University Nashville, Tennessee and Ann B. Morse, M.Ed., Nashville, Tennessee.
Description: Baltimore: Paul H. Brookes Publishing Co., [2019] | Includes bibliographical references and index.
Identifiers: LCCN 2018032013 (print) | LCCN 2018045687 (ebook) | ISBN 9781681252391 (epub) | ISBN 9781681252407 (pdf) | ISBN 9781681252315 (pbk.)
Subjects: LCSH: Language arts (Early childhood) | Children—Language. | Early childhood development.
Classification: LCC LB1139.5.L35 (ebook) | LCC LB1139.5.L35 D53 2019 (print) | DDC 372.6—dc23
LC record available at https://lccn.loc.gov/2018032013

British Library Cataloguing in Publication data are available from the British Library.

2023   2022   2021   2020   2019

10   9   8   7   6   5   4   3   2   1

Contents

About the
Downloads and Videos

Purchasers of this book may download, print, and/or photocopy the rubrics summarizing information about specific literacy support programs for professional use. These materials are included with the print book and are also available at www.brookespublishing.com/downloads with (case sensitive) keycode 34ckDaD1k for both print and e-book buyers.

Purchasers of this book may access the videos of adult–child interactions for professional use. These materials are referred to within the print book and are also available at www.brookespublishing.com/downloads with (case sensitive) keycode 34ckDaD1k.

Videos include

- Video 1, Tanya and Eliza

- Video 2, Janna and Vera

- Video 3, Liza and Vivian

About the Authors

David K. Dickinson, Ed.D., Associate Dean for Research and Strategic Initiatives and Margaret Cowan Chair of Education, Peabody College of Education, Vanderbilt University, PMB 818, 230 Appleton Place, Nashville, Tennessee 37203

David K. Dickinson received his doctorate from Harvard University's Graduate School of Education after teaching elementary school in Philadelphia, Pennsylvania, while earning his master's degree at Temple University. For more than 30 years, he has studied early language and literacy development among children from low-income backgrounds. Using observational and intervention research, he has sought to understand factors that foster short- and long-term development of language and reading comprehension and to improve the quality of support children receive. He has coauthored the widely used preschool curriculum *Opening the World of Learning (OWL)* (Pearson), coauthored three volumes of *The Handbook of Early Literacy Research* (Guilford Press), authored or coauthored more than 100 peer-reviewed articles, and spoken to practitioner and research audiences around the world.

Ann B. Morse, M.Ed., Nashville, Tennessee 37215

Ann B. Morse earned her master's degree in education with a focus in early childhood from Lesley University. For more than 30 years, she has worked on behalf of young children from low-income backgrounds and their families. Through the Head Start National Training and Technical Assistance Network, she provided professional development to programs related to supporting children with disabilities and enhancing literacy skills. She coached pre-K teachers to enhance children's language and literacy skills through intervention research projects at Vanderbilt University. She was a contributing author of the language and literacy-based curriculum *Opening the World of Learning (OWL)* (Pearson).

Foreword

David Dickinson and Ann Morse have made important contributions in this volume. First, they have rewritten the study of child development through the lens of language. They review familiar developmental domains (discussing attachment, executive function, socioemotional development, risk factors that imperil healthy development), making the case that language development is not just another in that list of domains but, rather, central to all of them: the site where differences in parenting show up most powerfully, the mechanism by which parents promote attachment, executive function, socioemotional development, and cognition, as well as a tool children can wield in their own regulation of attention, management of emotion, involvement in social relations, and ongoing acquisition of knowledge.

This insight leads them to a reanalysis of programs meant to improve child outcomes by influencing parenting practices. Some such programs think of their mission as improving the child's language environment in order to promote better/richer/faster language development. Others place their explicit emphasis on the social/emotional aspects of parenting, on responsiveness to child initiations. Yet another group of interventions provides access to books as the primary mechanism for improving children's developmental outcome. Dickinson and Morse locate improvement of language interaction at the center of all these approaches, whether that is an explicit goal or an unintended consequence, and argue that effects on language interactions constitute the active ingredient in any successful preschool parenting intervention.

A valuable aspect of this volume is its efficient summarization of information about more than 15 different programs designed to support young children through improved parenting and access to enriching experiences. The book offers a template for the presentation of such information—a template that should be exploited to guide those interested in selecting, initiating, or expanding efforts to support families. The programs included range widely in design and emphasis, defining a landscape onto which other programs not included here could usefully be mapped. For example, the approach of providing families with children's books is being replicated in a community wide public-private partnership initiated by the iREAD Foundation in Shenzhen, China (Chen & Snow, 2017). The iREAD approach also incorporates some of the community-based parenting support characteristic of Save the Children and Bookstart as well as use of text messaging to parents like that implemented by Háblame Bebé. Similarly, home visiting programs such as the Parent-Child Home Program (https://www.parent-child.org/home/proven-outcomes/key-research/) and explicit parent instructional programs such as the parent-instruction intervention evaluated by Leech, Wei, Harring, and Rowe (2018) share many but not all of the features implemented in the programs described here, and they offer important potential contrasts that would be informative to existing and new efforts. Ultimately we might envision a comparative analysis of many such programs with overlapping as well as contrasting components, as way of exploring how much the various components contribute to the overall impact.

The big message is that any effort that supports the quality and quantity of parent–child communication will have long-lasting positive impacts on children's development. Dickinson and Morse have documented the effectiveness of many approaches to ensuring the desired improvement, and in the process they provide reassurance that we know what to do to improve child outcomes and that enhancing language interactions will be implicated in any such efforts. The challenge is to coordinate resources and talent to ensure we can make steady progress by using the full array of effective practices where they are needed most.

Catherine E. Snow, Ph.D.
Patricia Albjerg Graham Professor of Education
Graduate School of Education
Harvard University

REFERENCES

Chen, S. & Snow, C.E. (2017, May). *Experimental Impacts of a large scale shared book reading intervention in China on children's vocabulary development and parental literacy beliefs.* Annual meeting of the American Educational Research Association, San Antonio, TX.

Leech, K., Wei, R., Harring, J. R., Rowe, M. L. (2018). A brief parent-focused intervention to improve preschoolers' conversational skills and school readiness. *Developmental Psychology, 54*, 15–28.

Preface

What do parents of newborns most want for their child? Here are some hopes expressed by parents at a family child care center in Columbus, Ohio (Zelman, 2008):

- "To be a happy and healthy child."

- "To know that she is loved."

- "To be successful at whatever he chooses to do in life."

- "Enjoy a profession and excel."

- "May she be fortunate enough to have sincere friendship in her life."

All parents hold similar dreams for their children, and they expend enormous amounts of love and energy preparing them for the lives that await them once they leave home. In this book, we argue that the chances those hopes and dreams will be realized are partly determined in the child's first 5 years, and language, and the interactions that nourish its development, play a pivotal role.

As parents nurture their infants, toddlers, and preschool-age children, some live in financial security, buffered from many of life's stresses, whereas others struggle day to day to ensure their child is fed, safe, and healthy. There is huge variability in parents' financial circumstances; the cultural and religious traditions that give their lives meaning; the languages they speak; and the educational, emotional, and personal resources that adults can draw on as they parent their child. Despite this bewildering variability, there are commonalities in what parents provide their infants, toddlers, and preschool-age children that help improve the odds that they will move into the world with confidence and with the competences they need to be successful in school.

Parents from all backgrounds have the potential to nourish their child's early development, despite the odds they face. But many are less successful. They may struggle to engage in the responsive, loving relational dances that nourish children's growth due to their personal histories. They may hold unexamined beliefs about how adults should interact with infants, or they may be unaware of the importance of frequent, language-infused interactions with their infant and, later, their toddler. Others might lack financial resources to purchase the books that are a potent starting point for these interactions that bolster long-term development. This book is intended to offer support to those parents. We hope it also can reassure and encourage those who are supplying their children with the nurturing experiences that decades of scientific studies have determined are critically important. Most important, this book is for the professionals, programs, policy makers, and community members who are reaching out to lend assistance to families and children in need.

Children's lives go in many directions as they enter the world of schooling and beyond. The chances that parents' and children's dreams will be realized depend, in part, on the emotional, social, linguistic, and intellectual supports that adults provide in the first 5 years of their child's life. During those years, developmental foundations are laid that have a potent impact on later emotional, social, linguistic, and academic functioning. Separate strands of development are intricately and inextricably woven together during those first years. This book explores those multiple, interwoven strands of emotional, social, neurological, and language development between birth and age 5.

OUR APPROACH

We draw on the breathtaking range of discoveries since the late 1970s to describe how early development is profoundly shaped by adult–child interactions, which set in motion a spiral of mutually reinforcing linguistic, affective, and intellectual development. Language is central to all the strands of development that we examine—attachment, executive functioning, theory of mind, and literacy. Drawing on literally thousands of studies, we argue that language is central to healthy development for two reasons. First, language is nourished in the context of responsive, sensitive, and loving adult–child exchanges that also are the birthplace of attachment and executive functioning ability. Second, the linguistic competencies that children acquire are a tool that they use to control themselves, interact with others, and learn about the world. Language is also the wellspring that nourishes children's literacy development.

As we lead readers through a mass of research, we make the abstractions of science come alive with videotapes of adult–child interactions that illustrate key features of interactions that scientists are studying. These vignettes are both described in words and are available for viewing at www.brookespublishing.com/downloads with (case sensitive) keycode 34ckDaD1k. They are referred to multiple times because one can see multiple aspects of development being fostered during 30 seconds of engaged parent–child interaction. We also draw on personal experiences to illustrate key points.

Although we strive to bring science to life, we also seek to draw readers into the world of developmental science. We introduce and explain profoundly important concepts such as mediation, bidirectional causality, epigenesis, and many more. We frequently summarize the findings of meta-analyses that are reviews of many studies of a single topic and then illustrate major findings by discussing a single study in some detail. Our goal is to help the reader gain insight into how scientists study development by gaining understanding of the methods they use and the behaviors they are examining.

PROGRAM PROFILES

At the core of this book is the conviction that countries around the world can and should take steps to help families as they rear their young. To make concrete what some of those efforts look like, we describe programs around the world that are making a difference in the lives of children. There are countless programs designed to help parents. We have chosen to place a spotlight on those that either have a specific focus on language or that work with parents in ways that have a high probability of supporting early language development.

Exciting advances are being made in which coaches encourage parents to adopt interactive and positive parenting strategies and provide them with supportive feedback. In two programs we discuss, Play and Learning Strategies (PALS) and the Video Interaction Project (VIP), feedback is supplied as coaches and parents view videotapes of parent–child interactions. Two other programs combine informational coaching guidance with feedback to parents about adult–child conversations that occurred in a day.

In two other projects, parents are supplied information by home visitors who follow a prescribed curriculum using program materials. One such effort is the Early Childhood Education Development initiative of Save the Children, which is found in countries around the world. The other project is the well-known Home Instruction for Parents of Preschool Youngsters (HIPPY).

Book distribution programs have become extremely popular, and this book describes such programs. First, we consider the widely implemented Reach Out and Read, in which pediatricians give parents books at well-baby visits, along with the advice that they should read to their child. Then we introduce three efforts that distribute millions of books—Dolly Parton's Imagination Library, which is primarily based in the United States; Bookstart, which is used throughout Europe; and programs in Israel, Sifriyat Pijama ("Pajama Library") and Maktabat al-Fanoos ("Lantern Library"), that provide books to Hebrew- and Arabic-speaking Israelis. We conclude this section by discussing a hybrid approach—Family Reading Partnership in Ithaca, New York. It uses several strategies to distribute books while also seeking to raise community awareness of the importance of reading.

In the final set of program profiles, we briefly discuss a number of novel emerging approaches. One area of active effort is development of applications that run on smartphones, created to give parents tips and encouragement designed to help them enrich how they use language with their child. We then discuss large networks that might provide readers with points of contact for programs. Our final program profile, Five Steps to Five, bears testimony to how a few dedicated individuals can create an initiative that benefits many local families.

We have not included programs that use center-based delivery, such as Early Head Start. They are a critical part of the system of care for young children. Although we do not profile any such programs, Chapter 5 discusses research conducted in center-based programs and affirms the importance of those efforts, especially for children who are learning a new language.

LANGUAGE DIFFERENCES VERSUS LANGUAGE DEFICITS

A simmering debate around issues that are central to this book has been sparked by a major research study authored by Betty Hart and Todd Risley (1995). Data came from videotaped observations in the homes of children from vastly different economic backgrounds that were highly correlated with children's racial backgrounds. Hart and Risley reported that on average children between the ages of 12 months and 3 years in the most educationally and economically advantaged homes hear 30 million words more than some children living in homes with parents with the least educational and economic resources. They described many details of the homes' language environments, revealing the interlocking connections between the quantity and quality of talk and the impact of early variability on later school success (Walker, Greenwood, Hart, & Carta, 1994). Because of the intense time demands required to transcribe and analyze audiotapes, the study had a very small sample drawn from one community. Data were collected by observers in the homes, a method that might have had subtle but pervasive effects on family interactions. Given its small sample drawn from one location, the results of this study cannot be broadly generalized, but that has occurred. Those generalizations sometimes have perpetuated negative stereotypes that language used in the homes of certain groups of people is deficient (Dudling-Marling & Lucas, 2009).

Fortunately, an important effect of the Hart and Risley (1995) study is that it rang a loud warning bell that other researcher teams heard and have responded to. Multiple subsequent studies that we discuss also have found substantial differences in the amount and content of adult–child interactions that correlate with social and economic assets. These studies found great variability among families from the same backgrounds, just as Hart and Risley did. Education and income do not determine the parenting one will provide. There is no basis for describing any group of parents as deficient in their language or in how they support development. However, considerable evidence shows that there are major differences in the extent to which home-rearing practices equip children with language abilities and ways of using language required of them in school. Studies find that certain kinds of experiences consistently bolster language development, which is of central importance to this book and for those working with families. The findings of many meticulously conducted detailed studies have laid bare some of the building blocks of emotional, social, linguistic, and academic success. They all are linked to how language is used in homes, child care centers, and classrooms. These findings come from around the world, from varied cultures, and from parents from diverse social and economic backgrounds.

HOW THIS BOOK IS ORGANIZED

This book is organized into three sections.

Section I provides a detailed overview of development—social-emotional, executive function, theory of mind, and brain development—with an emphasis on the role of language. We conclude with chapters focusing on language, how adults support its development, and its contributions to literacy. This section also presents guiding principles for intervention that can support early language development.

Section II presents profiles of various programs that support early language and literacy development in diverse ways, such as educating and coaching parents and providing books for young children. The profiles include U.S.-based as well as international programs.

Section III concludes the book by exploring larger economic and policy issues related to early language and literacy development.

Section I is comprised of six chapters. Chapter 1 discusses attachment and executive function as foundations for later development. Chapter 2 discusses how the brain develops during the first few years of life and explores the relationship between brain development and language. Chapter 3 examines the early origins of language, how children acquire and begin to use language, and how this acquisition connects to other abilities young children are developing at this time, including the capacity for understanding symbolic representation, the ability to establish shared or joint attention to objects and experiences, and the awareness that other people have thoughts and feelings that differ from their own. Chapter 4 describes the major strands of language ability and touches on how each is affected by experience. Chapter 5 examines the multiple dimensions of environmental support for first and second language learning. We examine how different settings affect language use, illustrating how children benefit from interacting with varied people in diverse settings. We conclude with discussion of reading development, emphasizing the foundational role language plays. Chapter 6 continues the discussion of the larger context in which children develop language and literacy skills and identifies guiding principles, grounded in current research, for how best to support language and literacy development.

Section II examines specific community programs that help foster language and literacy development. This section begins with profiles of programs that supply coaching to parents of children from birth to age 5; these programs help facilitate the thoughtful, sensitive adult–child interactions that are so important to early development, including language development. Next, we present profiles of book distribution programs that help ensure young children have regular access to new books as they begin developing foundational literacy skills. Section II concludes with a review of other emerging programs, including technology-based projects as well as national coalitions and local projects. The profiles presented throughout Section II include U.S.-based as well as international programs; for easy reference, each program profile begins with a rubric summarizing key details about the program's mission and scope and includes a section outlining the research support for that program. Finally, Section III reconsiders the issues discussed throughout the book in a broader social and economic context in Chapter 7.

Throughout the book, the text refers to several brief videos that serve to illustrate the concepts discussed. These videos can be viewed at www.brookespublishing.com/downloads with (case sensitive) keycode

34ckDaD1k. The previously described program profile rubrics also are available at www.brookespublishing.com/downloads with (case sensitive) keycode 34ckDaD1k. Review "About the Downloads and Videos" for more information about the components available online.

CONCLUDING THOUGHTS

We attempt to make a wealth of scientific knowledge available to many who are preparing to work with or study families in need of support or those who already are engaged in such efforts. The research we explore points to the kinds of experiences that nourish development, but it does not specify how or where supports can be provided. It provides starting points for programs and parents to generate creative methods for helping to ensure that infants, toddlers, and preschool-age children receive the kind of linguistic and intellectual stimulation they require for optimal development. It is up to those working in many fields to devise new and effective ways to support families from all backgrounds, to devise programs and delivery systems capable of providing wide delivery of services, and to marshal the willpower needed to fashion public policies that will enable countries to meet the pressing needs of their most vulnerable and precious citizens—their infants and young children.

REFERENCES

Dudling-Marling, C., & Lucas, K. (2009). Pathologizing the language and culture of poor children. *Language Arts, 86*(5), 362–370.

Hart, B., & Risley, T. R. (1995). *Meaningful differences in the everyday experience of young American children.* Baltimore, MD: Paul H. Brookes Publishing Co.

Walker, D., Greenwood, C., Hart, B., & Carta, J. (1994). Prediction of school outcomes based on early language production and socioeconomic factors. *Child Development, 65,* 606–621. doi:http://dx.doi.org/10.2307/1131404

Zelman, S. T. (2008, August). *Parents share hopes, dreams for children.* Retrieved from http://www.columbusparent.com/content/stories/2008/08/30/cp_rs_education_edge.html

Acknowledgments

We would like to thank the many programs who warmly welcomed us, spent time introducing us to their efforts, and provided feedback on our draft descriptions of their programs. We thank Susan Landry from Play and Learning Strategies (PALS) and Blanca Quiroz, Melissa Sanchez, and Vanessa Hernandez from the Austin, Texas, PALS affiliate; Alan Mendelsohn, Adriana Weisleder, and Anne Seery from the Video Interaction Project in New York; Dana Suskind and Snigdha Gupta for assistance with the Thirty Million Words Project; Elisabeth Bruzon and Renée LaHuffman-Jackson from the Home Instruction for Parents of Preschool Youngsters (HIPPY) program in Fairfax County, Virginia, and Donna Kirkwood from HIPPY USA; Marianne O'Grady and Krista Kruft for assistance with Save the Children and Julee Allen and Sara Dang from Save the Children, Nepal; Aly Evans and Katrina Morse from the Family Reading Partnership, Ithaca, New York; Jeff Conyers from the Dollywood Foundation (which includes Dolly Parton's Imagination Library), Theresa Carl from the Governor's Books from Birth Foundation, and Carolyn Brasel (Tennessee); Dr. Rebecca Swan from the Vanderbilt University branch of Reach Out and Read, Nashville, Tennessee; Adriana van Bus for assistance with BoekStart in Leiden, Holland; Galina Vromen for assistance with Sifriyat Pijama and Maktabat al-Fanoos in Tel Aviv, Israel; Kent Warner, Mary Ellen Warner, Allen Clark, and Emma Rodriguez for assistance with the Five Steps to Five project, Port Chester, New York; Caitlin Molina for assistance with the Providence Talks project, Providence, Rhode Island; and Dale Walker for her assistance with projects being developed at the Juniper Gardens Children's Project in Kansas.

We thank the teachers, parents, children, and support staff who contributed invaluably to our visits.

We thank colleagues who read portions of this book and provided expert guidance and feedback. These include Roberta M. Golinkoff for feedback on the language chapters; Allyssa McCabe and Jeannette

Mancilla-Martinez for assistance related to first and second language development; Alan Mendelsohn, Kimberly Nesbitt, and Susan Landry for assistance related to attachment and executive functions; Paul Yoder for assistance related to parental support for infant–toddler language development; and David Zald for assistance related to neural development and functioning.

Finally, we thank Tess Hoffman for her efficient, skilled, and supportive oversight and editing of the manuscript.

To our fathers, Selden C. Dickinson and Arthur D. Morse,
whose warmth, humor, intelligence, and love nurtured
us and our desires to improve the world and who were
models for us through our lives and as we worked on this book

I

Research on Early Development, Language, and Literacy

1

Laying the Foundations
Attachment and Executive Function

Imagine the following scene, which you can view in Video 1, available with the downloadable materials for this book at the following link: www.brookespublishing.com/downloads with (case sensitive) keycode 34ckDaD1k. It is bedtime, and Tanya and her 18-month-old daughter Eliza are preparing to read a book, *Eggs, Eggs!* (Yoon, 2008). Eliza steps to the foot of the bed where there are two large pillows and turns around as Tanya offers her the book, "You hold it." Eliza opens it and vocalizes with pleasure as her mother sits next to her and says, "Ready?" Eliza hands the book back to her. The following exchanges occur during the first 60 seconds of this book reading.

1. Tanya: The title . . .

2. Eliza [as she points to the cover]: Eh!

3. Tanya: Yeah, it's a niño. [Tanya is bilingual and is using Spanish and English with Eliza.]

4. Tanya: . . . *Eggs, Eggs!* It's the title.

5. Eliza: Eigh! [She points, still focusing on the book.]

6. Tanya [as she looks at Eliza]: Eggs!

7. Eliza [carefully, as she points to a picture]: Whey dah?

8. Tanya: Is that a flower? Yeah, look at him. He looks like he's looking for eggs. Eggs.

9. Eliza [as she points to a picture]: Bah.

10. Tanya: Um hmm. It does look like a ball, doesn't it? [She looks at Eliza and pauses.] It's an egg though.

11. Eliza: Bah! [She points again.]

12. Tanya: Um hmm. [She turns to the first page and looks at Eliza as she asks a question.] Shall we start?

13. Tanya [reading the text]: Hooray, it's Easter, a day of fun. There are eggs to find for everyone. Let's grab our baskets, ready-set-go! Search here, search there, search high up, low. . .

14. [As Tanya reads, Eliza reaches for a flap on a page and opens it. Mom continues reading as Eliza opens another flap.]

15. Tanya: Look it. There's niño [points] . . . and they are looking for eggs. [She points to pictures as Eliza watches.]

16. [Eliza opens a flap and vocalizes.]

17. Tanya [pointing]: Remember you and Helly looked for eggs on Easter and put them in your basket [looks at Eliza with slight pause] on Easter? [long pause]

18. Eliza [sitting very still and focusing on the picture as her mother speaks, then opening a flap]: Ba- ba- . . .

19. Tanya: Basket. But are there any eggs? Look it. [She points.] . . . No eggs! Okay! Shall we turn the page? [She pauses.] Wanna turn the page? [She pauses and looks at Eliza.]

20. [Eliza reaches for a page to turn.]

21. Tanya: Good girl!

In this charming scene, we see a carefully choreographed interactional dance between a mother and child. Each is attending to the words and gestures of the other as, together, they enjoy a book they have read on many prior occasions. In lines 4 and 6, Tanya responds to Eliza's pointing and utterances with information—the title of the book and the name of the object (eggs). In lines 7–10, we see Eliza's initial comment result in a series of back-and-forth exchanges, in which Tanya affirms Eliza's thought that the picture shows a ball but gently informs her that it really is an egg. Only after these initial conversations does Tanya suggest, in line 12, that they start reading. At that point, parent and child continue to be closely attuned to each other, with Tanya monitoring Eliza's attention and allowing her time to explore the book. At the same time, Tanya begins to play a somewhat more directive role. Her comment, "Remember you and Helly looked for eggs on Easter and put them in your basket?" is particularly interesting. Here she draws on a shared memory and encourages Eliza to connect it to the book. As will be evident in later chapters, such talk that moves beyond the pages of the book, into the past and future, is powerful. It plays a role in supporting the child as she constructs a sense of her own history and her connections with her family and community.

We begin with this scenario because it exemplifies the type of parent–child interactions that support all facets of development that we will investigate in this book. Tanya and Eliza are engaged in a warm, sensitively tuned interaction that suggests they have a secure attachment relationship. Tanya is helping Eliza develop her ability to regulate her own attention and actions while also fostering Eliza's language and early literacy development. All within 60 seconds! This is the marvel of effective parenting. Joyful minutes spent together, marked by loving, responsive, and language-rich exchanges, can help lay the emotional, linguistic, and conceptual foundations for a lifetime of literacy experiences. Such harmonious and intellectually and cognitively rich moments also nourish brain development during the early months of life that are marked by explosive neural growth. Exchanges such as these can be characterized as responsive adult–child interaction, from which other intertwined aspects of development in early childhood— attachment (and social-emotional development), executive function, theory of mind, language, and ultimately literacy—emerge. This relationship is depicted in Figure 1.1, which we will revisit periodically throughout this book as we explore early development in depth. (Note that sensitive and responsive interactions can occur in homes, centers, and community settings. Optimal environments are free from violence; toxins; food insecurity; and hostility based on race, ethnicity, or religion.)

In this chapter, we first consider parent–child attachment, which is a fundamental building block of emotional and interpersonal health. We explain the concept, discuss factors that foster it and sad cases in which strong bonds are not established, and note the long-term consequences for early development. Then we turn to executive function, explaining what it is, describing early interactions that foster its development, and discussing long-term impact on early development. For both constructs, we highlight the role of language and emphasize the similarities in the patterns of adult–child interaction that give rise to these capacities. We close by considering some interventions that have been found effective and summarizing factors that bolster early development.

ATTACHMENT

It has long been recognized that the nature of a child's early relationship with his or her primary caregiver, usually the mother, can have a profound and lasting impact on how she engages with others and handles the challenges of everyday life. This understanding is known

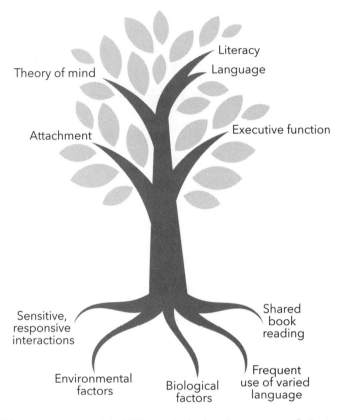

Figure 1.1. How responsive adult–child interaction leads to the emergence of other intertwined strands of development in early childhood: social-emotional development, executive function, language, and ultimately literacy.

as *attachment theory*. This section provides an overview of attachment theory and distinguishes between secure and insecure attachment; see Rees (2016) for a practitioner-oriented review of attachment.

Overview of Attachment Theory

Attachment theory was first developed by Bowlby (1969) and was based on observations of the bonding that occurs among animals—with geese and apes being of particular interest. Bowlby also drew on experimental studies of the traumatic effects on young monkeys as a result of being raised in cages where they lacked the comfort of a mother. Such animals displayed great distress, and they were unable to relate to other monkeys or parent their young appropriately later in life. He postulated that there is an instinctual need to form a bond with a (maternal) parent, and such bonds enable the young to explore the environment without excessive anxiety and lay the groundwork for their later ability to nurture their own young in a sensitive, loving manner. This theory was refined and tested by Mary Ainsworth, a colleague of Bowlby. (See Bretherton [1992] for a discussion of the development of attachment theory.) Ainsworth found striking variability in how mothers cared for their children during a series of careful observational studies of patterns of mother–infant interactions in different countries. Some were very responsive and sensitive as they adjusted their pace and their requests of the infant to the child's interests and attention. We note this in Tanya's reactions to Eliza.

Eliza [carefully, as she points to a picture]:   Whey dah?

Tanya: Is that a flower? Yeah, look at him.

Tanya has quietly allowed Eliza to guide the interaction, and she has patiently waited as her infant studied the book and then vocalized. Once Eliza vocalizes, Tanya interprets it as a question and responds accordingly and with approval. Note also Tanya's warm, gentle, and pleasant facial expressions and the physical contact between parent and child.

In the course of learning about the parent-coaching programs profiled in Section II of this book, we were given the opportunity to view videotapes made during home visits. We will discuss one gentle interactional dance between a mother, whom we will call Perla, and her three-month-old infant, whom we will call Rosalita, who was seated in a baby seat. During this visit Perla handed her baby a toy that contained small parts that rolled around as the toy was moved from side to side. Perla quietly held the toy so Rosalita could study it. After roughly 30 seconds, Perla turned away slightly and vocalized. Perla interpreted this as flagging interest and gently removed Rosalita from the baby seat.

In both of these mother–child interactions, the mother gently allowed her child time to examine an object and responded quickly and appropriately to her child's actions and vocalizations. Also, both mothers accompanied their actions with talk, supplying language to express what they believed their child might be saying, thinking, or feeling.

Long-Term Effects of Early Attachment

A history of such interactions during the first 2 years of life typically results in a secure attachment (Ainsworth, 1979, 1989; Rees, 2016). Such security allows the toddler or young child to explore the world, returning to the mother or other attachment figure when reassurance is needed. In this way, attachment provides a secure base for exploring the world. In contrast, very young children who experience distant, unresponsive, or harsh parenting fail to develop such secure attachments. They exhibit anxiety and fearfulness and may resist efforts of the caregiver to soothe them. They lack the security needed to fully engage with the world and the trust needed to accept loving support when it is tendered to them.

Attachment Styles and Behavior   Researchers elaborated this theory and found three basic types of attachment—secure, anxious/avoidant, and anxious/resistant (e.g., Ainsworth, 1989; Bretherton, 1992; Siegel, 2012). In this book, we only focus on the contrast between children who are securely attached and those who exhibit less secure patterns of attachment (i.e., anxious/avoidant, anxious/resistant) in order to clearly communicate broad patterns of findings. The nature of children's attachments has been studied by putting an infant or toddler in a strange room with her mother, toys, and a stranger. A securely attached child will happily play with toys while her mother is nearby but will become distressed if her mother should leave. The distressed child seeks reassurance and quickly settles when her mother returns. Children who have mothers who are distant, unresponsive, or harsh, however, tend to develop an insecure attachment. Children placed in a strange situation may ignore their mothers and show no response when their mothers leave or when they return. Others may express anger mixed with avoidance when their mothers return.

Longitudinal studies have examined the extent to which early attachment is predictive of later patterns of feeling and action. Looking at the association between attachment and later evidence of internalizing behavior is one way researchers have considered the effects of attachment. *Internalizing behavior* refers to behavior patterns in which a person turns emotional distress inward, resulting in depression, fearfulness, and withdrawal. (In contrast, externalizing behaviors, further discussed next, are those that express in an outward manner a person's emotional distress, resulting in aggressive and hostile behavior.) A meta-analysis that included more than 4,600 children from 42 samples found that secure early attachment had a tendency ($d = .15$)* to help protect children from later internalizing behaviors (Groh, Roisman, van Ijzendoorn, Bakermans-Kranenburg, & Fearon, 2012). Another meta-analysis examined studies that followed children from age 12 months into later life, with one study tracking them until age 22. After taking into account the factors that shape one's life later in adulthood, such as illness and parental loss, the study found that the attachment mea-

---

*Cohen's *d* describes the size of the effect of an intervention. It standardizes differences between groups in a way that allows for comparisons among studies with different-sized samples.

sured at 12 months was a good predictor of later patterns of interacting with others (Waters, Merrick, Treboux, Crowell, & Albersheim, 2000). The results from a single study by Waters et. al. (2000) provide particularly striking evidence of the nature of this long-term stability. Attachment was assessed for 60 Caucasian, middle-class infants at 12 months, and the children were followed for 20 years. When the children were reassessed as young adults, the researchers found that 72% received the same attachment classification as when they were infants. Only 18 of the young adults had shifted in classification. These shifts in classification were most likely (8 of 18) if they had experienced a traumatic life event (e.g., loss of a parent, divorce, life-threatening illness, parental psychiatric disorder, physical or sexual abuse by a family member).

The nature of attachment at an early age clearly has lasting implications for a child's emotional and social functioning. Even though the nature of early attachment is a strong predictor of later functioning, parent support programs provided after this critical early period can still improve attachment relationships. Parents can change, and their infants and toddlers can reap the benefits.

Effects of Attachment on Social Functioning　　Infants and toddlers experience patterns of interaction that lead them to anticipate how others will respond to them. These early cognitive-emotional patterns and expectations operate below the level of conscious awareness. Although they are based on interactions with primary attachment figures, they are generalized to others (reviewed in Fearon, Bakermans-Kranenburg, van Ijzendoorn, Lapsley, & Roisman, 2010). Infants and toddlers who develop secure attachments expect sensitive, supportive, and loving responses, and this assurance enables them to explore the world in a focused manner. This can be seen in Video 1, when Eliza studies the book and later joyfully turns flaps to reveal hidden pictures. Her mother supports this by quietly allowing her to explore and then responds approvingly to Eliza's actions and words. The same pattern of supported exploration, followed by a response to the child's initiatives, was visible between Perla and Rosalita when we observed them. A history of emotional support over time enables children to move into the broader world and engage with other people and experiences with relative confidence. In contrast, those with less secure attachments may withdraw or express hostility.

To what extent does early attachment affect how children later engage with others? This question has often been addressed. Given the numerous studies of attachment, meta-analyses are available that provide a solid base for considering the effects of attachment on interpersonal behavior. One such effort looked at the effects of early attachment on later *externalizing* behaviors (Fearon et al., 2010), which are behaviors directed outward such as fighting, cheating, lying and stealing. It included 69 separate research samples and nearly 6,000 children. Attachment was evaluated early in the child's life, and the observation of externalizing behavior occurred by age 5 in most cases. The researchers found that children who exhibited externalizing behaviors were less likely to have formed secure early attachments. This association was moderately strong (d = .31), and boys were somewhat more likely to exhibit externalizing behavior.

Examining the extent to which a child forms friendships is another way to consider his social competence. Having friends is one of the most important aspects of life to many children, so the ability to get along with peers is very important. A meta-analysis examined effects of attachment on children's later peer relationships (Groh et al., 2014). It drew on 80 studies that included 4,441 children, with some studies including adolescents. It found a moderate association (d = .39) between security of attachment and peer relationships. Remarkably, this association was similar regardless of the child's age when attachment was initially assessed. This finding provides further evidence of the enduring importance of attachment.

Associations Among Attachment, Language, and Cognitive Ability   Not only is attachment closely related to later social-emotional development and interpersonal relationships, but it is also associated with language development, cognitive ability, and future academic outcomes. These associations come together in the parent–child activity with which we opened our discussion—book reading.

Language Development   The quality of children's attachment relationship is associated with their language development. Tanya's warm and sensitive interaction with her child included considerable talk; the language she used was often too complex for Eliza to understand, but Tanya engaged her as a conversational partner. Likewise, when we observed Perla and her infant, Rosalita, we noted that precisely the same qualities characterized their interaction. Such exchanges foster language growth. This association between attachment and language use results in children's improved language ability, as revealed by longitudinal studies that have found that secure attachment and language growth are positively related. A meta-analysis of 32 studies found a modest association (d = .28) between attachment and language (Van Ijzendoorn, Dijkstra, & Bus, 1995). This was replicated by a study that followed 99 children from age 24 to 36 months (Spieker, Nelson, Petras, Jolley, & Barnard, 2003). The analysis of the National Institute of Child Health and Human Development (NICHD) Child Care data by Belsky and Fearon (2002) also found that expressive language measured at 36 months was related to attachment. Interestingly, children from modest social and economic backgrounds who were securely attached had language abilities that were on par with those of more affluent peers. This finding of parity is contrary to the many studies we discuss later that find slower rates of language growth in this population. This important finding suggests that parents from all economic and educational backgrounds can provide good support for their children's language growth between birth and 36 months if they also have habitually engaged in the responsive interactions that foster and result from strong attachment relationships. The role of socioeconomic status (SES) is further explored next.

Cognitive Ability and Academic Outcomes   In general, studies of early development find relatively little evidence of association between attachment and general cognitive ability (Belsky & Fearon, 2002; Spieker et al., 2003; Van Ijzendoorn et al., 1995), but there is a small, long-term association between attachment and academic skill. A study that followed 1,023 children from age 24 months to fifth grade evaluated attachment at 36 months and tested reading and math skills in fifth grade (McCormick, O'Connor, & Barnes, 2016). After controlling for many background variables, the researchers found that securely attached children did slightly better on the academic tasks. Interestingly, this improvement was partly accounted for by the fact that more securely attached children were better able to stay attentive to tasks. Note what we saw watching Eliza. She experienced moments of highly focused attention to the book as her mother responded to Eliza's interest and patiently held the book so she could study it. Similarly, Rosalita experienced moments of highly focused attention to an object as her mother responded to her interest and patiently held the toy so she could study it. Caregivers who are sensitive to children's interests and assist them as they explore novel objects are not only deepening emotional bonds, but they also are fostering their child's attentional capacities.

Book Reading   Book-reading time between Tanya and Eliza was very conducive to fostering close emotional bonds. Researchers have taken advantage of that fact and used book reading as an activity in which to observe how attachment affects mother–child interaction. Adriana Bus and Marinus van Ijzendoorn observed middle-class Dutch mothers and children ages 1½, 3½, and 5½ years as they read a storybook and looked at a booklet with letters and words. The researchers determined the nature of the child's attachment relationship at 18 months. As mothers and children read books, children who were more securely attached needed less discipline to maintain their focus and more often tried to read on their own and examine illustrations (Bus & Van Ijzendoorn, 1988). Mothers of securely attached children tended to provide more literacy instruction, and children who received such tuition had stronger literacy knowledge. In a subsequent study, these researchers examined book reading among four groups—parents with either low or high SES who reported they read to their children either frequently or infrequently (Bus & Van Ijzendoorn, 1995). Securely attached children were much more likely to be from homes in which reading was common. This finding indicated that securely attached children are better able to engage in literacy-related activities. Mothers with a history of responsive, emotionally rich book reading use it as an opportunity to deepen attachment bonds while also fostering language growth (e.g., Tanya and Eliza).

Conversely, children who have an insecure or anxious attachment relationship may be harder to engage in book reading, making it a less pleasurable activity for the mother or child. Although this pattern may naturally emerge, it is possible to change. For mothers whose infants and toddlers are difficult to engage, it may be possible to help the infants learn to engage more successfully in activities such as play and book reading. This might improve the quality of the attachment bond while also building language, which is what many teams of researchers and educators have attempted. We will discuss these interventions after we have reviewed research on executive function.

EXECUTIVE FUNCTION

Establishing a strong emotional bond with a nurturing adult is fundamentally important to children. Learning to regulate one's actions, feelings, and thoughts is a second fundamental developmental challenge. This is needed if one is to interact with others in a socially acceptable manner and focus on tasks. Different terms are used to refer to the abilities drawn on to control one's attention, behavior, and emotions— *executive function, self-regulation,* and *cognitive control.* We will use the term *executive function.*

Importance at School Entry

To grasp the importance of executive function for school success, imagine a teacher with 25 6-year-olds in her classroom. When the teacher is reading a story to the group, she notes that four or five children frequently become distracted and play with their shoes or try to engage their friends. They also are prone to blurt out answers rather than waiting to be called on. Those who attend to stories are more likely to engage in sustained focused play during independent activity time, creating elaborate structures with blocks or assembling puzzles. Yet, a few flit from one activity to the next and occasionally pose management problems. Children who have trouble sustaining attention in groups or engagement in tasks fit the profile of those with weak executive function skills. Their patterns of participation in the classroom mean that they lose out on opportunities to gain the skills and knowledge being taught and honed in school.

Measuring Executive Function

One way to evaluate a child's executive function skills is to ask teachers to rate the extent to which a child can engage in and stay attentive to tasks in school and comply with classroom expectations and social norms. Teachers are able to distinguish among children when making ratings, and the ratings assigned by a teacher one year tend to correlate reasonably well with teachers' ratings the following year. That stability suggests that the capacity is somewhat stable and different teachers respond in a similar manner to questions used to assign these ratings. Teacher ratings as a measure of children's executive function skills have some limitations, however. Researchers also need measures that can be used before children attend school; moreover, different teachers may have different expectations for behavior. As a result, a host of clever methods have been devised to directly test children's executive functioning.

To understand how these tasks measure executive functioning ability, it is helpful to reflect on what is involved when one regulates one's own behavior. In order to comply with a classroom expectation, such as learning to raise one's hand before talking, children must translate the teacher's words into meaning, store this message as a cognitive representation, retrieve it at appropriate times, and use it to restrain the overwhelming urge to share some exciting piece of information (e.g., "I have a hamster too!") without first raising one's hand and waiting to be called on for an answer. Also, children engaging in a sustained activity, such as building a city using blocks, must formulate a plan and hold it in mind while dealing with the challenges of placing one block at a time. They need to monitor their own behavior and also check on whether they are complying with classroom rules (e.g., "No buildings taller than you"). Finally, they need to monitor their interactions with peers (e.g., "I'm building the tower, and you are working on the fence"). These complex tasks require memory, the use of language to formulate and communicate plans, and the ability to regulate one's emotions and impulses (Kopp, 1982).

What makes self-regulation so complex is that it is not a purely cognitive enterprise. Emotions color all people's interactions with the world. For example, fear or anxiety may lurk below the surface of awareness while a child is interacting with peers as memories of past engagements with caregivers are triggered and activate emotional responses deep in the brain (Blair, 2002). Strong emotions may burst forth as a building made of blocks suddenly collapses or another child bumps a carefully constructed tower and sends it crashing to the floor. At such a moment, emotion-driven urges to strike out, cry, or yell may be dampened if the child recalls socially approved responses, inhibits her immediate emotion-laden impulse, and acts in a socially approved manner. For example, the tower builder may say, "You messed up my tower. Why did you do that?" instead of hitting other children.

One type of assessment of executive function evaluates children's ability to resist temptation and delay gratification. Performance on these tasks is said to measure hot executive function ability—the use of executive control in the face of emotions or desires. One amusing hot executive function task is the wrapped gift task. The experimenter brings a gift and wrapping supplies for the child. The child is asked to sit with his back to the experimenter and not to peek while the experimenter spends 1 minute wrapping the present. The experimenter puts the gift on the table and leaves for 2 minutes to get a bow. The child is told not to touch the gift. The child's score is based on the number of times he turns, peeks, or touches the gift. Tasks such as these have been used with children as young as 22 months old (Kochanska, Murray, & Harlan, 2000). Performance on such tasks relates to teacher ratings of children's ability to engage in classroom activities in ways that reflect use of executive function ability (Fuhs, Nesbitt, Farran, & Dong, 2014; Nesbitt, Farran, & Fuhs, 2015).

A second type of executive function task assesses what some researchers call *effortful attention* (Kochanska et al., 2000) and others refer to as *cool executive function*. The name is designed to contrast with the challenges posed by the hot executive function tasks. Cool executive function tasks draw on a child's memory and attentional focus to a complicated task, rather than the child's ability to resist doing something he wants to do. In cool executive function tasks, children are given a rule to guide their behavior, tested to see if they can follow it, and given a second rule that requires a shift in focus. For example, in the dimensional change task, children are given a set of cards that have star and truck shapes in blue and red. Children first are asked to sort a set of cards according to one dimension, color (red vs. blue), and then according to shape (star vs. truck). Head-Toes-Knees-Shoulders is another popular cool executive function task in which children are told to touch their toes when the assessor says to touch their head and to touch their heads when the assessor says to touch their toes.

Executive Function and Academic Achievement

Acquisition of strong executive function abilities is a slow process that draws on emerging intellectual and language skills. Between birth and school entry, caregivers support its emergence in ways that are similar to how caregivers foster attachment. Children who develop strong executive function abilities early in life reap long-term benefits in the form of better subsequent peer relationships. These abilities also tend to translate into stronger academic performance.

Kindergarten teachers realize the importance of children's ability to regulate their attention and behavior. When kindergarten teachers were asked to rate the most important factors that contribute to a child's readiness for school (U.S. Department of Education, 1993), the top two responses were being physically healthy and well rested (78%) and being able to verbally communicate their needs and wants (64%). Close behind these responses were a cluster of behaviors associated with executive function, including being curious as indicated by engaging well in new activities (57%), not being disruptive (60%), following directions (60%), sitting still and paying attention (42%), and finishing tasks (40%).

Teachers are right to rate these as key indicators of readiness to learn. Multiple large longitudinal studies have explored the associations among children's academic, social, and intellectual abilities in kindergarten and later school success. One study sought to identify the behaviors and abilities measured at school entry that predict later school success. The researchers combined results from six large longitudinal studies conducted in the United States, Canada, and the United Kingdom (Duncan et al., 2007). The combined sample included more than 36,000 children. These studies provided data from school entry through fifth grade and included teacher interviews about children, direct assessments, and observational data. In their analyses, the researchers took into account information about children's parents and economic circumstances. They found that early attentional skills (cool executive function) made a significant, small ($d = .10$), but educationally important contribution to the prediction of reading and math skills in fifth grade. Surprisingly, challenging behaviors were not predictive of later academic success. Both teacher ratings of attentional skills and assessments of these skills predicted later achievement, a finding that lends support to the value kindergarten teachers place on behaviors that reflect self-regulatory ability. Further evidence of the unique importance of cool executive function came from a study of 173 kindergarten children (Brock, Rimm-Kaufman, Nathanson, & Grimm, 2009). These researchers used measures of hot and cool executive function and explored the effects of children's ability to maintain attention on their math growth and learning-related behaviors. They found that it was the cool executive function measures that were predictive of math achievement.

At the same time that children are acquiring executive function, they are also gaining linguistic and cognitive abilities. How are these emerging competencies related? We discuss research that tries to answer this challenging question in the next section. We will pause and discuss two concepts that are needed as the complex interrelationships among competencies that develop between birth and school entry—mediation and bidirectional effects—are explored.

Mediation and Bidirectional Relationships   Mediation is the process that occurs when the improvement in an ability, such as reading, is related to earlier experiences, such as book reading, and to improvement in another ability, such as oral language development. Book reading may foster later reading skill because it improved children's language abilities. We will discuss the results of a study conducted by Kimberly Nesbitt, Mary Fuhs, and Dale Farran (2015) to help you understand mediation and how it applies to development of executive function.

Nesbitt and her colleagues (2015) examined how the executive function ability of preschool children affects their growth in math and reading. They assessed the executive function, literacy, and mathematical abilities of 1,103 children in 80 prekindergarten classrooms in the fall and spring. (In Figure 1.2, executive function is represented

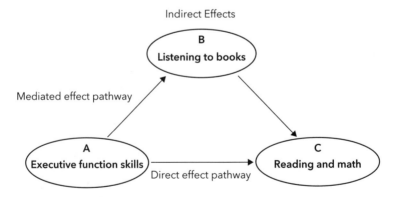

Figure 1.2.   Direct, indirect, and mediated effects in the relationship among executive function skills, listening to books, and reading and math skills.

by A, learning-related behaviors by B, and literacy and mathematical abilities by C.) They hypothesized that the strength of a child's executive function skills in the fall (A) would be predictive of the child's reading and math skill in the spring (C). They also anticipated that stronger executive function ability (A) would enable children to effectively engage in learning-related activities (B), and engagement in these activities would help predict growth in academic skills (C). That is, they anticipated that executive function (A) would have direct effects on reading and math (C), and learning-related behaviors (B) would also help predict later academic skills because these behaviors would enable children to engage in the classroom in more productive ways. That is, they expected learning-related behaviors would mediate the association between fall executive function and spring academic skills.

They tested this theory by collecting detailed descriptive information about children's classroom behaviors. They observed children as they engaged in routine activities three times during the year. Each child was observed for 3 seconds using a snapshot technique, after which the researcher coded for four types of learning-related behaviors: 1) the child's level of involvement; 2) engagement in a task that included multiple steps (e.g., doing a puzzle, reading a book, playing make-believe); 3) participation in a social activity; and 4) disengagement or disruptive behavior. They also asked teachers to report on children's learning-related behaviors. Teacher reports were reasonably well correlated with the direct observations. Nesbitt and colleagues (2015) used statistical methods that allowed them to take into account information about the children's backgrounds and academic and executive function competencies in the fall. They found that 1) fall executive function predicted spring academic abilities, 2) fall executive function predicted learning behaviors during the year, and 3) learning-related behaviors predicted spring academic skills.

To put these results in technical terms, fall executive function was directly related to spring academic skills. Fall executive function was also indirectly related to spring reading and math because some of its effects were mediated by the child's participation in learning-related behaviors in the classroom. Children with strong executive function skills were more able to engage in learning-related behaviors in the classroom and able to benefit more from classroom instruction. Learning-related behaviors mediated the effect of fall executive skills on spring academic abilities.

Bidirectional relationships between emerging abilities are another important phenomenon that will be repeatedly encountered as early development is explored. When two abilities are related to each other, it can be hard to determine the nature of the association between them.

Consider the relationship between a child's interest in hearing books and her oral language skills. A researcher might well find that growth is correlated across both areas; interest in listening to books improves at the same time that oral language grows. This could be because strong interest in books helps fuel language growth or because strong language ability fosters interest in books. And there is a third option—both may be happening. Interest in listening to books may foster language growth that increases interest in books, and increased book reading may lead to language growth. Such a pattern would reflect bidirectional effects. It is important to be aware of this possibility because reciprocal effects can increase the potency of both of the two related capacities.

An example of bidirectional effects comes from an analysis of the emergence of executive function and academic skills in preschool. Fuhs and her colleagues (2014) were interested in further understanding the association between growth in executive function and children's engagement in learning activities in preschool. In our discussion of mediation, we noted that stronger executive function at the beginning of preschool increased the chances that children would engage in beneficial behaviors; that engagement enhanced learning. Could children who engage in productive learning activities improve their ability to sustain focus while engaged in an activity, thereby improving their executive function skills? Fuhs and her team addressed this question using data from 2 years. Children were tested at the beginning and end of preschool and again at the end of kindergarten. Executive function predicted growth in academic skills and language. In addition, the researchers found a bidirectional relationship—improved math and language skills also supported growth in executive function. Thus, strength in executive function can support growth in an academic area as children begin their schooling careers, and stronger academic abilities can foster growth of executive function.

Long-Term Effects of Executive Function on Later Academic Competencies   Evidence is accumulating to indicate that executive function ability has beneficial effects on academic abilities beginning at school entrance and continuing through the primary grades. A long-term study was carried out by Smith, Borkowski, and Whitman (2008), who followed children from ages 3 to 14. They assessed children's IQ, receptive vocabulary, and reading readiness at school entry, and they assessed children's reading comprehension and IQ at age 14. Teachers rated students' cognitive and social-emotional self-regulation (part of executive function skills) when they were 10 years old. As expected, later reading was predicted by early vocabulary and reading. Also, early reading helped predict executive function at age 10, which itself was correlated with reading comprehension at age 14. When age 10 executive function ratings were taken into account, the association between reading skills at age 5 and at age 10 was reduced. These findings indicate that age 10 executive function partially mediated the effects of early reading on later reading comprehension.

Bidirectional associations have been found between executive skills and academic abilities in preschool and kindergarten (Fuhs et al., 2014). Will that continue to occur once children enter school and engage in formal educational activities? That is the question posed by researchers who followed 379 children who were being reared in low-income homes. Children's reading skills were first assessed in kindergarten or first grade and then again in third and fifth grade (Stipek, Newton, & Chudgar, 2010). At each time point, teachers also rated children's ability to engage in work-related tasks. As expected, reading scores were moderately correlated with each other over time, and teacher ratings were generally consistent across the three time points. More important, teacher reports of children's work-related behaviors in kindergarten and first grade predicted reading in third grade, and third-grade teacher reports predicted fifth-grade reading. There was no evidence that literacy ability in kindergarten and first grade fostered growth in work-related skills in third grade, but third-grade literacy did contribute to work-related skills in fifth grade. Thus, the ability to productively engage in school learning at school entry sets children on a path to reading success. They continue to benefit from the ability to sustain engagement in academic learning tasks through the primary grades. In addition, as children gain skills as readers and receive teacher approval for their efforts, their ability to remain engaged in learning tasks improves.

Summary of Connections   Children are positioned to benefit from school if they enter with good executive function capacity and reasonably strong academic skills. Executive function abilities appear to have bidirectional effects in the more informal learning environments of preschool and kindergarten. Engagement in activities such as listening to stories, looking at books, writing, and playing with math manipulatives builds academic and self-regulatory capacities. Children with strong executive function skills continue to benefit more from school than those with weaker skills, and academic success begins to translate into improved executive functioning by the later grades. All of this raises the question: What early experiences equip some children with strong executive function skills by the end of their preschool years?

The Emergence of Executive Function Abilities

Caregivers are constantly responding to infants' and toddlers' entreaties to interact and play with them, their resolute efforts to master skills such as walking and eating, and their unrelenting desire to explore the world. As children play with objects and interact with others, they must focus and maintain their attention. Recall how, in Video 1, Eliza studied the pictures in the book and stayed engaged in the reading activity. (We observed similar focus and engagement when we watched how Rosalita intently examined the objects moving about in the toy her mother held for her.) Also, as they enter into the social world, children need to learn to express their needs and desires in acceptable ways. Research is beginning to find that the way parents respond to and support children's efforts to master skills has an impact on children's emerging executive function abilities. Interestingly, the caregiving behaviors we will highlight are similar to those associated with attachment.

Caregiving and Executive Function: Perla and Rosalita   To consider the many subtle ways in which caregivers engage infants that have implications for the growth of executive function, we will consider the interaction between Perla and Rosalita that we mentioned earlier and describe it in somewhat greater depth. When we met Perla, she was playing with Rosalita, her 3-month-old infant, in an infant chair. The entire interaction was possible because Rosalita was positioned so she could see her mother and the object her mother gave her, and Rosalita's mother was fully engaged with her. This arrangement provided the context that enabled them to share the following experience. Perla handed her infant a round plastic toy with objects that slid around under a transparent cover whenever the toy was moved. It was somewhat heavy, and when Rosalita grasped it, she held it up to her face, covering her face. As we observed, Perla paused, peeked behind it quietly, and then said, "Oh, where are you?" as she initiated a kind of hide-and-seek game. She then took control of the toy and held it at a slight angle so the infant could see the objects move around. The infant heard the sound and looked down. The mother held the toy for about 30 seconds, moving it slightly so the objects moved around. The infant attended closely as Perla commented on what was happening. Eventually Rosalita lost interest, grunted, and strained forward in her seat. Perla immediately stopped playing with the toy and interpreted Rosalita's grunt and movement as a request to get up. She said, "Oh! You wanna get up?" as she removed her from the chair and held her.

Perla was gentle, warm, and keenly attuned to all of Rosalita's signals throughout the interaction. She noted what interested Rosalita and immediately responded. She helped Rosalita explore the toy by moving it slightly. She did not press her own agenda in an intrusive manner; rather, she allowed her daughter to look at the moving objects and listen to the sounds they made. She also used language to narrate her interpretations of the infant's desires by asking "Oh, where are you?" when the infant's face was covered. As Rosalita looked at the toy, Perla said, "That's fun. It's got sea animals, yeah." Finally, when Rosalita tired of the toy, Perla said, "Oh! You wanna get up?" Perla helped Rosalita to explore the world in these few moments of play. This support for Rosalita's actions is called *scaffolding*, a concept further explained in the next section.

Perla gave Rosalita some control of objects, the activity, and her own location. By so doing, she gave her daughter autonomy support. She was able to support her autonomy because she was highly responsive to Rosalita's verbal and nonverbal signals. What she did not do was abruptly engage Rosalita, forcing an activity on her or insisting that she continue after she became bored. Such negative interactions are referred to as *being intrusive* or *controlling*. Perla also accompanied her actions with language that mapped directly onto the activity. She also put into words what she believed were the child's mental and emotional states. This was most clear when she said, "You wanna get up?" This effort to understand the child's mental state is called *mind-mindedness*. That is, she was attentive to the child's mind and verbalized what she believed Rosalita wanted and was thinking. Finally, Perla was gentle and loving during her interaction with Rosalita.

Rosalita was encouraged to be cognitively and linguistically engaged while also feeling loved and safe throughout the entire time. Various studies found that these caregiving strategies foster development of executive functioning (Bernier, Beauchamp, Carlson, & Lalonde, 2015; Grusec & Maayan, 2010).

Parental Scaffolding of Children's Engagement   Parents begin to have an impact on their child's emerging executive function skills from an early age as they help their infants sustain attention to objects and events. This process of supporting a child's ability to carry out a difficult task has been referred to as *supplying scaffolding* for the child, a construct initially formulated by Vygotsky (1978). Vygotsky advanced an influential theory of child development and proposed that the development of children's higher cognitive abilities is the result of their gradual internalization of their culture's ways of interacting, acting, and learning what he called their *culture's tools* (Wertsch, 1991). Language is one of society's most powerful tools that plays an important role in children's development of executive function abilities. According to Vygotsky, adults initially provide strong guidance for children as they learn the skills and behaviors required of them. Those supports are gradually reduced and removed as children gain competence and can function without assistance. The guidance adults provide is called *scaffolding*, evoking the construction metaphor in which buildings are supported until they are strong enough to stand on their own.

The metaphor of scaffolding may also apply to children's acquisition of executive function. Evidence suggests that children's ability to regulate their own attention and actions can be viewed as a shift from being regulated by others to being regulated by themselves, which reflects gradual internalization of the culture's ways of acting. Caregivers may help children acquire executive function skills by providing strong guidance toward methods that are less directive and are designed to help children maintain their engagement in tasks.

To understand how mothers foster early development, consider how Perla assisted Rosalita. Perla provided strong scaffolding for Rosalita's attention throughout the brief interaction that we witnessed. She positioned Rosalita so she could see the toy, held it in a way that ensured Rosalita would look at it, and moved it to draw her attention to the moving objects. Perla was sensitive to her daughter's involvement and held the toy still to help Rosalita maintain her attention and study it intently. She quickly shifted the activity when Rosalita became tired. Similarly, Tanya provides scaffolding for Eliza's attention in Video 1. When Tanya reads with Eliza, we see that Eliza has internalized the routines associated with book reading. She knows what will happen as she reads with her mother, where to sit, how to look, and the kind of conversation in which to engage. At several points, she initiates playful interactions around the book. Tanya takes a directive role at times. She points to pictures and asks questions that are meant to prompt specific responses, and she moves the activity forward by turning pages. Yet, she also helps Eliza maintain her attention and engagement, pausing and holding the book still as Eliza looks at pictures and following Eliza's comments and questions in a way that encourages continued attention to a picture or idea. This kind of scaffolding helps very young children learn to direct themselves and regulate their own attention and actions.

Research on the Effects of Scaffolding   Susan Landry and her colleagues studied this process of movement from being other-directed to self-directed (Landry, Smith, Swank, & Miller-Loncar, 2000). They drew on Vygotsky's (1978) approach to development and hypothesized that very young children would benefit from having parents who helped them direct and maintain their attention as they learned to engage in activities and acquired skills needed to carry them out. They hypothesized that there would be a slow shift in the extant mixture of strategies that would be helpful. During the study, as each of the parents played with their own child, the researchers coded parents' behaviors for help they offered children in maintaining their attention to an activity or object. Strategies that Landry et al. found included offering children choices through verbal methods, such as questions or suggestions, or nonverbal methods, such as pointing. The researchers also coded times when the caregiver directed the activity, including verbal or nonverbal strategies that offered children little choice, such as verbal requests (e.g., "Point to the birdie") or showed the child the specific desired behavior. The researchers expected that children would always benefit from assistance maintaining their engagement, but highly directive supports would decrease in utility because they sometimes force the child to shift attention away from what the child was doing or interrupt a child as she was starting to do something different from what the adult wanted the child to do.

Landry and her team (2000) tested these hypotheses by following 289 children and primary care providers from age 2 to 4½. They tracked children's language and cognitive development and observed how their caregivers played with them. They also coded children's participation in activities at age 4½ for the extent to which they initiated and sustained actions when they were playing with their parents. A caregiver could strive to help a child maintain focus and direct the child's attention. Thus, the researchers found that maintaining and directing behaviors are beneficial. They found that children at all ages benefitted from parents who used strategies that helped them maintain their engagement. These benefits showed up in enhanced cognitive and language abilities. In addition, those improved cognitive and language skills that were acquired by age 3½ were indirectly linked to a child's ability to initiate and sustain an activity at age 4½. Directives had different effects. When children were 2½ years old, caregiver directives were associated with children's enhanced cognitive and language growth, but at age 3½ parental directives were related to less independent activity for children at age 4½. Thus, as children become more able to regulate their own attention, they benefit from engaging in sustained activities, and directives tend to interrupt such engagement.

The ability to initiate and sustain activity is a strong indicator of the emergence of executive function. Therefore, this study provides good evidence that caregivers play a role in supporting the emergence of executive function from the time children are 2 years old. Support for a child's capacity to sustain engagement is beneficial throughout early childhood. Directives are helpful when very young children initially need heavy scaffolding, but they decline in value as children get older.

Replicating findings is critical in science and is rather rare in social science. It is therefore interesting to note that other results consistent with Landry's findings have been reported. Bindman, Hindman, Bowles, and Morrison (2013) studied 127 children between age 3 and the age just before they entered kindergarten. They assessed children's language, cognitive, and executive function skills. The summer before children entered kindergarten, researchers observed parents and children as they prepared for a pretend birthday party. They found that parents of children with stronger executive function abilities used hints and suggestions, actions that served to sustain the child's engagement, and less directive language.

Fine-Tuning Adult Scaffolding   The study by Landry and colleagues (2000) indicated that children benefit when parents help them sustain engagement in an activity. But what enables them to do that? Why are some better than others? A longitudinal study that followed 80 children from age 12 months to 26 months examines this question (Bernier, Carlson, & Whipple, 2010). Children's homes were visited four times, mothers were videotaped, and children were assessed for their executive function, memory, and cognitive abilities. The mothers' interactions with their children were coded for three features of parenting that the researchers surmised could help children's emerging executive function skills:

- *Sensitivity:* mothers' gentle responsiveness

- *Mind-mindedness:* indications that mothers were attempting to understand their child's mental and emotional states (e.g., "You really don't like that, do you?")

- *Autonomy support:* instances when mothers helped their child carry out a task

The researchers found two patterns of results on the executive function tasks, referred to as *two dimensions of ability.* One dimension reflected use of hot executive function ability and the other included cool executive function. Sensitivity, autonomy support, and mind-mindedness measured before children were 2 years old all predicted cool executive function at age 26 months. None of these predicted hot executive function. These features of parenting are related. Mothers who are tuned into their child's mental and emotional states (mind-mindedness) are able to help them accomplish tasks (autonomy support). Sensitive parents are attentive to the child's rhythms and respond in a gentle, supportive manner that can foster autonomy. This finding aligns with the videotaped interaction between Tanya and Eliza and the interaction the authors observed between Perla and Rosalita.

Language: Private Speech   Vygotsky (1978) hypothesized that language is a tool society passes on to children. As we discussed earlier, it is woven into the parent–child interactions that build strong attachment bonds and is a means for parents to convey the norms and behavioral expectations of their group (e.g., "Use your inside voice in school." "You need to listen and wait your turn"). Language also is used for cognitive purposes, such as when individuals make plans and carry out complex tasks ("Okay, I turn left at the first light . . ."). Adults direct infants' and toddlers' actions by showing and telling them what to do. Children slowly internalize these expectations and the associated talk. As children strive to do things, the role of language sometimes is evident when children quietly talk to themselves. This is called *private speech*. Vygotsky hypothesized that it is a manifestation of children's incorporation of societal norms and evidence that language is being used to help regulate actions. With time, this vocalization disappears because children have fully internalized the use of language. A charming example of this process was conveyed to me by a preschool teacher. One child often arrived at school in an agitated state. The teachers found that when he was having trouble settling and focusing, they could take him aside; look him in the eyes; say, "Matthew, focus;" and encourage him to say "focus" as well. This helped him settle and gave him a strategy to use independently.

Researchers have explored Vygotsky's (1978) hypothesis about private speech. They do so by observing children as they engage in complex tasks, recording their vocalizations, and determining if there is an association between private speech and success in completing the task. Two longitudinal research studies used this approach, one with children between ages 3 and 4 (Berk & Spuhl, 1995) and one with children from first to third grade (Bivens & Berk, 1990). In each case, researchers found that children used private speech. Its use among the preschool children was associated with better performance on the task they were asked to do, and its use among the older children doing a math task was associated with stronger mathematics performance the following year (Bivens & Berk, 1990). An investigation done with 5- and 6-year-olds found that use of private speech increased as tasks got harder, and its use was related to better performance on the task (Fernyhough & Fradley, 2005). Winsler, Diaz, Atencio, McCarthy, and Chabay (2000) followed children from age 3 to 5, half of whom had been identified as having challenging behavior. All of the children used private speech, but those with challenging behavior were more likely to use it. Consistent with Vygotskiian theory, researchers found a decrease in use of private speech as children got older. In addition, they found an association between the use of private speech and results on measure of executive skill.

A theory advanced by Zelazo (2015) has added precision to Vygotsky's (1978) theory. Zelazo also posited that individuals control their attention and direct actions to accomplish tasks using language to formulate and hold in mind rules and goals, and he described the neural activation patterns associated with planning and regulating action.

Language Development and Executive Functioning   Language ability has effects on children's ability to regulate their thoughts and actions that goes well beyond use of private speech. Indeed, there is strong evidence that language plays a major role in supporting the emergence of executive functioning from a very early age. Pointing is an early and important means by which children engage others in attending to objects of interest and eliciting information about them (see Chapter 3). It is therefore interesting to learn that a large study that included 1,117 children found that infants' gesturing at 15 months was correlated with language at age 2 and 3 (Kuhn, Willoughby, Wilbourn, Vernon-Feagans, & Blair, 2014). Early gesturing also was associated with executive function at age 4. The effect of early gesturing was mediated by children's language at age 2 and 3. This finding is a preview of findings in discussed in Chapter 3, showing continuity between preverbal communication and later language. It also calls attention to the deep connections between language and emerging executive functioning capacity.

Vocabulary has been found to have a particularly strong association with executive function. Catherine Ayoub and colleagues found that it serves both cognitive and social functions (Ayoub, Vallotton, & Mastergeorge, 2011). They were interested in its role in supporting emerging self-regulatory skills. They pursued that question by examining data from an evaluation of Early Head Start. Data from nearly 3,000 children, collected at 14, 24, and 36 months of age, included measures of language and self-regulation. Children's vocabulary at 24 months contributed to predicting the growth in self-regulation between that age and age 36 months. Also, children with larger vocabularies at 24 months performed slightly better than others on the self-regulation measure at later points. Receptive vocabulary was found to be correlated with 4- and 5-year-olds' performances on assessments of hot and cool cognition (Carlson & Wang, 2007). It also was related to parents' ratings of their children's abilities to control their impulses (e.g., "Does the child think before he or she acts?") and regulate their emotions (e.g., "After receiving a disappointing gift from someone, how likely is your child to pretend to like the gift?").

Additional evidence of the central role of vocabulary came from a study that followed children from age 15 months to 60 months, the point when most were beginning formal schooling (Kuhn, Willoughby, Vernon-Feagans, & Blair 2016). Vocabulary predicted improving executive function throughout this time span. It is interesting to note that the rate of growth between 15 months and 36 months was an especially strong predictor because this is the period when children are beginning to display symbolic ability and make rapid progress in language learning (see Chapter 3). The complexity of language among older children, measured in terms of the length of sentences they used, began to be an important predictor. This shift reflects that growing ability to use language for more complex cognitive tasks, a topic discussed in Chapter 4.

Associations between language and self-regulation have also been found among bilingual children, and the relationship is bidirectional. Researchers followed a mixed-income group of monolingual and bilingual children from the beginning of preschool at age 4 through the end of kindergarten (Bohlmann, Maier, & Palacios, 2015). Self-regulation was tested in the child's dominant language. In an analysis of children's English receptive vocabulary, the researchers found that language scores predicted later self-regulation and, in turn, self-regulation supported later language growth. This finding echoes the finding discussed early among primary grade children.

Clear lines of association can be drawn among parenting practices, language, and development of executive function abilities. Longitudinal studies have followed children during the toddler and preschool years to assess the effects of parenting on language and self-regulation. Researchers in one study visited homes when children were 15, 24, and 36 months old (Matte-Gagne & Bernier, 2011). They observed as mothers helped children play with toys and complete tasks they supplied. They found that mothers of 15-month-old children who used language as they helped children complete tasks had children with stronger language development at age 24 months. Children who performed best on self-regulation tasks a year later at 3 years old were more likely to have had good vocabulary scores a year earlier. Vocabulary at age 2 mediated the effects of early parenting on later development of executive function ability. Other studies that used similar methods also found that enhanced language mediates the effects of parenting, measured at age 2, on later self-regulation (Bernier, Carlson, Deschenes, & Matte-Gagne, 2012; Hammond, Muller, Carpendale, Bibok, & Liebermann-Finestone, 2012).

One final study merits discussion because it examined naturally occurring events in the home, unlike other studies discussed. Also, its sample was drawn from families with a diversity of backgrounds in low-income households. Landry and colleagues observed 70 minutes of routine interactions between mothers when children in the home were 3 and 4 years old (Landry, Miller-Loncar, Smith, & Swank, 2002). They coded for occasions when mothers supplied verbal scaffolding. These were times when they supplied conceptual links among objects, people, or activities (e.g., "Where is the shirt that goes with those shorts?" "That's a giraffe." "You saw one at the zoo." "Hit the nail. It's the one that's round on top"). The researchers tested children's language when they were age 4 using the Clinical Evaluation of Language Fundamentals–Preschool (CELF-P;) and their problem-solving and memory skills using an intelligence test; they assessed executive function ability at age 6. When they were 4 years old, children whose mothers supplied more verbal scaffolding had stronger language and nonverbal skills (i.e., problem solving, memory). At age 6, those who performed well on the self-regulation task were more likely to have done well on the nonverbal task. Also, language ability at age 4 had an indirect effect on later executive function skills. Finally, those with strong language at age 4 also did better on the nonverbal tasks, and enhanced nonverbal ability helped boost later executive function ability.

SUMMARY: ATTACHMENT, EXECUTIVE FUNCTION, AND EARLY DEVELOPMENT

This chapter charted the development of children's emotional attachments to their caregivers and their emerging capacity to regulate their thoughts and actions using their growing executive function abilities. Parents play a central role by providing the emotional support and responsiveness needed to form secure relationships, by scaffolding children's attention to objects and engagement in activities, and with verbal enrichment that builds children's language abilities. There are profound long-term consequences of this early development on later emotional, social, cognitive, linguistic, and academic abilities. The consistent and strong message that early patterns of caregiver–child interactions can play a significant role in shaping later development is particularly important. The place of language in these interactions is of pivotal importance. Simply put, children benefit enormously when their parents are responsive and sensitive and engage with them using informative language as they guide, direct, and respond to the children. In the short term, such exchanges lead to improved parent–child attachment bonds and stronger language. These enhanced abilities set in motion a cascade of later benefits because early abilities lead to later strengths that then fuel later growth. Early language and executive functioning are related to children's developing ability to understand the thoughts and feelings of others—their theory of mind (see Chapter 4). Language will again be encountered as a potent force that fuels development as this fascinating aspect of development is explored.

2

The Brain and the Developing Child

The previous chapter reviewed evidence demonstrating the lasting impact of early experiences on children's later social-emotional functioning. Understanding how specific experiences affect later development is important to parents, care providers, and policy makers. That knowledge sheds light on the kind of experiences that are vital and those that may have lasting negative consequences. Even deeper insight into the effects of early experience is beginning to emerge from neuroscience research. (See Nelson & Bloom [1997] for a clear discussion of methods used to study brain functioning.) Thanks to the efforts of scientists from around the world, researchers are learning a great deal about the structure, functioning, and development of the brain. Given that our focus is on how caregivers and teachers affect children's development, we focus on research that examines 1) the effects of experience on how a child's brain processes those experiences and 2) how early experiences can shape future behavior. But we need to briefly describe the architecture of the brain and some basic information about how the brain functions. We then discuss neural development, emphasizing the remarkable possibilities for learning that nature makes available during the first years of a child's life. Finally, we discuss research that focuses on self-regulation and attachment. Later, as we discuss language (Chapter 3) and the effects of negative experiences and the benefits of interventions (Chapter 5), we briefly consider those topics from the perspective of neuroscience.

BRAIN BASICS: NEURAL STRUCTURE AND FUNCTIONING

Before delving into the complexities of how the brain develops in young children, and the relationship between language development and early neural development, it is necessary to establish a basic understanding of the brain's major structures and functions. An overview of these topics is provided next.

Structure

The brain has multiple subdivisions and three major areas—the cerebrum, which is divided into two hemispheres; the cerebellum; and the brainstem (see Figure 2.1). The cerebrum is where most of the brain activity related to self-regulation, attachment, language, and academic achievement occurs. The large frontal lobe is particularly well developed in humans and is used for planning, problem solving, governing emotions, logic, and mathematics (Tsujimoto, 2008). For most people, the left temporal lobe is used for language and memory. The parietal lobe is associated with vision and movement, and, in combination with the language areas, it plays an important role in reading and connects visual input with language.

Deep within the cerebrum is the limbic system, sometimes called the *emotional brain*. It is an evolutionarily old system that is well developed in mammals and also found in reptiles. The limbic system includes the thalamus, hypothalamus, amygdala, and hippocampus, which are important for regulating emotions and storing and retrieving memory (Blair, 2002). The regions of the limbic system are connected to the frontal cortex, which governs planning, and also to the language areas in the temporal lobe (Nolte, 2002).

This quick review of distinct regions of the brain greatly simplifies the activities occurring within each region and the ways that capaci-

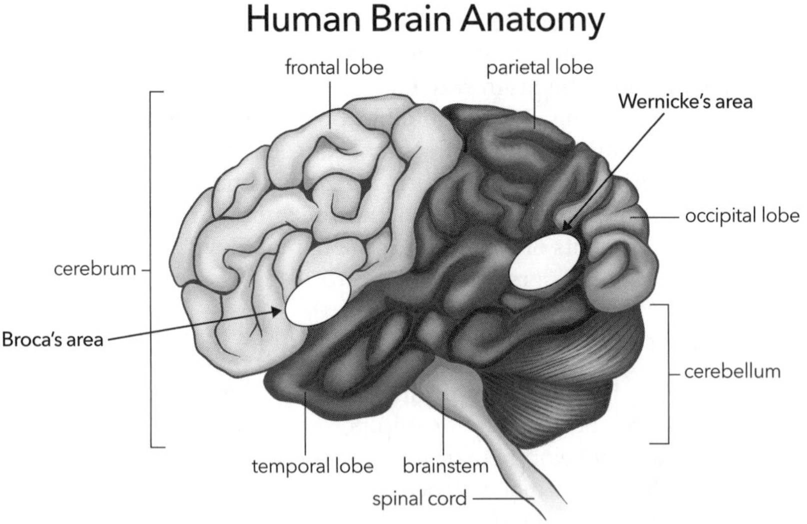

Human Brain Anatomy

Figure 2.1. The major areas of the brain (cerebrum, cerebellum, and brainstem); the four lobes (frontal, parietal, temporal, and occipital); and their correspondence to language areas. (Adapted from "The human brain–Illustration" © iStockphoto/[blueringmedia].)

ties such as the ability to understand and use language draw on complex connections with regions of the brain beyond the temporal lobe. For example, a meta-analysis of 120 neuroimaging studies examined the semantic system, which is the processing system that helps people understand the meaning of words. This meta-analysis found involvement of seven different regions of the brain (Binder, Desai, Graves, & Conant, 2009). In particular, linkage with the visual area in the parietal lobe is critical for reading. Thus, although different regions are critical for processing specific kinds of information, their interconnections are vital because they enable people to integrate different sources of information.

Functions

The brain is able to carry out an incredible number of complex tasks because of the massive number of interconnections among its roughly 100 billion neurons, or cells. Each prefrontal cortex neuron can have up to 100,000 of these points of interconnection, known as *synapses* (Huttenlocher, 2002), which are described next. Each neuron collects information through one of its many dendrites, which are small branching structures like the roots of a plant, and transmits this information to other neurons through a larger part of the cell called an *axon*. Information is transmitted from the external world to the brain, and from one region of the brain to another, when one neuron connects with others at synapses. Synapses are locations where the activation of one neuron's axon leads to the release of a neurotransmitter, which is a type of chemical. The neurotransmitter then makes contact with the dendrite of another neuron, where the neurotransmitter may increase or decrease the target neuron's readiness to fire. At the same time, the newly activated neuron may receive excitatory and inhibitory input from many of its other dendrites, so the impulse it receives may not be simply conveyed to another neuron. Rather, the receiving neuron may incorporate input from multiple sources before firing and activating other neurons (Huttenlocher, 2002).

The connections among neurons develop over time, with patterns of activation becoming increasingly predictable and rapid as they are repeatedly used. Thus, experience helps shape the flow of information by fostering the interconnectivity among neurons as networks of neurons become increasingly specialized in responding to specific types of input (Johnson, 2011). Over time, these tightly linked networks become associated with more distant networks as the brain gains the capacity to process increasingly more varied and complex forms of input (Hoff, Van den Heuvel, Benders, Kersbergen, & De Vries, 2013; Johnson, 2011).

BRAIN DEVELOPMENT

In the first years of life, the brain rapidly grows in size, and the density of connections among neurons explodes as these neurons develop countless additional dendrites (Fox, Levitt, & Nelson, 2010). The size and complexity of dendrites also dramatically increases, vastly enhancing opportunities to form synaptic connections among neurons. Many of these rapidly developing dendrites come in contact with others and form synaptic junctions as neural impulses are passed from axons to dendrites. Repeated activation of synaptic connections ensures the maintenance of those synapses. However, billions of synapses are not activated and they wither away because there are so many dendrites (Huttenlocher, 2002). This dying off of dendrites with the resulting loss of synapses is called *pruning* and is associated with increased efficiency as the synapses that are retained are being used.

Another important structural change that occurs in the early years is development of the myelin sheath, which is a protective layer of insulation over neurons that are carrying electrical impulses. A fatty protective sheath is formed around the axons that carry information from one neuron to the next. Myelin sheaths act as insulators, like electrical cables that are insulated, and they enable more efficient transmission of electrical impulses from the neuron's body to synaptic junctions. Thus, the myelin sheath enhances the conductivity of neurons, speeding transmission of impulses, and it may contribute to behavior changes such as the rapid improvement in language abilities (Pujol et al., 2006) that occurs somewhere between 18 and 24 months of age. Although development of neural structures is most rapid in the early years of life, important changes continue into early adolescence, including changes in the thickness of the different regions of the cortex and development of increasingly prominent folds in the tissue of the brain (Tsujimoto, 2008).

Sensitive Periods of Development

The density of synapses associated with different systems peaks at different times, with vision preceding areas associated with language. Figure 2.2 shows the pattern of development and pruning of three areas associated with language—Heschl's gyrus, which processes auditory input; Wernicke's area, which is important for linking meaning to sounds; and Broca's area, which is central to planning and producing sounds. All three areas reach their maximum synapse density at age 3, the time when children's grammatical structures are becoming more sophisticated, their word learning is quickly progressing, and they are

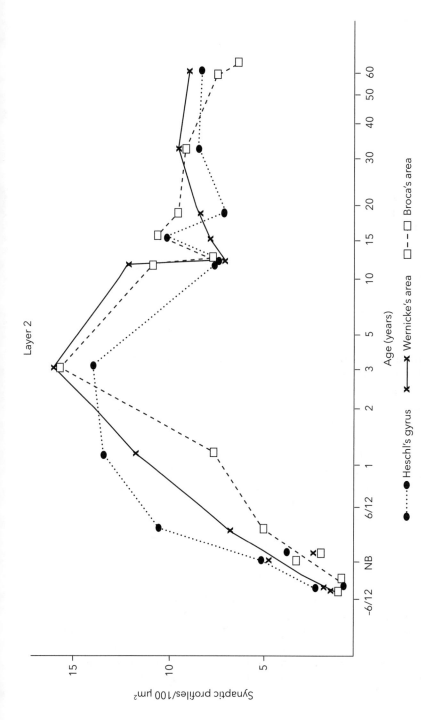

Layer 2

Synaptic profiles/100 µm²

Age (years)

● ⋯⋯ ● Heschl's gyrus   ✕ —— ✕ Wernicke's area   □ – – □ Broca's area

Figure 2.2. Synaptic density in three areas associated with language—Heschl's gyrus, Wernicke's area, and Broca's area. These areas reach maximum density around age 3. (From NEURAL PLASTICITY: THE EFFECTS OF ENVIRONMENT ON THE DEVELOPMENT OF THE CEREBRAL CORTEX, by Peter R. Huttenlocher, Cambridge, Mass.: Harvard University Press, Copyright © 2002 by the President and Fellows of Harvard College.)

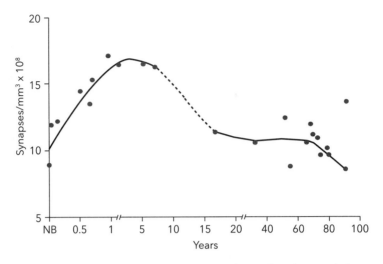

Figure 2.3. The increase and decline in synaptic density of the prefrontal cortex, which is associated with planning, problem solving, emotion regulation, and logic. Peak density occurs around ages 4–5. (From NEURAL PLASTICITY: THE EFFECTS OF ENVIRONMENT ON THE DEVELOPMENT OF THE CEREBRAL CORTEX, by Peter R. Huttenlocher, Cambridge, Mass.: Harvard University Press, Copyright © 2002 by the President and Fellows of Harvard College.)

beginning to speak in a more fluent and understandable manner. In all of these areas of the brain, there is a slow decline in the density of synapses through the elementary school years, followed by a leveling off in early adolescence.

After language areas peak in synaptic density, they are followed by the frontal cortex, which develops over a much more prolonged period. The proliferation of synapses followed by pruning is illustrated in Figure 2.3, which shows the increase and decline in the density of synapses in the prefrontal cortex, which is the area most associated with planning, problem solving, emotion regulation, and high-level activities such as logic (Huttenlocher, 2002). The period of peak density occurs around ages 4–5 years, the time when most children in the United States enter formal schools.

The previous section described the process of myelination, which occurs early in life and speeds the transmission of electric impulses from neurons to synaptic junctions. Myelination occurs rapidly in the language area between the ages of 5 and 18 months and has been suggested as a physiological change that helps govern the pace of early language development (Pujol et al., 2006). Myelination continues to occur in regions relevant to language until at least early adolescence, another indication of the slow rate at which brains develop.

The Role of Early Experiences

An age-old question is whether human development is governed more by genetic factors (nature) or by experiences (nurture). It is increasingly apparent that development involves a complex dance in which people's genetic endowment plays a key role in laying the foundation, but experiences shape how the brain functions and how it is structured. As the fetus develops and in the earliest weeks of life, much of the brain's development is governed by genetically determined sequences that provide a blueprint for the construction of the mature brain (Fox et al., 2010). Even though genes lay the foundation for development, experience plays a key role in sculpting the developing brain from the beginning (Quartz, 1999; Quartz & Sejnowski, 1997). The brain is optimally responsive to the effects of experience during the early weeks, months, and years of life when rapid development is occurring because patterns of activation of neurons help shape the network of connections that are being established (Fox et al., 2010; Haartsen, Jones, & Johnson, 2016; Huttenlocher, 2002). In particular, children's early experiences with language and social interaction are important influences on brain development.

Language

The emergence of language has been studied in detail and the results of these investigations provide an ideal way to see the interplay between genetic and environmental factors in children's development—an interplay that enables language to develop in similar ways in all children while also incorporating the subtle distinctions that are found across languages and cultures. Humans come into the world primed to be social animals, with language being a powerful tool, honed through evolution, that is used for social purposes.

Even as the fetus develops in its mother's womb, it is beginning to process linguistic input by using specific regions of the brain that have been adapted to handle the type of information language systems employ (e.g., fine-grained and fast discrimination among similar sounds). Hearing becomes active in the second half of gestation. At that time, the fetus's developing speech recognition systems begin processing speech as it is filtered through the uterine wall. This input provides newborns with a start on language acquisition at birth. One study examined electrical activation patterns in newborns as they listened to language. The study found that the newborns responded differently to variations in pitch, intensity, and duration found in the language they had heard in utero but did not respond the same way to these variations in other languages (Abboub, Nazzi, & Gervain, 2016). Their responses are associated with development of areas of the brain specifically tuned to processing language. Findings report that shortly after birth the left temporal lobe, the area most strongly associated with language among adults, displays stronger responses to speech than the right lobe (Friederici, 2006). Adults continue to process words and grammatical features in left temporal areas, whereas the right temporal lobe processes prosody, which are the pitch contours of speech that are critical to understanding sentences. That same part of the right temporal lobe has been found to be specially responsive to such prosodic input among infants as young as 3 months old (Friederici, 2006).

This early sensitivity to language helps explain newborns' responses to different sounds. They tend to show a preference for their mother's voice (Decasper & Fifer, 1980) and respond more positively when hearing passages that were read to them during the third trimester than when listening to passages they had not previously heard (Decasper & Spence, 1986). They also respond differently to the language they have been hearing in utero than to an unfamiliar one (May, Byers-Heinlein, Gervain, & Werker, 2011). Later in the first year of life, infants are sensitive to the contours of language, including its rhythm, pitch, and stress and the frequency with which sounds occur, and they use these subtle cues to segment the speech stream into words (Johnson & Jusczyk, 2001; Jusczyk, Houston, & Newsome, 1999). Anyone who has listened to a foreign language should be impressed by this because it can be very hard to know when one word ends and the next begins.

People are clearly biologically prepared to attend to and make sense of the sounds of language. As people are exposed to these sounds, networks of neurons begin responding in predictable patterns that reflect consistencies in the input they are receiving. Thus, experience tunes the function of neuronal networks, and using these networks that are primed for language may even affect the development of the brain itself. Remarkable evidence of this impact of experience on neural development comes from a study of the effects of experience on development of the auditory cortex (Webb, Heller, Benson, & Lahav, 2015). Infants born prematurely often have hearing loss that is attributed to being thrust into a relatively noisy world at a point when the auditory system is still rapidly developing. In this study, half of a group of infants born extremely prematurely (at 25–32 weeks) were randomly placed into two groups. For roughly 3 hours a day, the intervention group heard audio recordings of maternal sounds produced to mimic the intrauterine sound environment of the mother's voice and heartbeat. Others heard the routine noises of the hospital environment.

After around 23 days of exposure, the infants who heard maternal sounds were found to have a significantly thicker auditory cortex, a measure that reflects more robust development. The authors theorized that the auditory climate surrounding the developing fetus and new-born helps to shape neural development in ways that may affect later language development.

Other Social Stimuli   Infants enter the world programmed for social interaction. Recognizing and interpreting faces is vitally impor-tant. Faces signal emotions and intentions; distinguishing among faces enables infants to distinguish between their caregivers and others. Infants are attracted to faces and begin life with a tendency to tune into them. Studies of infants' developing ability to recognize faces reveal that although they are genetically primed to attend to faces, facial rec-ognition skill develops with experience. Some evidence indicates they can recognize familiar faces by 1 month (Nelson, 2001), but the founda-tion for that ability is laid much earlier. In one study, infants who were 1–5 days old were shown videos of women who moved their eyes and mouths and videos of mechanical objects that moved. Their brain activ-ity was detected using functional near-infrared spectroscopy. This is a noninvasive method of monitoring blood flow in the front part of the brain that measures changes in near-infrared light. The study revealed that the social videos led to increased activity in the area of the brain associated with face recognition (Farroni et al., 2013). The strength of activation increased with age, suggesting that the area became increas-ingly sensitized to social input between 1 and 5 days after birth. Even though they were only days old, the older infants showed stronger responses to the social stimuli, suggesting they were already becom-ing specially attuned to faces.

Young infants quickly notice whether their caregiver is looking at them. For instance, in one study, 4-month-old infants were shown videos in which a person either looked directly at them or slightly to one side. Only when the person looked directly at them was there increased activity in the areas of the brain activated by social activity (Grossmann et al., 2008).

Infants clearly enter the world with sensory systems attuned to human voices and faces, which is the most powerful means by which social information is communicated to infants. Their early social expe-riences activate chains of neurons that become increasingly efficient at recognizing previously experienced sounds and sights. The brain's ability to adapt to experiences and stimuli is an important aspect of brain development discussed in the next section.

Neural Plasticity

An impressive feature of the human brain is that it continues to change in response to experiences. This capacity to adapt to change is called *plasticity* (Huttenlocher, 2002; Nelson & Bloom, 1997). Plasticity is evident in the way the brain adapts to experiences with language and reading and other kinds of sensory stimuli. Studies of the hippocampus, the area of the brain that establishes memories, have furthered researchers' understanding of neural plasticity.

Reading and Language   Studies of reading development clearly reveal the impact of experience on brain functioning. Huttenlocher (2002) noted that language, like other neural functions, may initially be represented relatively diffusely within the brain. As language is repeatedly used for specific tasks, such as reading, this function becomes restricted to particular language areas. This hypothesis has been supported by neuroimaging studies showing that beginning readers draw on widely distributed neural systems when processing print, but this language function becomes increasingly localized and efficient with use (Pugh, Sandak, Frost, Moore, & Mencl, 2006). When children learn to read, regions of the brain that process words, syntax, and visual input are activated and, with practice, usually develop highly efficient pathways of communicating. With time and practice, patterns of activation shift as children progress from the effortful sounding out of words to fluent silent reading. Studies of children with reading disabilities illuminate the importance of the ability to create efficient pathways because children with serious reading problems are less likely to display patterns of brain activity that reflect consolidation of processing skill than skilled readers. They are slower to create highly efficient associations between the neural areas that process visual input and the areas that govern pronunciation of words (Pugh et al., 2006).

Sensory Systems   Studies of brain development of humans who are deaf, hard of hearing, or blind have found remarkable evidence of the resilience of the brain. Although specific areas of the brain are genetically programmed to be responsive to particular kinds of sensory input, the brain can make remarkable adaptations if the intended stimulation is not received. This adaptability testifies to the brain's malleability, particularly early in life. An example is children who are born with sensory hearing loss and receive cochlear implants, which are devices that transmit speech sounds by directly transmitting electrical impulses to the auditory system. The input provided is different from natural speech in several respects, but children who receive cochlear implants at very early ages make more rapid progress in learning language than those who receive the implants at later ages (Tomblin, Barker, Spencer, Zhang, & Gantz, 2005). This finding reflects the greater neural plasticity that is present at early ages. The early differences in auditory processing that are associated with age of implantation diminish over time, however, and these differences are not statistically significant by later elementary school (Dunn et al., 2014). This demonstrates the brain's continuing capacity to respond in new ways when it receives novel input. The sample used was small, however; a study with a larger sample might find statistically significant differences because means on language scores for the children who received cochlear implants later in life were relatively lower.

Another example of how the genetic blueprint interacts with environmental stimulation comes from studies of the development of babbling among children who are hearing and children who are deaf or hard of hearing. All children begin to babble, but children who are deaf or hard of hearing begin to do so significantly later, and their babbling has different sound properties than children who are hearing (Eilers & Oller, 1994). Thus, babbling is a biologically driven development, but environmental input plays a role in its onset and characteristics. Further indication of the interplay between environmental input and genetically based processes is the finding that children who are deaf or hard of hearing and are exposed to signing begin to babble in sign language (Petitto & Marentette, 1991).

A final example of the interplay between the genetic blueprint and environmentally guided development comes from research on children who are born blind. The visual areas of the brain that typically process visual input have been found to become responsive to auditory and tactile input. Studies of animals also have found that auditory and visual stimuli are necessary for development of neural connections used to receive and interpret sensory input (Fox et al., 2010).

Memory and the Hippocampus Studies of adult animals have found plasticity in the hippocampus, which is the area of the brain associated with establishing memories. The hippocampus is involved in recall of events, general knowledge, and spatial learning. It has connections to other brain regions involved in recording and storing fear-inducing events (McEwen, 2000). The function of the hippocampus and related brain regions is influenced by hormones that are responsive to stress; these hormones are released when people are excited or frightened or experience other forms of stress. As the brain readies the body for physical activity, such as running or fighting, it also activates networks of neurons in areas of the brain associated with memory and executive function. When traumatic events happen, they activate responses in the hypothalamic-pituitary-adrenal axis, which, in turn, releases hormones that can affect regions of the brain associated with attention, emotional arousal, memory, and executive function.

Repeated and sustained exposure to stressful events, such as those associated with living in poverty or being subject to neglect or abuse, also activates these connections. Such exposure is associated with shrinkage of the hippocampus (reviewed in McEwen, 2000) and an increase in reactivity. *Reactivity* in this context refers to the propensity to experience an elevated level of emotion and attention in response to a life event (reviewed in Blair, 2002; Blair, 2010). Research examining the hippocampus of animals found reductions in the length and branching of dendrites after 21 days of exposure to adrenal steroids, but these effects can be reversed by stopping exposure to the adrenal steroid and providing drugs that counter the negative effects (McEwen, 2000). Living in poverty and rearing children while experiencing the stresses that often accompany such a lifestyle have adverse effects that can be traced to patterns of neural functioning set in motion by the natural way of responding to stress (see Chapter 5). The good news that is of central importance to this book comes from a review of research by Clancy Blair (2010). He reported evidence of the benefits of interventions designed to counteract early adverse experiences. These effects may not result in reversal of damage to brain structures, but there is evidence of resilience in how the brain functions. Blair concluded, "A functional reversal of the effects of early stress in which environmental enrichment leads to compensatory neurobiological changes, perhaps associated with changes in frontal cortex, which alter the behavioral and cognitive consequences of high reactivity" (p. 185).

SUMMARY: BRAIN DEVELOPMENT IN EARLY CHILDHOOD AND BEYOND

The human brain is a marvel of nature. It enables people to experience and integrate a bewildering assortment of sounds, feelings, sights, and experiences. It ensures similarity among all humans with genetically determined early establishment of basic brain structures and organization—a blueprint for the brain. Yet, its responsiveness to environmental input enables people to become distinct individuals with separate cultures, languages, and personal competencies. Early experiences play an especially powerful role in shaping the course of later development, but the brain continues to be shaped by experience.

3

Joining the Community of Language Users

In 5 short years, children develop from helpless but endearing creatures into willful, creative, and curious individuals. Infants respond to immediate sights, sounds, and feelings; gain understanding of the world through their senses as they interact with objects and people; and communicate with sounds and actions but without conscious intent. They inhabit a world limited by their own experiences in the moment. In contrast, 5-year-olds can move beyond the immediate sensory world as they communicate and learn using the symbolic representational systems of their culture—the language, music, dance, and rituals of their society. These systems enable children to acquire the knowledge, customs, and beliefs accumulated by their culture over generations.

In this chapter, we provide a broad view of early development. We start by putting it into an evolutionary context as we argue that the capacities of particular interest to humans—symbolic representations and language—are simultaneously a product of, and a contributor to, the evolution of the species. We discuss research on different types of symbolic development. We examine research to see how children are able to join their linguistic community as we consider how infants and adults establish shared attention to objects and experiences. We discuss children's development of a theory of mind—that is, awareness that other people have perceptions, feelings, and thoughts that are different from their own. We see that this capacity has important implications for children's social competence. We conclude by turning to vignettes of mother–child interactions to illustrate how parents support their child's development of multiple competencies in the course of simple, everyday interactions.

THE EVOLUTIONARY ROOTS OF LANGUAGE

Humans have long wondered about their origins. Who were their ancient ancestors? In what ways are humans like or different from them? What makes humans different from animals? The effort to trace the roots of *homo sapiens* continues, but it is safe to say the process of the species' evolution has spanned at least 3.5 to 4 million years. Anthropologists now believe that evolution occurs within niches that include physical features such as the climate, nutrients, and the geographic location where a species lives (Christiansen & Kirby, 2003; Fuentes, 2015; Pinker, 2010; Whiten & Erdal, 2012). The niche for humans includes the culture constructed and sustained through language and other symbolic systems.

Humans evolved in niches, but the fact that they exist in social groups that create cultures (i.e., sharing patterns of action, speaking, believing) is unique to the species. Many anthropologists believe that aspects of humans' physical evolution, such as increases in the size of the cerebral cortex, changes in the vocal tract (Fitch, 2005), and the evolution of language, have partly occurred as a result of participation in cultural niches (Christiansen & Kirby, 2003). The capacity to use language has evolved along with the species. Over many centuries, physiological capabilities that are critical to language have evolved in ways that are finely tuned to its characteristics. The articulatory system enables humans to rapidly produce a huge variety of sounds, and the auditory system enables humans to notice very subtle distinctions among the sounds they can produce. The human brain has areas that are especially efficient in processing language and linking linguistic input to other stored information. Of particular importance is the fact that language is extremely well suited to communicating symbolic information.

Thus, a host of physical changes have made it possible for humans to represent their feelings and thoughts in symbolic forms, including language, and to use language to communicate. These symbolic capacities have helped humans organize themselves into cultural groups (Fuentes, 2015). The relatively recent emergence of the capacity to use symbols such as pictures and words to communicate feelings, wishes, and thoughts has greatly accelerated cultural evolution over the past 50,000 years (Nelson, 1996). Through spoken, pictorial, and inscribed symbols, humans have been able to communicate, store and pass on information across the generations.

SYMBOLIC REPRESENTATION

Symbols are defined as sounds, actions, or objects created by people that are intended by their creator to stand for or represent something else—an object, action, thought, emotion, or belief. Language is a powerful system for communicating a vast array of symbolic meanings.

Think about the word *hot* to understand what it means for a word to function symbolically. It is produced by combining a specific sequence of sounds: /h/ /ŏ/ /t/. A child might first hear *hot* used as a warning as he is about to touch a pan on the stove, thereby linking a specific situation, emotional state, and physical sensation to the word. That type of learning need not carry symbolic meaning; it could simply trigger those associations and function in roughly the same way as an alarm call produced and responded to by a startled flock of crows. *Hot* can be used in other contexts, however, in which the meaning is detached from the direct experience. A parent could later talk about the importance of not touching a hot pan, and *hot* could be used to refer to light bulbs, hair dryers, and the sun on a bright day. The child will gradually come to abstract a core set of meanings from those varied uses, and the word will begin to function as a symbol detached from a specific event or object. With time, *hot,* like any word, can even function metaphorically. For example, when a child is hunting for a hidden object, an adult could give the clue, "You are getting hot" to indicate she is close to the object. Such extensions of the meanings of words are a central design feature of language (Lakoff, 2003) and are the result of tacit agreements among groups who speak the same language.

The evolution of language and humans' use of it to convey symbolic meanings helps explain why *homo sapiens* are so distinct from other higher primates, even though humans share 99% of their DNA with them (Nelson, 1996). Studies of primates and other animals find they have many remarkable abilities to understand and recall experiences and some rudimentary ability to use tools (Fuentes, 2015; Tomasello & Farrar, 1986). Only humans create and use complex symbolic systems as they enact, teach, and reflect on their culture's norms, beliefs, rules, accumulated knowledge, and shared history (Geertz, 1973; Turner, 1967). It is amazing that between birth and the age when children begin formal schooling, they acquire the power to use language to communicate and understand information, beliefs, and advice.

As children acquire symbolic systems, they begin to serve as potent intellectual tools (Wertsch, 1991). Symbols enable one to capture and hold fleeting thoughts, feelings, and experiences by transforming them into symbolic representations that can be recalled, shared, and recorded. A surge of energy associated with seeing a favorite toy can come to be known as *excitement;* the magical combination of movement and music can be called *dance;* and the mysterious transformation of ice into water can be called *melting.* By symbolically representing experiences, objects, feelings, and ideas, people gain the opportunity to hold onto them and thus understand them by linking them to similar experiences, objects, feelings, and ideas. People also can learn what others in their society think, feel, and believe about something they have seen or experienced.

Many profound aspects of culture are communicated by using symbolic means (Geertz, 1973; Goffman, 1971). For example, religious beliefs are represented by images and enacted through rituals (e.g., prayer, weddings, worship services). Patterns of displaying respect are enacted through the forms of address used, the extent to which people express their opinions directly (Brown & Levinson, 1987), and the formality of the language used. Language is the most potent means that people use to represent the world symbolically.

Language enables children to join their culture as they come to share its ways of interacting, thinking, and knowing. It empowers children to expand their understanding of the world exponentially by talking with and learning from others. Language also supplies children with a tool for understanding and controlling their own feelings and thoughts. For example, as children learn the word *excitement* to describe a fleeting emotion experienced in a particular situation, and they learn the same word applies to other such occasions, they can use the word *excitement* to help them become aware of the similarity in their feelings across different situations. By labeling that feeling, children can better recognize it when it occurs. They also can become more competent at managing their own behavior when they are excited. (Notice how this skill relates to both social-emotional development and executive functioning.) Adults support this learning as they tell children they are excited, inform them of the culture's expectations for how one should behave when excited, and give them strategies for dealing with situations that make them feel excited.

Also, as children hear others talk about being excited and observe expressions of excitement, they can begin to recognize that others have similar feelings and can begin to build an awareness that other people have minds and emotional states distinct from their own. This insight is referred to as the acquisition of a *theory of mind*, discussed further in the second half of this chapter. Before a child can learn language or begin to construct a theory of mind, however, he needs to join others in attending to and thinking about the same thing. This capacity for joint attention is critical for a child to develop in order to join the social world.

THE ROLE OF JOINT ATTENTION IN SOCIAL INTERACTION

One widely accepted view of how infants learn language is that it emerges as a result of a convergence of capacities that enable infants to learn from others (Tomasello, 1999, 2000, 2016). Children learn by noting what other people are doing, and they are particularly attentive to people's intentions—what they are attempting to do. They also learn by collaborating with others on shared tasks, and they learn what others intentionally teach them. Woven through these modes of learning is children's desire to join the group and learn to act in ways that align with their culture (Tomasello, 1999, 2000, 2016). Children learn by being part of interactions with others and observing what others are doing; intentional instruction accounts for only a small portion of the teaching done by parents, caregivers, siblings, and others.

Learning from others draws on the capacity to attend to the same things as another and engage in joint attention to the same thing. The vague term *same thing* is used intentionally because infants and toddlers and their caregivers initially engage in joint attention to physically present objects, such as toys, pets, and books, and to ongoing activities. Joint attention to concrete things sets the stage for far more complex sharing of attention to things that are not physically present— memories, plans, and ideas. A 14-month-old might engage in play with his brother using toy farm animals, whereas those same toys might launch a 3-year-old and her older sibling into recollections of a visit to a zoo or farm. In that case, they are attending to a thing that exists only in their minds.

Before we turn to the research on this foundational and somewhat complex process, consider Perla's interactions with Rosalita that were described in Chapter 1, as well as the vignette discussed in the same chapter and shown in Video 1: Tanya's interaction with her toddler Eliza. Perla was entirely in control of constructing an occasion when she and Rosalita could attend to the same toy. She gave Rosalita the toy she had selected because its sounds and appearance were likely to be interesting. Perla positioned the toy so Rosalita could see it and held her infant's attention by moving the object gently and speaking softly. Rosalita responded to what was presented to her, but the event was created and controlled by her mother, who accompanied the moments of shared focus with language that helped her infant stay engaged. There was no indication that Rosalita was aware that her mother was looking at the same toy that she was studying.

Tanya and Eliza engage in a far more complex interactional dance in their book reading. Eliza, who is 18 months old, is a partner in creating and maintaining shared attention. First, there is the setting and the book. Eliza sits in a location where she and her mother can attend to the book. Tanya hands her the book, and Eliza makes a sound indicating pleasure and opens it. These simple acts have created an occasion that enables them to attend to pictures and words—symbolic representations. They both look at the book, and Eliza points to the cover, saying,

"Eh." In that moment, she moves beyond simply attending to the same general object as her mother and directs her mother to attend to a specific element within it. Tanya obliges and this leads to four back-and-forth exchanges during which they are intently focused on pictures and print as Tanya imbues them with symbolic meanings. The writing is something called a *title* and the pictures reference things in the world—a child (niño) and eggs.

Tanya:	The title . . .
Eliza [as she points to the cover]:	Eh!
Tanya:	Yeah, it's a niño. [Tanya is bilingual and is using Spanish and English with Eliza.]
Tanya:	. . . *Eggs Eggs.* It's the title.
Eliza:	Eigh! [She points, still focusing on the book.]
Tanya [as she looks at Eliza]:	Eggs!
Eliza [carefully, as she points to a picture]:	Whey dah?
Tanya:	Is that a flower? Yeah, look at him. He looks like he's looking for eggs. Eggs.
Eliza [as she points to a picture]:	Bah.
Tanya:	Um hmm. It does look like a ball, doesn't it? [She looks at Eliza and pauses.] It's an egg though.
Eliza:	Bah! [She points again.]
Tanya:	Um hmm. [She turns to the first page and looks at Eliza as she asks a question.] Shall we start?
Tanya [reading the text]:	Hooray, it's Easter, a day of fun. There are eggs to find for everyone. Let's grab our baskets, ready-set-go! Search here, search there, search high up, low . . .
	[As Tanya reads, Eliza reaches for a flap on a page and opens it. Mom continues reading as Eliza opens another flap.]

| Tanya: | Look it. There's niño [points] . . . and they are looking for eggs. [She points to pictures as Eliza watches.] |

[Eliza opens a flap and vocalizes.]

| Tanya [pointing]: | Remember you and Helly looked for eggs on Easter and put them in your basket [looks at Eliza with slight pause] on Easter? [long pause] |

| Eliza [sitting very still and focusing on the picture as her mother speaks, then opening a flap]: | Ba- ba- . . . |

| Tanya: | Basket. But are there any eggs? Look it. [She points.] . . . No eggs! Okay! Shall we turn the page? [She pauses.] Wanna turn the page? [She pauses and looks at Eliza.] |

[Eliza reaches for a page to turn.]

| Tanya: | Good girl! |

At this age, Eliza certainly does not know what a title is and may not fully understand the connection between the image of eggs and actual eggs, but her mother is laying the foundations for those insights. Near the end of their exchange, Tanya attempts to create a remarkable new type of joint attention when she says, "Remember you and Helly looked for eggs on Easter and put them in your basket . . . on Easter?" Here we see Tanya seeking to draw Eliza's attention to a past event, evoked through symbolic means, using only words and memories associated with eggs. Eliza may not have made the mental leap from looking at pictures with her mother to recalling something that happened several days ago, but it is remarkable that language makes that shift possible.

Think how vastly different this interaction is from what might occur in an interaction with a favorite lap cat. You and your cat might have a shared routine in which she waits until you sit in the perfect chair and provide an inviting place to sit on your lap. She will arrange herself, and you both can experience pleasurable moments of connection as you pet and she purrs. In these moments, you are connected through physical contact, but you will attend to the same external event only if your cat happens to become alert to a sound or sight, in which case you might look in the same direction. You might comment on what you are seeing, "Oh, look at that squirrel!" Your words might convey some emotional state, but those words will never carry symbolic meaning. Your cat cannot attend to something you comment on or point to and will never intentionally draw your attention to something.

ENTERING THE SOCIAL WORLD

Infants come into the world prepared to be social and connect with their parents, caregivers, and siblings. At birth, infants exist in their own world of sensations and needs. They slowly begin to interact with others. By the end of their second year, they have become social beings—they coordinate their actions and feelings with others, they come to understand the feelings and thoughts of others, and they learn from others. In this section, we explore how children gradually enter the social world during the first and second year of life and how this socialization process relates to language development.

Attention and Social Development in Infants' First Year

This long process of social development begins in the first months of life. By the time they are 3 months old, infants stay engaged in periods of mutual gaze with their caregivers (Adamson & Bakeman, 1991). Caregivers and infants begin to coordinate their attention and actions with each other as they connect in this manner. During these intervals of shared attention, sensitive caregivers, such as Perla, provide interesting things for children to attend. These intervals are brief because sensitive caregivers modulate the level of stimulation to avoid overwhelming the baby. Through these episodes, infants and caregivers synchronize their actions and emotions. One expression of this developing mutuality is when infants imitate others' facial expressions (Meltzoff, 2007). Remarkably, infants who are deeply engaged with someone who makes an interesting expression can mimic it. They are taking a first tentative step toward being able to experience the world as others do. This very early form of imitation puts infants on the path toward being able to learn from others.

Responding to Joint Attention   By about 6 months of age, infants develop another type of joint attention. They become less interested in simple direct engagement with their caregivers; rather, they begin to join others in attending to interesting objects and events in the world. Whereas they previously interacted with another person or gazed at interesting objects, they now begin to coordinate their own attention to objects and people with others' attention to these environmental stimuli (Adamson & Bakeman, 1991). They use the gaze of another person as an indication that there may be something interesting for them to look at. This type of joint attention is referred to as *responding* to joint attention and is present by the time infants are 6 months old (Mundy et al., 2007; Mundy, Sullivan, & Mastergeorge, 2009). This awareness is of great importance. As the infant and his caregiver attend to the same thing, they are seeing and responding to the same object. They are developing a history of shared actions, feelings, and images. This responding to joint attention is called *outside-in* attention because it is driven by the efforts of adults and by other outside stimuli that capture the child's attention. Infants also make strides in learning to imitate others as they copy how another person uses an object. This capacity is the next step toward acquiring the ability to learn from others.

Initiating Joint Attention   At about 9 months, infants reach another milestone. They begin to initiate episodes of coordinated attention. Infants initiate joint attention by looking at objects and vocalizing, pointing, and gesturing. These initiations reflect the infant's beginning ability to draw others into her sphere of activity. These efforts to initiate joint attention can be classified in two categories—protodeclaratives and protoimperatives. Protodeclaratives occur when an infant calls attention to an object or event of interest. Protoimperatives occur when an infant enlists others in achieving her goals. Protodeclaratives are especially powerful because they engage others in enjoying something that interests the child and are accompanied by positive emotions. This is less often the case for protoimperatives (Henderson, Yoder, Yale, & McDuffie, 2002), which are used to control others. When an infant engages another person using a protodeclarative, she creates a teachable moment. At the very moment the infant is interested in something, the adult or sibling can provide information about it. That person might name it, show how it moves, or make some comment about its appearance. The infant is primed to take in such information because she initiated the interaction. The payoff from such encounters comes as children begin using language. Those who initiate joint attention more often and use protodeclaratives display faster growth in early language learning (reviewed in Henderson et al., 2002; Mundy et al., 2009).

What Neuroimaging Reveals About Joint Attention in Infancy
Studies of patterns of electrical activity in infants' brains showed the differences between the ways that infants coordinate attention with others. Responses to joint attention, which emerge around 6 months of age,

are accompanied by increased activity in the posterior, or rear, areas of the brain that are associated with areas that regulate the development of reflexive orienting to biologically meaningful stimuli (reviewed in Mundy et al., 2007). In contrast, the frontal areas of the brain are activated during the initiations of joint attention that emerge around 9 months of age (Henderson et al., 2002; Mundy et al., 2009). Episodes of joint attention associated with frontal lobe activation occur as infants and toddlers use protodeclaratives to comment on the world, drawing others' attention to things that interest them. The activated areas are related to emotion regulation, and the frontal lobe is associated with higher cognitive activity that includes planning future actions.

Attention and Social Development in Children's Second Year

Children have repeated shared experiences as they engage in countless occasions when they and others attend to the same thing; the things they see and the emotional responses they have are like other people. These experiences contribute to infants' realization that others are "like me" (Meltzoff, 2007). Evidence that children understand others by drawing on shared experiences comes from studies that examine times when children do and do not follow the eye gaze of others. By age 12 months, infants are skilled at looking at the same things as others. Do they realize that what their own eyes are seeing is the same information being registered by the other person's eyes? Do they see their own visual experience as being like that of their play partner?

Beginning at about age 12 months, the answer is "yes." Researchers found although infants could follow another's head movements, they did not follow head movements that typically accompanied shifts in eye gazing if the other person's eyes were closed (Meltzoff, 2007). Even stronger evidence that toddlers are using their own experiences to understand others comes from a more complex blindfold activity conducted with 18-month-olds. Some toddlers were given a typical blindfold to wear, and others were given a trick one that they could actually see through. Those who had worn the trick blindfold and saw someone wearing it tracked his head movements; those who had worn the standard blindfolds did not (Meltzoff, 2007). They could use their own experience wearing the trick blindfold to determine that someone else wearing the same blindfold could actually see ("like me") and that the person's head movements were therefore worth following, despite the fact that the person appeared to be blindfolded.

Awareness that others are "like me" seems to include awareness of shared emotions and motivations. Indeed, infants have been seen as mind readers (Tomasello, 2000). Infants realize that human actions result from an intention to do something, and there are plans and goals. Human actions, unlike those of a ball or a balloon, occur because someone wants to accomplish something. By the age of 10 months, infants realize that people have plans, and infants seek to understand why people are doing things—to interpret their intentions (Tomasello, Carpenter, Call, Behne, & Moll, 2005). During the second year of life, children gain skill in understanding and predicting others' actions using knowledge of their likely intentions (Tomasello, 2000, 2016; Tomasello et al., 2005), which enables them to join with others in increasingly complex shared efforts to accomplish the same goal. Such an interaction is aptly illustrated in Tanya and Eliza's book reading. Eliza took the book from her mother, seated herself, opened the book, and initiated the activity. She clearly understood that her mother intended to join her in a pleasant book-reading interaction.

During play with peers or adults, having a shared goal allows a toddler to move beyond simply taking turns rolling a ball or putting blocks on top of each other. The toddler and a play partner can begin to work together to accomplish a shared goal. For example, when building a block tower, the adult and child might take turns, and the adult might hold the building steady while the toddler places blocks. By engaging in such a dance of shared goals and actions, toddlers are being drawn into their culture as they acquire its patterns of goals, actions, and emotions.

Toddlers have made remarkable progress toward learning to understand and collaborate with others by the time they are a year and a half old:

- They can attend to the same events and objects as others and engage others in attending to things in which they are interested.

- They interpret the actions of others as reflecting motivations and revealing feelings that are like those that they themselves experience.

- They are able to collaborate with others as they seek to achieve a shared goal.

The array of developments tied to children's growing ability to join their social world is dramatic. Even more remarkable is the complex interweaving of other powerful strands of development during this period—language, self-regulation, and the capacity for symbolic representation discussed earlier in this chapter.

Joint Attention, Language, and Self-Regulation   The ability to establish joint attention has important implications for language learning. Let's return to the example of the word *hot,* adding the insights acquired by considering a child's capacity to understand others' intentions. As a toddler is about to touch a hot object, he might hear his mother say, "Hot!" with alarm. He would experience the unpleasant burning sensation in that moment. Hearing his mother say "Hot!" with alarm would trigger memories of previous occasions when his mother expressed fear in that tone of voice. Also, he would understand that his mother's motivation was to warn him about the imminent danger. Recalling these experiences and relating them to himself will help him associate *hot* with a particular kind of situation. Whereas *hot* uttered in the tone used to label things (e.g., "Doggie!") might lead the child to think the word referred to the object he touched, the tone of voice signaling his mother's motivation and fear would lead him to associate the word with the physical sensation and associated emotions instead.

Skill in this kind of mind reading seems to contribute to children's early language development. One longitudinal study found infants who were adept at following the gaze of an experimenter and sustaining attention at 10 and 11 months of age displayed more advanced vocabulary at age 2 years. During the first year, those who gestured when responding and sustained shared attention learned more than twice as many words as those who were low in gesturing and sustaining attention (Brooks & Meltzoff, 2008). Similarly, a longitudinal study followed 50 children from different socioeconomic backgrounds from age 14 months to 54 months (Rowe, 2012). At 54 months, children from more advantaged backgrounds had stronger receptive vocabularies. Toddlers whose parents used more gestures and conveyed different meanings used more gestures themselves. The use of gestures helped to predict the size of a child's later receptive vocabulary development. There may well be a self-reinforcing cycle at work. Parents who are tuned into their infants engage them in cycles of joint attention using gestures, pointing, and eye gaze. Their infants gain skill engaging in episodes of joint regard and experience pleasure from those cycles of engagement. They then learn that they can draw their caregivers and siblings into such interactions through gesturing, which gives them opportunities to learn language as they learn about the world.

Some evidence also suggests that joint attention may be related to early development of self-regulation. This association makes sense if one recalls that efforts to initiate joint attention draw on planning ability, which involves activation of the frontal lobe of the brain. Self-regulation also draws on those same neural circuits as it requires one to make an effort to refrain from doing something or an effortful plan to stay focused on a task. One study assessed how quickly 12-month-olds responded to an adult's effort to engage them in jointly attending to an object. At 36 months, these children were given tests of self-regulation that required them to wait for a snack (Van Hecke et al., 2012). Those who were quick to respond to the attention requests at 12 months were better able to wait for the snack at 36 months. The relationship between self-regulation and early attention regulation has been found to extend to school entry among children who attended Early Head Start. Children whose mothers reported their child more often gestured or used other motions to communicate at 14 months were more likely to perform well on school entry assessments (Martoccio, Brophy-Herb, & Onaga, 2014).

This remarkable set of accomplishments associated with the maturing of children's joint attention ability also contributes to children's symbolic development and their ability to understand how others perceive the world. We discuss those topics later in this chapter. First, we briefly discuss research on autism spectrum disorder (ASD) because it helps make apparent the complexity and importance of early developments related to coming to view the world through the eyes of other people.

Autism Spectrum Disorder and Joint Attention   The profound importance of the early developments previously described has become evident as researchers studied the early origins of ASD. ASD is a complex condition that includes impairment in a person's capacity for social engagement. Children with ASD experience difficulty coming to understand the world through the eyes of others.

The challenges these children experience start early in life. Studies of the early origins of this disorder have found distinctly different early patterns of engagement. Infants who are later diagnosed as being on the autism spectrum are slow to initiate episodes of joint attention (reviewed in Mundy et al., 2009). They can respond when encouraged to attend to something but are less likely to encourage others to attend to something that is of interest to them. Children with ASD try to draw attention to something they want; they request objects or actions with sounds or actions; and they issue imperatives, essentially saying, "Give me that!" What they are much less likely to do is to simply call attention to something that they find interesting—to name it or ask another person to share their interest in it (Harbison, McDaniel, & Yoder, 2017). That is, they use protoimperatives far more often than protodeclaratives. Protodeclaratives create opportunities for infants and adults to attend to the same thing, creating opportunities for infants to learn from others. Protoimperatives are less likely to create such occasions (Harbison et al., 2017).

Brain researchers interested in ASD propose that the normal course of development of joint attention involves integration of neural processing in the posterior regions with processing that occurs in the frontal regions (Mundy et al., 2009). Activity in the posterior regions may reflect the infant's representation of the world as she experiences it. Activity in the frontal lobe may be associated with recognition of other people's experiences, motivations, and plans. In the latter part of their first year, children who are developing normally begin to coordinate these (i.e., they map their own experiences and feelings onto others). They come to see others through their experiences. Unfortunately, infants who are at risk of developing ASD may be less successful in developing these associations. The posterior and anterior regions of the brain may not communicate efficiently, and the shift toward entering fully into the social world may be delayed.

A broad array of developments is associated with the capacity for joint attention. Being aware of this array helps one understand how deficiencies in development of this capacity, associated with ASD, result in such far-reaching effects on overall development.

A CLOSER LOOK AT SYMBOLIC DEVELOPMENT

We previously discussed how infants begin to develop the ability to communicate using symbolic systems—specifically, language. They come to associate hearing a certain word (e.g., *hot*) with certain sensations, objects, or experiences (e.g., the feeling experienced when touching something very warm, heated objects such as a frying pan or the sidewalk on a summer day, being outside in the sun). We return to this topic as we introduce another transformative development that occurs during the second year of life—the capacity for symbolic representation. This capacity draws on children's growing ability to join others in attending to the world and collaborate to accomplish shared goals. As toddlers learn to play with others and understand the world through the eyes of their culture, they learn the symbolic forms their group uses to represent those objects, actions, and experiences. Whereas infants understand others by mentally mirroring their actions and feelings, 2-year-olds begin acquiring the ability to accomplish this mind-melding using symbolic representations.

Using Symbolic Representations: Pictures and Models

Symbolic ability is evident in children's penchant for interpreting pictures as symbolic representations of objects. This is present by the time they are 2 years old (Preissler, 2004). An example of how this insight has been determined comes from a study in which an experimenter showed a child a picture of a whisk. This kitchen tool was new to the child. The experimenter pointed to the picture and called it a *whisk*.

Later, the child was shown the same picture and an actual whisk and was asked to point to the whisk. On average, children selected the object and not the picture. Experiments completed with children from three different cultures indicate this development is universal. Children in remote areas of India and Peru, as well as children in Canada, were shown pictures that communicated information about where objects were hidden (Callaghan, Rochat, & Corbit, 2012). Children across all cultures successfully completed the tasks, but those in Canada did so at a somewhat earlier age. The concentrated exposure to symbols available in Western urban societies may speed the ability to interpret pictures but is not necessary for it to occur.

Another game-like task has been used to assess symbolic understanding. A child is shown a toy, such as a teddy bear, that can be hidden in different places in a room. She is also shown a model that is an exact duplicate of the room where the toy will be hidden. The experimenter then uses the model to show the child where the toy is hidden within the room and then asks him or her to find it in the actual room. If a child grasps the notion that the model represents the room, then she can use the information to find the bear. Children who are able to use the information this way are deemed to be capable of using a symbolic representation (the model) to understand the world. By age 3, children are typically successful with this task (DeLoache, 2004). If the experimenter explicitly notes that she is using the model to help the children find the toy, then children are successful even earlier (Sharon, 2005). This finding reflects the power of the child's ability to recognize the experimenter's intention. The child learned what was being taught because she understood that the adult intended the child to see the model as representing the room and showing where the bear is hidden.

Using Symbolic Representations: Early Writing

Symbolic development during the early preschool years also is manifest in children's emerging ability to use marks as symbolic forms to convey meaning. Two- and three-year-old children use marks that represent something. They may not realize, however, that others cannot assign the same meaning to their markings. They slowly improve in their awareness of the need to create representations that others can understand. By age 4, a child can change pictures to help her audience know what is being represented (reviewed in DeLoache, 2004). This awareness of the power of marks to convey information, combined with the realization that only particular kinds of marks can be understood by others, is centrally important in the emergence of writing. When children come to realize that marks can convey meaning and want to communicate information with their marks, they are moti-vated to learn conventional ways to use inscriptions to communicate.

Careful analysis of the writing behaviors of children from around the world has revealed universal sequences of acquisition of writing ability (reviewed in Harste, Woodward, & Burke, 1984; Levin, Both-De Vries, Aram, & Bus, 2005; Rowe & Wilson, 2015). A fundamental starting point is the intention to communicate words and ideas using marks, as opposed to simply enjoying the activity of making interest-ing marks or seeking to create an appealing visual display. One must then master the many conventions governing how one forms letters and places marks on paper—alignment, spacing, verticality, and size (Rowe & Wilson, 2015). At the same time, children must isolate distinct sounds from the speech stream and associate them with one or more letters. This is an enormously challenging step that draws on phonological awareness, a capacity discussed in the next chapter. Yet, as any student knows, after all these critical basic skills have been mastered, there is the challenge of organizing one's thoughts and putting them on paper in an organized and rhetorically compelling format. That final phase of development draws on advanced language competencies that continue to be acquired throughout one's life. Although these competencies are acquired over decades, the foundations are laid in the first years of life. A mother and her infant playing with and talking about toys and a father reading and rereading a favorite book with his toddler are moments that lay the foundation to enable the child to acquire language competencies needed to navigate her social, academic, and workplace worlds.

THEORY OF MIND

The capacity for mind reading builds on 1) the ability to engage in joint attention and 2) the ability to understand the physical world using rep-resentations created in the mind. These developments contribute to another remarkable conceptual advance. During the preschool years, children become aware that other people have thoughts, feelings, and motivations that are distinct from their own; that is, they develop a theory of mind.

Observing Theory of Mind Talk During Book Reading

Consider this conversation between Janna and her 4-year-old daughter, Vera, who are reading the book, *A Hat for Minerva Louise* (Stoeke, 1994). (Their encounter is depicted in Video 2, available with the download-able materials for this book atwww.brookespublishing.com/downloads with [case sensitive] keycode 34ckDaD1k) An adventurous chicken wants to explore the barnyard after a snowfall. She goes out exploring but is underdressed so she looks for things to wear—boots, a scarf, and a hat. She happens on objects that look somewhat like what she needs (e.g., she uses a hose as a scarf) and ends up wearing a very odd assortment of items. During the mother and daughter's reading of this story, the following exchanges occurred. Before the chicken heads outside, Janna has the following conversation with Vera:

Vera: I like staying outside. I want to go out all day long and even night.

Janna: You want to play outside in the snow all day and all night? Well, what do you need to do that? Can you just go out with your pajamas on?

Vera: No.

Janna: No? What do you need?

Vera: A coat and some boots and gloves.

Janna: Mmm-hmm. Gloves, yup. What about for the top of your head?

Vera: A hat.

Janna: That's what Minerva Louise says. "If I had some warm things like you [Janna quotes Minerva Louise speaking to a well-dressed snowman], I could go out and play. I could stay out and play." Now she's going to go out and look for some of those things.

[Janna then reads book text written from the point of view of Minerva Louise: "A scarf might help, but not this one. It's way too big." She pauses.] What does Minerva Louise think?

Vera: That water hoses are scarves.

Janna: That's pretty silly, isn't it? Is that a scarf?

Vera: No.

Janna: It's a water hose!

An illustration in the book shows four hats hanging up high where Minerva Louise does not see them as she continues looking for a hat. Janna has Vera count the hats, and then mother and child have this exchange.

Janna: Four hats. And does she see them?

Vera: No!

Janna: No! She just keeps going—there she goes.

One can see that there is more complexity to this seemingly simple book than is initially apparent. On one level, the child needs to understand that the animal depicted is not like real chickens because she has motivations and feelings like a child. She wants to go outside and explore the snowy world, and she can get cold so she needs clothing. But the humor lies in the fact that the child realizes that the chicken fails to understand that various objects that have some resemblance to clothing really are not intended to be used as such.

To find this book to be amusing, Vera needs to understand things from the chicken's perspective: She wants to be warm, and she see objects as being things that they are not (a hose is not a scarf). Janna sets Vera up to understand the book by reminding her of her own experiences going outside in the winter. She creates an understanding in Vera that Minerva Louise is "like me" with respect to enjoying cold, snowy days. Also, Vera must realize that the world as the chicken views it is not aligned with the real world. The humor comes from recognizing this mismatch—Minerva's understanding of the world and the child's understanding of how things actually are in the real world. Grasping the story from these multiple perspectives requires two critical insights: 1) others have feelings and perceptions that are like ours (i.e., wear clothes on cold days to keep warm), and 2) others may perceive things differently than we do (i.e., they have different feelings, thoughts, and motivations).

Examining a parent–child interaction during book reading helps people understand how a 4-year-old has developed a theory of mind. Researchers used various clever methods to determine what children understand about the perceptions and knowledge of others as they studied the development of this awareness.

Research Studies of the Development of Theory of Mind

Researchers explore children's construction of a theory of mind in varied ways. One kind of task that has been used tests children's ability to distinguish between appearance and reality. In one classic task, a child is shown a box of cookies and finds it actually contains pencils. This child is then asked what another child, who has not looked inside the box, will think the box contains. Younger preschoolers say "pencils;" older ones who have a better understanding of belief say "cookies" (see Flavell [2004] for a review of similar work).

Another task that is often used seeks to determine if children realize another person holds a belief that is false. The notion is that one must realize that people understand the world differently in order to understand that someone else has ideas that are false.

One such common task involves allowing a child to see an object being moved from one hiding place to another while someone else taking part in the study does not see this occur. For example, a child and his mother are shown a cookie being hidden under a cup. The mother leaves the room for a moment, and the researcher moves the cookie to another hiding place as the child watches. When the mother returns, the child is asked where she will look for the cookie. To answer correctly, the child must realize that the mother does not know about the changed location of the cookie; thus, correctly predicting that the mother will look under the cup is an indication that the child realizes what his mother knows is different from what the child knows. Increasingly complex methods are used with older children (see Slaughter, Imuta, Peterson, & Henry [2015] for a review). The ability to pass such false-belief tasks improves between the ages of 3 and 4 (Wiesmann, Friederici, Singer, & Steinbeis, 2017). Judging by her enjoyment of *A Hat for Minerva Louise* (Stoeke, 1994), it is safe to speculate that 4-year-old Vera would pass the hidden cookie false-belief task.

Social Competence and Theory of Mind   Think about your friends and people you admired when you were in elementary school. Try to recall whether they were people you would refer to as being considerate of others, sensitive, responsive, and friendly. This exercise might lead you to a conclusion that is aligned with many studies—awareness of others' thoughts and feelings is beneficial to one's ability to relate well to others. For example, a young child is building a tower with a friend in the blocks area. The friend bumps into the tower, and it crashes down. Was that an accident or on purpose? Recognizing the difference—which requires awareness of the friend's thoughts and feelings—has important consequences. The response of the child whose building was demolished might also be affected by the child's executive function skills. A child with a strong capacity to refrain from responding impulsively might be able to resolve the matter without conflict. Furthermore, having strong language skills might make the child more capable of engaging in a conversation about the event. These are the complicated interdependencies that psychologists seeking to understand development try to unravel.

An exploration of the complex interrelationships among emerging and interconnected strands of development was conducted by Rachel Razza and Clancy Blair (2009). They selected 68 children from low-income homes who attended Head Start and followed them as preschoolers and in kindergarten. The researchers were interested in how theory of mind and executive function might relate to each other and how the two might affect social competence development, taking into account executive function and language ability. In both preschool and kindergarten, children were given four different false-belief tests, tests of executive function, and a receptive vocabulary test. The researchers also asked preschool and kindergarten teachers to rate children for characteristics such as their ability to control themselves, their ability to understand others, and their confidence in social situations.

Razza and Blair (2009) found that the size of children's vocabularies in preschool related to kindergarten theory of mind and social competence. They removed the effects of language using statistical means. Executive function and theory of mind in preschool were related to higher ratings of social competence in kindergarten. In addition, children with stronger social competence ratings in preschool also performed better on theory of mind tasks in kindergarten. This finding of bidirectional effects, flowing in two directions, suggests these abilities are mutually reinforcing. Children with early awareness of others are more socially competent, and more socially skilled children are likely to increase their awareness of others. Similar results were found in a study of 212 preschool-age children in Turkey (Korucu, Selcuk, & Harma, 2017). Social competence was related to self-regulation and theory of mind, but theory of mind helped account for those ratings even after taking self-regulation into account.

The effects of theory of mind on social competence continue to be important into elementary school. A meta-analysis of 20 studies and more than 2,096 children from preschool through age 10 supports this assertion (Slaughter et al., 2015). On average, children between preschool and age 10 who perform better on tasks that assess theory of mind tend to be more popular. They are likely to be viewed as someone children want to be friends with and someone who is liked by others. This association is three times stronger among girls than boys, possibly because girls tend to value interpersonal intimacy more and athletic ability factors heavily in boys' social standing. Indeed, the association between theory of mind and popularity is not statistically significant for boys.

Language Ability, Executive Function, and Theory of Mind   In Chapter 1, we discussed the emergence of executive function and highlighted the role of language in its emergence. Language and executive function also play a pivotal role in the development of theory of mind. In this section, we briefly discuss studies that illustrate these relationships. Although executive function and language are both linked to development of a child's theory of mind, language plays a central role.

In one study, 82 children's executive function and theory of mind competencies were assessed at ages 2, 3, and 4 (Muller, Liebermann-Finestone, Carpendale, Hammond, & Bibok, 2012). Children's language

abilities were also tracked. Researchers found executive function predicted later theory of mind abilities through the preschool years. The
finding of most interest to our exploration of the role of language was
that a child's theory of mind abilities measured at age 2 supported
growth in language measured at age 3. The enhanced language competence, in turn, supported executive function skills at age 4. These
strands of development are interwoven, with effects flowing in multiple directions.

Theory of Mind and Parent-Child Conversations   Although
overall language growth plays an important role in theory of mind
development, the ability to label emotional states has a particular benefit. This insight is in line with research that knowledge of words that
refer to mental and emotional states is related to awareness of one's
own thoughts and feelings and those of others. When one talks about
remembering, knowing, and thinking, one is talking about things
that occur in the mind. When using words such as *angry, happy,* and
disappointed, one is talking about feeling states—aspects of one's own
internal state that are not visible to others. Conversations that use such
terms, called *mental state verbs,* draw attention to the internal states,
which may help children refine their awareness of the distinct internal
realities of other people.

Studies of the effects of language on children's knowledge of mental state found that the seeds of this relationship may be planted at
an early age. Researchers with an interest in attachment and theory of
mind assessed the mind-mindedness of mothers (Meins et al., 2002).
Infant–mother pairs were observed as the mothers played with their
6-month-old infants. They determined how often mothers made reference to their infants' mental and emotional states. The researchers
also noted if the mothers seemed to correctly reflect the child's mental
state. At 12 months, mother–child attachment was evaluated using the
strange situation (see Chapter 1). When children were 45 and 48 months
old, they were given theory of mind assessments. Researchers found
that children's performance was related to the mother–infant talk that
referenced their infants' emotional states when they were observed at
age 6 months. This association between mother–child interaction at 6
months and children's later theory of mind suggests that early patterns
of mother–child conversations are indicators of a mother's skill in tun-
ing into her child and her inclination to verbalize for the child what the
child might be thinking or feeling.

We can be more confident about the results of one study when
similar findings are reported by another research team. A study that
followed children from age 15 months to 33 months tracked mothers'

use of words referring to desires, thoughts, and knowledge (Taumo-epeau & Ruffman, 2008). More maternal use of mental state words at one time point predicted children's performance on tasks measuring understanding of emotions at the next time point. Another longitudinal study also found effects of mother–child talk about mental states and children's emerging understanding of others' perspectives. Mothers and children were observed talking about pictures on three occasions when children were between 3 and 4 years old (Ruffman, Slade, & Crowe, 2002). At the end of the study, children's theory of mind was related to their use of mental state words and the frequency of mothers' talk about mental and emotional states. This study found that the both mothers' and children's use of mental state words matters. Its results are consistent with other work examining mother–child reminiscences about the past (Fivush, Habermas, Waters, & Zaman, 2011). A similar finding came from a study in which researchers asked parents of 2- and 3-year-olds to identify words relating to state-of-mind words that their child knew. Children who heard more words at age 2 performed better on theory of mind tasks at age 3 (Carlson, Mandell, & Williams, 2004).

Syntactic Development and Theory of Mind   An interesting feature of mental state words is that they are almost always used in sentences that have a syntactic form called a *complement*. The initial clause such as, "She thinks," "He wants," or "I believe" is followed by a second clause that makes explicit what is wanted, felt, or believed. As children learn words that name mental and emotional states, the syntactic forms in which those words are used encourage the children to attend to those states. Support for that notion has been found in studies of children between 3 and 5 years old that find an association between linguistic skill and performance on theory of mind tasks (Lohmann & Tomasello, 2003). Evidence supporting this hypothesis came from a study by de Villiers and Pyers (2002), who followed 28 children ages 3–5. They tested children's performance on a set of theory of mind tasks. They examined children's understanding of language that included words referring to mental states (e.g., *think, know*) and their ability to explain beliefs in responses to prompts such as this:

> "He thought he found his ring, but [second picture] it was really a bottle cap. What did he think? [Pointing back at first picture.]"

To answer completely a child would need to use a complement clause such as, "He thought that it was a bottle cap." De Villiers and Pyers (2002) also tracked children's spontaneous language use for evidence that they could use advanced syntactic forms. Children's language abilities were generally more advanced than their performance on false-belief tasks, lending support to the hypothesis that emerging syntactic skills contribute to children's ability to understand alternative perspectives.

A final piece of evidence showing the impact of language on theory of mind comes from a study of children who were deaf or hard of hearing. Some children who are deaf are born to hearing parents and others are born to parents who are deaf. Parents who are deaf typically are fluent users of sign language, which is as complex and sophisticated a language as spoken language. In contrast, if parents of children who are deaf do not know sign language, they cannot provide their children with equally rich language. A study of children born deaf whose parents were also deaf found they performed the same as hearing children of the same age on tests of theory of mind (Schick, de Villiers, de Villiers, & Hoffmeister, 2007). Those whose parents were hearing performed more poorly, even if their parents had learned to use sign language. These findings suggest that early and continued exposure to the type of sophisticated syntax that includes talk about mental and emotional states supports skill in understanding these states.

Book Reading and Theory of Mind   Book reading is rich with opportunities to talk about mental states, which can be seen between Janna and Vera in Video 2. The story and pictures in *A Hat for Minerva Louise* (Stoeke, 1994) showed the chicken wearing silly objects and supplied opportunities to talk about Minerva Louise's false beliefs. Many books include starting points for engaging in such talk. An examination of 90 books written for 3- to 5-year-olds found they were rich with mental state words. Mental state words were found about every three sentences in books for each age group (Dyer, Shatz, & Wellman, 2000). Magalit Ziv and her colleagues (Ziv, Smadja, & Aram, 2013) asked mothers to enjoy books with their children in one of three ways: 1) reading the books, 2) telling the child the story from a book after they had read it to themselves, and 3) telling a story using a picture book without words. All three types of interactions resulted in considerable talk about thoughts and feelings. More than 20% of all the parent–child talk was of that type. Of particular interest to those who work with parents who may struggle with their own reading was the finding that both forms of telling the story resulted in significant amounts of rich talk. However, it is important to note that in this study, the subjects were well-educated and skilled in engaging in such conversations.

There is evidence that rich talk about thoughts and feelings while reading supports children's developing understanding of others' minds. Juan Adrian and colleagues asked parents of 34 4-year-olds to report how often they read with their child and observed them reading to their children (Adrian, Clemente, Villanueva, & Rieffe, 2005). Reports of how often they read and use mental state words when reading helped predict children's performance on theory of mind tasks. These are correlational data—exposure to presumably beneficial talk about books relates to improved theory of mind. There could be many reasons for this association, however. Parents who read more and use such talk while reading may talk with children at many other times of the day, and they may play a lot of games. If a researcher posits that a certain factor might cause children to develop some capacity more quickly, then conducting an experiment is a stronger way to test the association. That has been done with book reading.

The effects of book reading on children's understanding of mental states and ability to talk about thoughts, feelings, and emotions have been tested using experiments. Over a 4-week period, 4-year-olds heard six books read by teachers in large classroom groups, by a graduate assistant in a small group, and at home. All together, they heard books read about 70 times (Peskin & Astington, 2004). For all of the books, readers were told not to talk about the characters' thoughts and feelings.

Half of the group heard books in which the text made explicit references to mental states:

> Did you know that Fox would bump into a rake? Rosie heard the loud bump, but did she figure out that it was hungry Fox behind her? No, she didn't turn around. She doesn't know that he's behind her. Watch out, Rosie!

The other half heard no explicit talk about mental states:

> Fox is not careful and bumps into a rake. Rosie hears the loud bump, but does she turn around? No, she keeps her eyes right on the road. She doesn't look left and she doesn't look right. Watch out, Rosie.

These books all had pictures that graphically displayed the situations and clued children into the humorous events being described.

The results were somewhat of a surprise. As expected, after this intense period of hearing books being repeatedly read, children in both experimental conditions displayed equal growth in their ability to understand mental states and predict if a character would hold a false belief about a situation. Those who heard books that included mental state terms used more such language in follow-up tests but did not demonstrate better comprehension of the words. They apparently learned how such words are used but did not fully grasp their meaning. The biggest surprise was that the control group made even more growth than the experimental group in their ability to explain why a character might have a false belief. The authors speculated that the books heard by the control group, which did not include explicit reference to mental states, may have required children to more actively engage in figuring out why characters were doing things. Alternatively, it is possible that parents adhered less closely to the experimental design in conversations that occurred in the home. Books without embedded explanations could have encouraged more talk about the reasons for characters' behaviors. In any case, this study provides evidence that books that are carefully chosen to highlight events that involve mental states can support growth in children's understanding. It also suggests that giving children many occasions to think about why characters are doing things and how they are feeling may enable them to develop their theory of mind knowledge in the absence of adult guidance.

A second study that sought to test the effects of book reading used a design in which children from low-income homes heard books in one-to-one reading sessions in which the interactions that occurred were carefully controlled (Tompkins, 2015). At three different time points—prior to the experiment, 1 week after the experiment concluded, and 2 months afterward—teachers rated children's social competence, and children were given a battery of assessments of theory of mind and understanding of emotions. The children who participated were divided into three conditions. In the experimental group, each child was read three to five books a week for 5 weeks. During these one-to-one readings, the experimenter engaged the child in conversations about characters' feelings and their false beliefs. Meanwhile, in the first control condition, children heard the same books but without benefit of these conversations. In a second control group, children did not participate in any one-to-one readings.

In all three conditions, when children were assessed on the delayed posttest 2 months after the experiment concluded, their performance on tasks assessing their understanding of false beliefs had improved from the pretest. Immediately after the readings, children who simply heard the books without discussion performed better than those who heard no books, but 2 months later, those two groups performed the same. Children who engaged in talk about the books displayed more understanding, however, than the other two groups at the immediate posttest 1 week after the experiment concluded. Remarkably, 2 months later those children who had talked about the books were even slightly better at this than they had been at the conclusion of the experiment. There was no statistically significant effect on children's understanding of emotions or teachers' ratings of social skills. This finding suggests children who repeatedly engage in conversations about mental states may acquire the ability to better reflect on situations and understand beliefs held by others. Learning to use and understand words that refer to mental states seems to follow a different pathway that requires more time and possibly different kinds of experiences.

SUMMARY: LANGUAGE, BOOK READING, AND SOCIAL DEVELOPMENT

Between birth and school entry, humans make an extraordinary journey. They begin as helpless infants, living in their own world of immediate sensations and actions. With the benefit of genetically provided abilities and extensive parental support, they gain the ability to join their social group. They come to understand events and objects through the eyes of people living in their culture, and they gain the ability to represent the world symbolically and use symbolic systems for understanding and communicating. Language is the centerpiece of a culture's symbolic world and helps children draw on their realization of commonalities between themselves and others as they construct a theory of mind and an understanding of how their culture refers to mental events and feelings. These developments are intertwined and also draw on the executive functioning competencies discussed in the last chapter. Strong evidence shows that parent–child conversations play an important role in fostering development of this intertwined set of abilities. Furthermore, it is clear that books and book reading provide a means to expose children to the kind of language, conversations, and thinking that foster their developing understanding of others. Conversations, whether they occur during diapering, eating, or reading books, are powerful levers that parents, child care staff, and teachers employ to foster the growth of multiple interwoven aspects of development.

4

Language Systems and Development

Language is the quintessential symbolic capacity employed by humans which emerges remarkably quickly, drawing on perceptual, cognitive, and motoric capacities, and is nourished by humans' social nature. Children become members of their community and culture by acquiring language competencies. Chapter 1 discussed how the quality of language-enriched interactions contributes to the development of attachment relations. It also explored the role of language in children's emerging ability to regulate their feelings, actions, and thoughts. Chapter 2 examined language in the context of brain development and neural plasticity in early childhood. Chapter 3 explored the origins of children's social engagement with others and how language contributes to children's ability to understand the world through the minds of others. This chapter focuses specifically on different systems of language and the emergence of language in children.

In this chapter, we will consider language from a structural linguistic perspective as we discuss the different systems of language and related abilities that young children develop. We consider children's ability to produce sounds and order words using appropriate syntax and their acquisition of vocabulary. We also consider children's emerging ability to use language for varied purposes, including telling narratives and understanding stories. As we discuss each aspect of language ability, we describe the competence and briefly discuss major developments that occur between age 1 and 5. As we discuss universal features of the varied strands of language ability, we also will touch on individual variation among children, with particular attention to effects of differential home language environments.

THE MAJOR SYSTEMS OF LANGUAGE

Language has multiple systems that are woven together to produce a powerful and complex tool for communication. The discrete elements of language that are used (e.g., phonology, syntax, vocabulary, prag-matics) are consolidated and refined into fluent systems as humans use language to communicate (Lieven, 2016; MacWhinney, 2004; Tomasello, 2003). This approach is consistent with the usage-based view of neural development advanced in Chapter 2. Competencies emerge through use as networks of neurons are repeatedly activated in the service of different goal-directed activities. For example, knowledge of individual words and how they are used in phrases that children repeatedly hear is basic to development of syntactic knowledge (Lieven, 2016; Toma-sello, 2003). When we discuss early literacy development, we draw on this perspective, which views development as the result of activating related competencies that eventually function as distinct systems.

Before children learn to read and write, they acquire oral lan-guage, learning to communicate through speaking and listening. To understand oral language development, which is intimately linked with later literacy, we examine the competencies children must acquire in four major areas—phonology, words and morphemes, syntax, and pragmatics. Orthography, the graphic symbols used to represent lan-guage when people write, is a fifth system. Because our emphasis is on oral language, we do not discuss this fifth system in detail. That decision does not indicate that we view lightly the task of learning the orthography of one's language or how to associate spoken with written symbols. It simply lies beyond the scope of this book.

Impediments to Development

Children ideally master the complex array of linguistic skills required to communicate, read, and write at appropriate points in their devel-opment. Unfortunately, many children face obstacles. Some delays in development are caused by environmental factors, such as limited exposure to varied vocabulary. Other problems are more closely linked to biological factors. In some cases, language problems are a by-product of other developmental abnormalities (e.g., autism spectrum disorder, Down syndrome), whereas others are specific to the language sys-tem. Problems rooted in the language system range from those that are relatively mild and transient, such as an articulatory problem such as speaking with a lisp, to more severe problems, such as omitting words, failing to mark tenses correctly, and struggling to comprehend discourse. The long-term consequences of early language-related dis-orders are often associated with later academic functioning (National Academies of Sciences, 2016b). Indeed, one study followed children 15 years after an initial diagnosis and found 52% had lower academic achievement later (King, 1982). This high degree of lasting effect may reflect that children often experience problems related to more than one dimension of language.

Phonology: The Sounds of Language

Sounds are the gateway to understanding language. People need to produce sounds in a specific manner and with the correct stress and pitch to be understood. This complex system of sounds within a particular language is its *phonology.* Each language has its own set of regularities, referred to as *rules.* These are not rules in the sense of explicit rules that govern games because they are not explicitly stated; indeed, it requires considerable analytical acumen to describe these patterns. Phonological rules govern how people sequence the individual units of sound called *phonemes.*

Phonemes are sounds that mark the difference in meaning between two words. For example, the only distinction between *map* and *nap* is a subtle difference in how the initial consonant, or phoneme, is produced: /m/ rather than /n/. A phoneme is the smallest unit of speech sound that signals a difference in meaning in a language. For example, the syllable *bat* can be segmented into the phonemes /b/ /ă/ /t/, but /b/ is an indivisible unit of sound and so are /ă/ and /t/. A subtle change in the sound of any of these phonemes signals a change in meaning (e.g., /p/ instead of /b/, /i/ instead of /a/.)

Phonemes are not the same as letters because English often uses multiple letters to represent a single phoneme. For example, the word *light* is spelled with five letters but has only three phonemes: /l/ /ī/ /t/. The phonemic level of language is key to reading because children need to learn to translate letters into the sounds of their language. They need to map the sequences of letters they see to the phonemes these letters represent in spoken words. Making this connection unlocks the storehouse of knowledge associated with a word—how the word is pronounced, how it is used in sentences, and the web of conceptual knowledge related to the word. Between birth and the time of school entrance, most children learn the implicit rules of their language, enabling them to speak intelligibly and understand others (Fenson et al., 2006; National Academies of Sciences, 2016b). Gaining explicit awareness of the sounds of language is a more difficult task. Acquiring the ability to consciously attend to distinct phonemes is called *phonemic awareness* and is a major stumbling block to many beginning readers.

Individual Differences in Developing Phonological Skills   Significant numbers of toddlers and preschool-age children are identified as experiencing problems with speech and language development.

Early identification of these problems is important because it qualifies children in the United States to receive early intervention services.
Receiving such services at an early age can be important to setting a
child on a pathway toward more successful development. Articulating
words properly is a relatively common problem. One study estimated
such problems were found in 15% of 3-year-olds, with this declining to
about 4% of 6-year-olds (National Academies of Sciences, 2016b). Such
problems are twice as common among preschool-age boys as girls, but
this differential rate declines by the time children enter school. Biologically based problems that are specific to articulation do not seem to
significantly impede later literacy development (National Academies
of Sciences, 2016). Language delays often found in multiple language
competencies help explain why children with significant language
delays struggle with varied reading and writing competencies (Hoffman, 1997; Scarborough, 2001).

Dialect and Phonological Variation   Users of a given language
speak in ways that vary. Variations include how words are pronounced, syntax, and, to some extent, vocabulary (e.g., *bubbler* to refer
to a water fountain, *pop* to refer to the sweet beverage called *soda* in
some regions). Everyone speaks a particular version of a language,
called a *dialect*; thus, all speakers of English in the United States speak
one or more dialects of English (Adger, Wolfram, & Christian, 2007).
Dialectal variability in pronunciation and syntax is a potent marker
of identity because the dialect one speaks is determined by multiple
factors, including geographical region and social class. One's dialect
carries profound social meanings because the dialect spoken by the
dominant group in a society tends to be valued most highly, and dialects spoken by groups held in low regard may be disparaged. Because
the dialect one speaks is often associated with socially valued aspects
of identity, negative beliefs and attitudes related to those identity features may be triggered when a dialectal feature signals membership in
a less prestigious group.

In the United States, if an English speaker uses pronunciation and
syntax that reflect a dialect held in low regard, then other people often
view these variations as bad English. From the perspective of linguists,
however, these differences are simply the result of systematic, rule-
governed differences between a person's native dialect and society's
preferred language. They have nothing to do with intellect or the complexity of one's native dialect. Unfortunately, people often make inferences about one's intelligence based on the dialect one speaks, even
though all dialects are systematic and equally complex (Labov, 1972).

An example of this phenomenon occurred during my (David
Dickinson's) childhood. My family moved to Lincoln, Nebraska when

I was entering kindergarten. I played with friends whose families had lived in the area for generations and who were fluent speakers of that region's dialect. A feature of that dialect is the addition of a subtle /r/ after short /a/ so that *wash* becomes more like *warsh*. My mother, who grew up in Chicago where that pronunciation was not used, found that pronunciation particularly distressing. She, like the professor in the musical "My Fair Lady," sought to train me to adjust my pronunciation to match hers by repeating phrases using the vowels as she did.

For complex historical reasons, many people living in the United States who are of African heritage speak a dialect that sometimes is referred to as *ebonics* or *African American vernacular*. It affects how words are pronounced in multiple ways, and its use is often stigmatized because of the association between use of this dialect and racial stereotypes (Rickford et al., 2015). Children initially acquire the dialect used by their parents but later may be caught between a desire to gain facility using the language of the dominant culture and wanting to remain connected with their own peer group. A potent example of this occurred in a colleague's fifth-grade classroom in a low-income African American community in west Philadelphia. She had a math and science resource room that included two boa constrictors and mice, potent starting points for conversations. One day, Abdul, an articulate boy whose father had a job as a radio announcer, was engaged in an animated conversation about the snakes when a classmate suddenly cut him off saying, "Abdul, you talkin' like a white boy." Such exchanges lay bare the complex dynamics of power and racial identity that some students have to navigate.

Phonological Awareness and Literacy   The ability to become aware of the sounds of language apart from the meanings of words is called *phonological awareness* and is of pivotal importance to early reading. Indeed, the inability to attend to language sounds, especially to phonemes, has been a major cause of reading difficulty (National Early Literacy Panel, 2009; National Reading Panel, 2000; Stanovich, 1986). (To be clear, *phonological awareness* refers to several aspects of awareness of sounds—awareness of syllables, rhymes, and so forth; phonemic awareness is one critically important subskill within phonological awareness.) Awareness of the sounds of language is first revealed in children's ability to attend to the clusters of sounds in words and evidenced by their enjoyment in hearing and producing rhyming words. Phonological awareness begins to appear around age 3 (Chaney, 1992; Lonigan, Burgess, Anthony, & Barker, 1998; Silvén, Poskiparta, Niemi, & Voeten, 2007). The ability to attend to distinct phonemes, referred to as *phonemic awareness,* is more valuable to early reading. An early indication of its emergence is when a child can attend to the initial or final sounds of words (e.g., answering the question, "What is another word that begins with the same sound as *snake?*"). More advanced phonemic awareness tasks include answering questions such as, "What would the word *cup* be if I said it without /k/?" Another task involves giving children four words and asking which one has a different middle sound—*fun, bin, cup,* or *gum.* Phonemic awareness emerges during the first 2 years of formal schooling, with literacy instruction playing an important role in its consolidation (Anthony et al., 2002; Anthony, Lonigan, Driscoll, Phillips, & Burgess, 2003).

The rate at which children acquire phonological awareness, including phonemic awareness, is strongly affected by genetic factors, with one study finding that genetics accounted for 60% of the variation among preschool-age children (Samuelsson et al., 2005). In addition to those genetic factors, home language environments make a difference. Children from homes where parents are less economically advantaged and have lower educational levels often display slower rates of development (Burgess, Hecht, & Lonigan, 2002; Dickinson & Snow, 1987; Snow, Burns, & Griffin, 1998). Those with weak early phonemic awareness in the first two grades of school have difficulty making up ground in the later elementary years, and this contributes to later reading problems (Ehri et al., 2001; Torgesen, Wagner, Rashotte, Burgess, & Hecht, 1997).

Words and Morphemes: Units of Meaning

Words are the building blocks of language. Each word is made up of one or more meaningful elements, or morphemes. A *morpheme* is the smallest unit of language that carries meaning. For example, *paper* is one morpheme; *paper* also can be called a *root word* because it functions as a basic morpheme to which other morphemes can be added to create compound words, such as *newspaper* or *wallpaper.* The morphemes in this example—*paper, news,* and *wall*—are called *free morphemes* because each can stand alone as a meaningful unit of language. Other units of meaning, called *bound morphemes,* are bound to root words. For example, the suffix *-s* means "more than one" and *-ed* means "in the past." Neither *-s* nor *-ed* can stand alone as a word, but each is a meaningful unit of language when added to another word; adding *-s* to the noun *dog* changes the word to a plural, *dogs* (more than one dog), and adding *-ed* to the verb *howl* changes the word to *howled* (an action that took place in the past). Thus *-s* and *-ed* are bound morphemes. Other bound morphemes are used as prefixes or suffixes and change the meaning of the root word. For example, the prefix *un-* added to *able* reverses the meaning of the root word *able.*

During the preschool years, children learn an astonishing number of new words. One estimate is that by the time children enter school, they know about 5,000 words (Carey, 1978). Carey based her estimate on words that children might use and understand. Biemiller and Slonim (2001) used a more demanding approach and asked children to define words. They estimated the number of root words children know at different ages, thus they did not include the many additional words formed by adding bound morphemes such as -*ing* and -*ed*. They found that, on average, second graders know 5,200. They collected data from two samples, one of well-educated upper-middle class families and one from a sample that included families from all economic backgrounds. Those from more advantaged homes knew far more of the words on the word lists the researchers used—4,925 versus 2,669.

We can use Carey's estimate to think about how many of the 5,000 words known at kindergarten children learn each day. Assuming children begin speaking shortly after they are 1 year old, this means they need to add roughly 10 words to their vocabulary each day to reach this total. But that is not how word learning occurs; rather, it often is an incremental process. One typically hears words multiple times and slowly builds a sense of how they are pronounced, how they are used in sentences, and what meanings are associated with them. Bloom (2002) discussed word learning and described it not as learning 10 new words a day, but "learning one-hundredth of each of a thousand words" (p. 25).

Knowledge and Vocabulary   Sophisticated tools are available to assess the size of children's vocabularies, and researchers used them to determine competencies that contribute to reading and academic success. It is difficult to quantify how much a child knows about the world, however, and knowledge may play as important a role in reading and academic success as knowledge of specific words. Imagine a child is reading a book with her mother present. The book has a picture of a mother knitting. Knitting is a novel activity for the child, so the pair have a conversation in which the mother tells her son or daughter that the person uses knitting needles to weave the yarn into a piece of cloth that is then made into clothing, such as mittens. In subsequent conversations, the child may learn that yarn comes from different animals, with some discussion of that process. After learning that fabric is made of threads, the child may notice that her sweater is made of strands that a person or machine knitted together. All of this is part of the child's developing understanding of the word *knit* and related concepts. If tested for word knowledge, the girl could respond in a way that showed she knew the word *knit,* but the profound spreading network of associated concepts would be invisible. Those associated networks of knowledge that are activated when children read help account for the powerful associations between the size of a child's vocabulary and reading comprehension. Of course, it is extremely difficult to disentangle the two, but researchers have asked whether a measure that tests for the depth of knowledge children have about words, after one takes into account how many words they know, makes additional contributions to predicting their reading skill. The answer is yes. Deeper knowledge makes additional contributions (Proctor, Silverman, Harring, & Montecillo, 2012). The close association between vocabulary knowledge and vocabulary supports a concern that some experts have raised; namely, there is a substantial knowledge gap between people from different social strata in society (Neuman & Celano, 2006).

Another way to think about this issue is through the lens of what is called the *funds of knowledge.* This approach calls attention to the sources of strength and knowledge in communities where families may have limited incomes but have rich cultural and community traditions and other knowledge sources (Moje et al., 2004). This perspective argues that interventions should seek to identify the strengths of families and use them to support learning.

In one case, researchers used children's ability to tell interesting stories. Preschool children from low-income homes were randomly assigned to either a control condition in which they received no special attention or an intervention condition (Peterson, Jesso, & McCabe, 1999). For the intervention condition, the preschool children were paired with college students, who engaged the children in telling them stories an average of 26 times. The researchers asked open-ended questions, introduced related vocabulary, and wrote down the story the child told. The children then heard their own stories read back to them. Children's receptive vocabulary and their narrative ability were tested, and they showed substantial growth in both areas and outpaced the control group. In a follow-up project, McCabe (personal communication, February 27, 2018) worked in homeless shelters using the same approach and found that children were delighted to receive the books with their stories and eagerly used them as a basis for recalling the events they had told. A separate study also used the funds of knowledge approach and worked with mothers who were staying in a homeless shelter with their children. Researchers introduced them to strategies they could use to support their child's reading and found they exhibited great creativity (Di Santo, Timmons, & Pelletier, 2016).

The funds of knowledge approach has the potential to support families in a respectful and effective manner. Recognizing the benefits of this approach, however, does not contradict the broader concern we have raised—children who come to school with limited knowledge of the language assessed on standardized measures have a pressing need for opportunities to learn words and acquire knowledge associated with the words. Their funds of knowledge enrich their lives and enable them to function in their homes and communities, but for them to succeed in school, that knowledge needs to be broadened to include the range of knowledge valued in schools.

Long-Term Continuity: Gestures, Social Interaction, and Language

We discussed the preverbal roots of language learning in Chapter 3. Language begins developing in the first year and develops rapidly during the preschool years as children become adept at using multiple sources of information to quickly determine the meanings of words (Hirsh-Pasek & Golinkoff, 2008; Hirsh-Pasek, Golinkoff, & Hollich, 2000). Remarkable continuity has been found between children's early use of gesture to comment on the world and invite adults into conversations and their early vocabulary development (Rowe & Goldin-Meadow, 2009). To understand this continuity, think of a 12-month-old who is not yet talking but wants to call her father's attention to their cat who is scratching a post. She points, verbalizes, and looks at her father and then at the cat. Her father obliges by looking and commenting that the kitty is scratching the post. That interaction lays the groundwork for future exchanges when the child will use words along with gestures, and later still, may simply comment verbally. Recall that socioeconomic factors are related to the use of gestures. Those findings call attention to ways adult–child interactions in the first year of life contribute to later vocabulary development. They are early warning signs of the potential negative affect that factors associated with poverty may have on language development.

Language relies on highly efficient mental processing to translate speech sounds into meanings. Reflect on your mental activity in the following case. Imagine that someone said the word *expedite* in a sentence: "I want to expedite the payment." You need to hear the word and link it to a stored meaning, which might take a bit of effort because it is a relatively uncommon word. That capacity to quickly link sounds to meanings is refined as children are exposed to language. It has been experimentally studied by showing toddlers two pictures and saying the name for one of them. Children naturally look at the item being named, and the speed with which they do that provides a measure of how quickly and accurately they link the sound of the word to its meaning. Studies using this method with children between their first and third birthdays have found that children who respond more quickly develop larger vocabularies (Fernald, Perfors, & Marchman, 2006; Fernald, Thorpe, & Marchman, 2010) and display more growth in grammatical ability (Fernald et al., 2006). These early differences have lasting effects, because speed of lexical access at 25 months predicts vocabulary at age 8 years (Marchman & Fernald, 2008). Similar results have been found for children who are learning Spanish as a first language (Fernald et al., 2006; Hurtado, Marchman, & Fernald, 2007). Early speed of access is largely accounted for by the amount of language children hear; it is driven by the environment, not by genetic factors (Hurtado, Marchman, & Fernald, 2008). This distinction between access determined by genetic versus determined by environmental factors is of major importance to educators because people have far greater ability to affect behaviors and competencies when their development is mostly driven by experience.

The rate of early vocabulary development is critical because long-term rates of growth are remarkably stable. Standardized measures of vocabulary in preschool (ages 3 and 4) and kindergarten strongly predict language ability through the primary grades (Dickinson & Porche, 2011; Farkas & Beron, 2004; Leseman & De Jong, 1998; Muter, Hulme, Snowling, & Stevenson, 2004; NICHD Early Child Care Research Network [ECCRN], 2005b; Storch & Whitehurst, 2002; Verhoeven, van Leeuwe, & Vermeer, 2011; Walker, Greenwood, Hart, & Carta, 1994). These predictions stretch into middle school and high school (Cunningham & Stanovich, 1997; Dickinson & Tabors, 2001; Snow, Porche, Tabors, & Harris, 2007). The studies previously cited primarily include monolingual speakers, but a longitudinal study that followed bilingual children who spoke Spanish in the home also found a similar pattern of results. It found lasting and strong effects of early vocabulary in each language on later vocabulary in the matched language (English–English, Spanish–Spanish) and effects of early English knowledge on English reading comprehension (Mancilla-Martinez & Lesaux, 2011a,b). The lag in early acquisition of vocabulary is linked to problems with reading comprehension years later (Dickinson & Tabors, 2001; NICHD ECCRN, 2000, 2005b; Snow, Barnes, Chandler, Goodman, & Hemphill, 1991; Snow et al., 1998).

Individual Differences in Vocabulary Development   Given the early age at which individual differences in language learning appear and the remarkably stable pattern of growth, one might conclude that some children are genetically endowed with strong word learning abilities and these account for differences among children. That turns out not to be the case. The International Longitudinal Twins Study followed the reading development of a group of more than 2,000 identical and same-sex fraternal twins from preschool through second grade (Olson et al., 2011). The children were from Australia, Colorado, and Scandinavia. Vocabulary was tested in preschool and at the end of second and fourth grades, and genetic factors accounted for only 15% of the variability between children. This is far less genetic influence than was found for phonological awareness (61%) or word recognition and decoding in second and third grades (78%–81%). Another study of twins followed children to age 16 and found strong effects of the environment on language and reading comprehension (Harlaar et al., 2014; Tosto et al., 2017). In contrast, genetic factors were found to be much stronger determinants of decoding (Olson et al., 2011) and reading fluency (Tosto et al., 2017). The finding that variability in language is heavily dependent on environmental factors has implications for people interested in intervening in the lives of young children. It means that experience matters greatly. The challenge is to identify the kinds of experiences that are critical and then devise strategies to bolster supports for families and children to foster growth of vocabulary.

Syntax: Meaningful Sentences

The order in which people use morphemes and words is governed by implicit rules. Although a toddler can communicate simple meanings with one or two words ordered in different ways to convey more complex ideas (e.g., "Milk! Mama;" "Mama, milk!"), words need to be assembled in a specific manner dictated by the syntax of the speech community. For example, "Ball red the throw dog the" is word salad, whereas "Throw the dog the red ball" is easily grasped. Syntax is a remarkable feature of language that ensures endless possibilities for people to combine words in novel ways. Sequences of words can be reordered while retaining the same general meaning. Note that the following sentences convey roughly the same meaning even though the words are in a different order in each sentence:

- The duck paddled quickly on the turquoise lake.

- On the turquoise lake the duck paddled quickly.

- Quickly the duck paddled on the turquoise lake.

Syntactic knowledge also allows people to add endlessly to sentences by embedding new clauses:

- The duck that had been flying overhead paddled on the turquoise lake high in the mountains.

Such transformations are beyond what most preschool children can handle, but they are learning a system that will later make it possible to use language in an endlessly creative manner.

Between birth and school entrance, children master rules that govern the common ways of sequencing words and use them to understand increasingly complex sentences. The syntactic forms they use change with age, reflecting shifts in how children use language. As they approach age 2, they use nearly twice as many imperatives as declaratives and few questions (Vasilyeva, Waterfall, & Huttenlocher, 2008). The pattern reflects the fact that very young children use language more to control others and meet their own needs than to gain information. By the time they are 3 years old, children use about three times more declaratives than imperatives and increase the number of questions used. This shifting pattern of use reflects the fact that children increasingly use language to talk and learn about the world rather than to express desires and demands.

By age 3, children from all backgrounds display skill using three basic English sentence structures: declaratives ("I see the cat."), imperatives ("Don't pet the cat!"), and questions ("Where is the cat?"). At this point, they also begin learning the more complex syntactic rules that are important for understanding and producing the more formal language that will be required in academic settings. Roughly speaking, a 3-year-old's sentences average about three to four words and those of 4-year-olds average between four to five words. Longer sentences allow for more grammatical and syntactic complexity. For example, compare the three-word sentence "Throw the ball" with the five-word sentence "Throw me the blue ball."

Individual Differences in Syntax   Children in all cultures acquire the language of their society, and all languages, including manual languages used by the deaf, are equally linguistically complex. Biology predisposes people to acquire language by providing a multitude of cognitive, perceptual, and motoric capacities as well as a social nature that fuels people's desire to use language to communicate. Debates about the environment's relative role in driving language development have been particularly intense with respect to syntax. Some experts view syntactic development as the result of innate language learning principles (Pinker, 1994). We adopt the usage-based approach that views it as an emergent system grounded in cognitive capacities and nourished by environmental supports. This position has been supported by careful study of ways in which language experience is related to children's developing ability to use different syntactic structures (Lieven, 2016; MacWhinney, 2004; Tomasello, 2003). Further support for this point of view is the fact that only 21% of variance in syntax among individuals has been found to be explained by genetic factors (Byrne et al., 2005).

Differences in children's syntactic development have been found with respect to their SES. One study asked parents to describe their children's language use using a well-validated tool used with children between 16 and 30 months—the MacArthur-Bates Communicative Development Inventories (CDIs; Fenson et al., 2006). Compared with national norms, 70% of the children from low-income homes scored below the 50th percentile (Arriaga, Fenson, Cronan, & Pethick, 1998). Parisi (1971) tested syntactic understanding of children who were between 3 years and 6 months and 6 years old who were from three different socioeconomic backgrounds. Using a tool that assessed many syntactic features (e.g., plural, past, relative clauses, passive sentences), he found only slight differences associated with economic background among the youngest group, but by age 6, the three groups diverged considerably. The lowest SES group made nearly four times more errors than those from the highest SES homes. Children from middle SES homes fell between the other two groups.

These differences in overall length are due to divergence in the rate at which children from more advantaged homes use complex syntax. By age 3, most children move from putting two and three words together in single clauses to constructing longer and more complex multiclause sentences. Researchers found that the frequency with which children use complex syntax varies with family background and preschool classroom language experiences (Huttenlocher, Vasilyeva, Cymerman, & Levine, 2002); the rate of growth in children's use of multiclause utterances was related to their mothers' and preschool teachers' use of complex syntax. Building on Huttenlocher et al.'s study, Marina Vasilyeva studied the syntactic development of children between 22 and 42 months (Vasilyeva et al., 2008). Children from all homes acquired skill using basic single-clause syntactic structures, but children from higher SES homes used longer syntactic structures more often. They used conjunctions such as *and*, and some began using relative clauses (the boy who had a dog) and complement clauses associated with mental state verbs (I wonder when I will get a puppy).

Differences in syntactic development associated with SES are associated with the variety of syntactic structures used by parents. A study of children's lexical and syntactic development between 14 and 46 months coded parents' speech for the number and variety of syntactic elements in each utterance (Huttenlocher et al., 2002). They found a strong correlation between children's development and the complexity of syntax used by parents, and the predictive strength of SES was reduced when that measure was included in an analysis that included SES. This finding points to the syntactic complexity of parents' speech as one factor affecting syntax development. Preschool teachers' syntactic complexity was also found to affect syntactic development among children from low-income homes (Huttenlocher et al., 2002).

Syntax and Reading Comprehension   To understand stories, one must be skilled at using syntax to know how to assemble words in ways that communicate meaning. It makes sense that syntactic knowledge relates to listening comprehension because stories include a higher density of complex syntax than everyday conversations (Kim, 2015). This effect of syntax on listening comprehension is important because listening comprehension plays a major role in reading comprehension (Tunmer & Chapman, 2012b; Tunmer & Hoover, 1992). Evidence of the effects of early syntactic knowledge on later reading comprehension comes from a longitudinal study. When children were entering school, Valerie Muter and colleagues (2004) gave them tests of language and reading. One task tapped syntactic knowledge by giving children three to five words in a mixed-up order and asking them to create a meaningful sentence. The complexity of the items varied from three-word, subject-verb-object sentences, such as *made cookies Mom,* to sentences with articles such as *the* and auxiliary verbs such as *was: Ben throwing was stones the.* The researchers also tested to see if children could add a correct final morpheme when given a phrase:

• Here is a tree. Here are three . . . (trees).

• This girl likes to ride. Here she is . . . (riding).

• This boy likes to write. This is what he . . . (wrote).

Performance on these tasks of grammatical knowledge helped predict reading comprehension 2 years later.

Long-term patterns in syntactic development have rarely been examined, but one study found moderate to strong correlations between spontaneous language measures at age 3 (e.g., length of utterance, number of different words) and performance on standardized language assessments in kindergarten through third grade (Walker et al., 1994). Others who have studied the syntactic ability of children in the middle elementary school years have found that those with strong syntactic abilities fare better on tests of reading comprehension (Cain & Oakhill, 2006; Craig, Connor, & Washington, 2003; Vellutino, Tunmer, Jaccard, & Chen, 2007). This finding also holds true for Spanish–English bilingual children (Swanson, Rosston, Gerber, & Solari, 2008). Conversely, those with significant weaknesses encounter comprehension problems (Catts, Adolf, & Weismer, 2006; Catts, Fey, Tomblin, & Zhang, 2002; Scarborough, 2001).

Pragmatics: Ways of Using Language

Pragmatics is the linguistic term for the use of language beyond the sentence. This term covers an enormous range of competencies, including social norms governing appropriate ways of talking and mastery of genres that range from telling jokes to writing essays. Learning to master different ways of using language is laden with cultural meanings; it begins in the preschool years and continues throughout life.

One pragmatic skill preschool children acquire is learning how to address adults in a respectful way. I (David Dickinson) experienced a humorous example of this in Nashville when our neighbor's 4-year-old daughter was speaking to me. In this region of the country, it is traditional to address adults as "ma'am" and "sir" to show respect. This girl was being raised by her mother and had frequent contact with her mother's female friends and her grandmother. When speaking as a 4-year-old to me, she addressed me several times as "ma'am," using the form of respect appropriate for a woman. She knew she needed to show respect, but had little practice with "sir," the form one uses with a male.

Other pragmatic skills include less desirable abilities, such as telling lies and teasing, and negotiating skills, such as making promises, expressing thanks, and apologizing. As they master these ways of using language, children demonstrate competence as members of their social group. Indeed, Katherine Nelson (1996) described the child's acquisition of the ways of using language shared by his culture's group, which occurs between ages 2 and 5, as the emergence of the cultural self.

Pragmatic Skills: Narrative   One important pragmatic skill is the ability to tell a story. Recall your first date or another time when you were just getting to know someone new. What did you do? Most likely, you told stories about yourself. Similarly, a favorite activity at family gatherings is to recall shared events or retell stories about when someone did something memorable. These examples make apparent the importance of narratives about personal experiences. Indeed, narratives have been called "the linguistic meeting grounds of culture, cognition, and emotion" (Champion & McCabe, 2015, p. 493). It is through narrative that people communicate to others who they are and celebrate their connections to others. Narratives also help people define themselves as a culture and nation. Indeed, history is a form of narrative, and schools everywhere require students to learn the stories that define their nation. People also use narratives to understand themselves. One of the tasks of psychotherapy is to help people recall and make sense of their personal histories, which give people greater awareness and control of emotions associated with past events (Siegel, 2012).

Narrative development can be examined using a cognitive and linguistic lens. That approach reveals steady growth of narrative competence, beginning around age 3 and continuing in the primary grades. By age 3, children begin talking about past experience, and they progressively enrich their stories over the next 2 years. By the time they enter school, children can recount several past events in the correct order, using correct tense, and connect them with connectives such as "and then." These stories often include settings, descriptive details, and an indication of the child's personal reactions to the events. This narrative development helps children connect with other people in their immediate day-to-day world and beyond. By age 3, children begin to understand connections among experiences in their lives and the links between their own lives and those of their family and social group (Fivush et al., 2011).

The way children and their parents tell stories is deeply connected to their cultural roots (Heath, 1983; Minami & McCabe, 1995). For example, Japanese children tell very brief narratives that have similarities to haiku, a culturally valued poetic form (Minami & McCabe, 1995). In the later preschool years, children begin recalling and sharing experiences through narratives (McCabe & Bliss, 2003). There are broad similarities in development of narrative skills among children in the United States. Particular attention has been paid to development of African American and Caucasian children's narratives, and patterns of development have been found to be similar (reviewed in Champion & McCabe, 2015).

Cultural Variation in Narrative Forms Among American Children
During the first few years in school, differences in narrative content and organization that reflect cultural variability become apparent. Narratives are used in all communities, but they are especially important in working-class communities in the United States (Heath, 1983). Personal stories told by working-class adults have been judged to be far superior to those of middle-class, more highly educated speakers (Labov, 1972; Miller, Cho, & Bracey, 2005). Two studies described by Miller et al. found rich storytelling environments that nourished children's narrative development, surpassing what is observed in middle-class homes. In one study, mothers from European American middle-class and working-class backgrounds were interviewed about their lives. During those interviews, the working-class mothers told more than three times as many stories as did middle-class mothers, and the

stories were longer and more complex than those of the middle-class group. These patterns reflected the rich use of storytelling observed in these homes. In addition, children in a working-class neighborhood of South Baltimore and in a middle-class neighborhood were followed from age 2 years 6 months to age 3 years. Those from working-class homes produced nearly three times more narratives than those from middle-class homes, mirroring the mothers' frequency of narrative use during the interviews (Miller et al., 2005). The stories told in these homes are rich with dramatic language; they include devices such as changes in stress, pitch, and volume to convey feelings; and often deal with negative experiences. Teachers of young children who are looking for explicit recall of events, preferably those dealing with positive experiences, might fail to fully appreciate such stories.

Narrative has been studied especially carefully among African American children in the United States. These studies have revealed that the content and structure of narratives varies depending on 1) whether they are being told to a group or a single person and 2) whether the story is created by the storyteller or is a response to a research task in which a child is asked to retell a story he has been read. In some cases, the narratives African American children tell to groups in classrooms are highly imaginative and organized around a single event or topic. These narratives are called *topic-chaining stories*. In topic-chaining stories, settings and characters may shift, and connections among events may be implicit. In contrast, when African American children tell stories to a single listener, they tend to adopt the form more commonly found among European American children. Narratives in this form are called *topic-centered stories*. They are brief; they orient the listener by explicitly providing information about the setting, characters, and time frame (known as *orientations*); and they describe a single event and make some evaluative comments about it (e.g., "It was fun"). Multiple studies have examined the relationship between narrative skill and literacy. African American children who tell better narratives that they create on their own tend to do better on reading assessments (Champion & McCabe, 2015).

Helping Young Children Develop Narrative Skills   Children can be helped to tell good personal narratives. They tell better stories if they have many chances to hear adults tell stories that are filled with rich descriptions of events, people, and places (Sperry, Sperry, & Miller, 2018). Children also benefit from being asked open-ended questions that encourage them to supply more detail and receive encouraging feedback (Fivush & Fromhoff, 1988). The benefit of such interaction was studied experimentally. Parents of 3-year-olds were encouraged to engage their children in conversations about past experiences and to use open-ended prompts (Peterson et al., 1999). A year after the end of the study, children who received such support told better narratives than those in the control group. Surprisingly, they also had stronger vocabularies after the first year of the study.

A second way that adults can support narrative is by engaging in pretend play with their child and helping him or her construct a story filled with interesting events and dialogue. As adults play with their child, they can offer gentle guidance to help move the story forward or clarify actors and actions. Such guided playful supports have been tested experimentally and found to be associated with narrative skill (Dansky, 1980; Saltz & Johnson, 1974) and reading comprehension (Kendeou, White, van den Broek, & Lynch, 2009; Oakhill & Cain, 2012; Pellegrini & Galda, 1982).

Pragmatic Skills: Academic Language   *Academic language* refers to a cluster of abilities associated with academic settings and literacy (Barnes, Grifenhagen, & Dickinson, 2016; Nagy & Townsend, 2012; Schleppegrell, 2001; Snow & Ucelli, 2009). This language is different from typical conversations because it is designed to communicate with an unseen audience who may not the share the same knowledge about events and information as the author. It also has been called *decontextualized language* because it is about events and objects that are not physically present (Snow, 1991; Snow & Dickinson, 1991). Such talk includes discussing future events, giving explanations, pretending, planning, and speculating about why things happen. Academic language can be thought of as a set of ways of using language to convey meaning solely through words rather than relying on gestures, physically present objects, or shared understandings of familiar events (e.g., language such as "Remember what we did yesterday," "Let's do that again," or "Please give me one of those" relies on such shared understandings). Such interactions may occur when telling a story about a past event or making plans for a future event. It can be used when talking about a book; for example, when discussing the feelings of the characters ("Why is Peter hiding in the box?") or speculating what they might do next and explaining their motivations ("Maybe Peter wanted to see if his dog Willie could hear him when he whistled").

Academic language tends to use relatively sophisticated words and more syntactically complex sentences. Conversations that call for use of academic or decontextualized language are relatively rare in the home, but they do occur (Rowe, 2012). Children whose parents and teachers engage them in such talk more frequently are better prepared to cope with the linguistic demands of schooling (Leseman, Scheele, Mayo, & Messer, 2007). These benefits may be partly due to the intellectual activity required to construct meaning from words, but it may also occur because the language used during such conversations is rich with varied vocabulary and complex syntax.

Evidence that exposure to academic or decontextualized language at an early age yields later benefits comes from a study of interactions between parents from low-income households and their children when the children were 30 months old (Demir, Rowe, Heller, Goldin-Meadow, & Levine, 2015). Researchers observed parent–child talk and coded it for use of decontextualized language. Recall that decontextualized language is talk that conveys meaning through words rather than gestures or reliance on shared knowledge. Speech that Demir and colleagues coded as decontextualized included explanations, pretending, and talking about the past or future. They also coded for syntactic complexity and the number and variety of words used. Conversations about decontextualized topics were found to have a richer mix of vocabulary and complex syntax. Children who participated in more of these conversations at age 30 months were found at kindergarten entry to have larger vocabularies, better syntactic skill, and stronger narrative skills. It was the quality of language used and the purposes for which it was used that mattered, and not the overall amount.

Academic talk is relatively uncommon in preschool classrooms (Dickinson, 2001; Dickinson, Darrow, & Tinubu, 2008; Dickinson, Hofer, Barnes, & Grifenhagen, 2014). In group settings, teachers need to hold the attention of the group, so encouraging one child to tell a personal narrative risks losing the group's attention. Also, discussions that probe the reasons why events in stories happen are challenging because children vary in their ability to sustain attention to such conversations. Although guided pretend play can foster language growth, pretending is best done with individuals or small groups, and it can be difficult for teachers to find time to engage small groups in this type of play (Hirsh-Pasek, Golinkoff, Berk, & Singer, 2009; Toub et al., 2018). Preschool teachers do provide children some exposure to academic language, despite these barriers (Grifenhagen, Barnes, Collins, & Dickinson, 2017). Such discussions are most likely to occur when discussing books or participating in group meetings when the current thematic topic is being discussed (Dickinson et al., 2014). They also can occur during one-to-one conversations as children are engaging in independent activities. Children whose teachers engage them in more such conversations show improvements in vocabulary (Dickinson & Porche, 2011; Dickinson & Smith, 1994).

SUMMARY: LANGUAGE IN THE FIRST YEARS OF LIFE

It is amazing to consider the varied and complex ways that children learn to use language between birth and school entry. As toddlers, they are struggling to understand and produce sounds and slowly beginning to learn words and put two or three together. In their second and third year, they have begun to master basic syntactic regularities and are learning vast numbers of new words. By the time they enter school, they are carrying on conversations and using language for an increasing variety of purposes. These accomplishments are achieved not only because people's biological endowment makes it possible, but also because people are reared in environments that foster language acquisition. In the next chapter, we consider the critical contributions of parents and other caregivers.

5

Language Environments
and Language Development

We now consider how the adults in children's lives support their development of language. In this chaper and throughout the book we refer to "parents" and "caregivers" often. We want to be clear that children's language and general development is nourished by multiple family members, by adoptive and foster parents as well as teachers, friends and community members. Researchers primarily have studied parents and teachers, but patterns of interaction we discuss are relevant to all who interact with babies and children both young and old. As we consider mechanisms by which adults support learning, we shed light on specific factors that help account for the variability in development found among children reared by parents with limited education and few financial resources. We also explore the strengths of these homes and examine variability among these families. Drawing on what is known about first language development, we briefly discuss language development among children learning two languages, referred to as Dual Language Learners (DLLs), and features of adult–child interaction that support their emerging languages. We then examine early literacy development and the role of language in its emergence.

Erika Hoff (2006b) drew on a vast body of research on the environmental factors that support language development and advanced a bioecological theory describing environmental sources of language support. Language acquisition reflects the child's biological capacities to process and learn language and the environmental factors that affect a child's opportunities to acquire language. More specifically, biological factors, such as a child's genetic endowment and language learning capacities, interact with ecological factors, such as income, education, culture, race, and ethnicity, that affect the language-based interactions a child experiences.

All children are equipped with the biological capacity to learn the language of their community, but environmental factors play an enormous role in how quickly children acquire language. There is great variation in how often children participate in language-based interactions, the nature of the language used during those events, and adults' approaches to interacting with children. Many of the factors that shape language growth are related to families' economic and educational backgrounds. They play a significant role in determining the extent to which children enter school primed for success and help explain why those who live in poverty are at elevated risk of encountering difficulties in school.

POVERTY AND LANGUAGE

Interactions between children and parents or caregivers are the most potent way that the environment affects children's early development. Despite the fact that we talk about poverty as a variable that accounts for variation in child outcomes, such as language and academic achievement, it is important to be clear that poverty in and of itself does not result in depressed achievement. Rather, poverty creates challenges in the daily lives of children and their caregivers that have negative consequences for children's opportunities to learn language. Parent–child interactions are shaped by powerful factors that lie beyond the home. Families who live in poverty may confront a host of stressful life experiences, including health-related challenges (Aber, Morris, & Raver, 2012); maternal depression, especially among African American and Hispanic women and mothers with less than a college education who are between 18 and 24 years old (Ertel, Rich-Edwards, & Koenen, 2011); violence; and physical and sexual abuse (Jackson & Deye, 2015).

Numerous studies documented the deleterious effects of stress on neural functioning and development. Research examining its effects at the molecular level even found effects of stress in DNA that shape behavior throughout the lifetime (Shonkoff, 2016; Shonkoff & Garner, 2012). In addition, poverty affects the lives of people in ways that shape how they interact with their children. Poor families often have limited access to high-quality books (Neuman & Celano, 2001), lack access to knowledge of the world (Neuman & Celano, 2006), or work long hours at menial jobs that provide limited intellectual enrichment for parents to draw on when interacting with their children (Leseman & De Jong, 1998). Thus, sizable differences in children's oral language abilities are associated with their home background, and these have lasting effects on literacy and school achievement (Chatterji, 2006; Durham, Farkas, Hammer, Tomblin, & Catts, 2007; Farkas & Beron, 2004).

You might consider how many risk factors associated with poverty you experienced when growing up and compare notes with others. This exercise can help make the challenges that some families face as they raise their children more concrete.

Although far too many children from marginalized homes enter school with language competencies that place them at risk of school failure, there also are many low-income parents who foster their child's language growth despite the multitude of challenges associated with the stresses that come with life in poverty. In this chapter, we probe the complex set of experiences that foster early language and identify those that reliably support development.

CAREGIVER-CHILD LANGUAGE AND LANGUAGE DEVELOPMENT

Society has the ability to remedy some of the systemic causes of poverty, but people who are working with families and children need to address the issues by understanding the specific interactional processes that foster language development. Researchers repeatedly found substantial differences in children's rate of vocabulary growth between ages 9 months and 3 years (Hoff, 2003, 2006a; Rowe, 2012; Rowe, Raudenbush, & Goldin-Meadow, 2012). By understanding features of parent–child interaction related to language learning, people can better understand particular interpersonal dynamics that foster learning.

Quantity of Child-Directed and Overall Language Input

One characteristic of language experience that is shaped by ecological factors is the nature and amount of language to which children are exposed and the extent to which the child is a part of the conversation. Children hear talk that is directed to them, and they also overhear talk because it occurs in their presence. Researchers have examined the quantity and type of talk that occurs between adults and children between the ages of 12 and 48 months. One study examined the language environments of families who varied in income and racial background (Sperry et al., 2018). It included one low-income African American community and one low-income European American community, as well as two working-class European American communities and one middle-class European American community. Sperry and colleagues recorded 420 hours of conversation in the homes of 42 children and divided it into three types—talk directed to the child by the primary caretaker, talk directed to the child by all adults, and all talk that occurred during the observation period. They compared the findings across the homes in their studies and included those of an often-cited study by Betty Hart and Todd Risley (1995) that described the language experiences of children between 12 and 36 months in homes that varied by SES. Across these 9 communities Sperry and colleagues found statistically significant differences in talk directed to children by caretakers only between the most and least advantaged groups in Hart and Risley's study. No differences were found among any other communities, but the samples were not equivalent. The communities studied by Sperry et al. lacked a high-income group and sampled more language from older children who might have been viewed as better conversational partners by their parents. These factors could have reduced the differences in language use found to be associated with social and economic factors.

When speech from all caretakers was tallied, one group of African American children in Alabama was exposed to far more speech than any of the other groups. They heard 3,203 words per hour, a 102% increase over the number of words addressed to them by their primary caregivers. The researchers also saw considerable variability among their families who shared the same demographic characteristics and noted that such variability has been found by others (Hirsh-Pasek et al., 2015; Hurtado, Marchman, & Fernald, 2008; Huttenlocher, Waterfall, Vasilyeva, Vevea, & Hedges, 2010; Weisleder & Fernald, 2013). For example, Weisleder and Fernald found that average daily talk in Spanish-speaking, low-income families varied in the amount of child-directed speech, ranging from 12,000 words per day to 700 words per day. Findings of variability among families with similar levels of education and income are an antidote to the tendency to make assumptions about home language practices based only on a family's background.

The findings of the Sperry et al. (2018) study lead us to wonder about the relative importance of child-directed speech as opposed to talk that children overhear. This question was examined in a study that compared children who were cared for by a single provider with those who were cared for by multiple providers (Shneidman, Arroyo, Levine, & Goldin-Meadow, 2013). The researchers examined children's language experiences at age 2 years, 6 months and predicted vocabulary development a year later. Children with multiple caretakers experienced more child-directed talk and were exposed to more ambient talk. Child-directed interactions with the primary caretaker were the best predictor of later language, and conversations with other caretakers also made contributions. In contrast, the amount of ambient talk did not predict vocabulary development. The same result was found in a study in a Mayan community in which adults directed relatively little speech to very young children (Shneidman & Goldin-Meadow, 2012). These children heard considerable amounts of talk among siblings and other adults, but it was the amount of child-directed speech and not ambient speech that predicted language at 35 months. Thus, overheard speech makes no measurable contributions to the development of children in the early stages of language learning.

Findings indicating the potency of child-directed interactions are consistent with the research on joint attention in Chapter 3. Additional evidence of the importance of the quantity of child-directed input comes from a study by Hoff and Naigles (2002), who videotaped mother–child interactions of 63 children from high- and middle-income families. Children were selected based on their language development. All were just beginning to combine words, and they varied in age from 16 to 31 months. Children's growth was observed, and increases in the number of different words children used were related to the number of words used by their mothers when conversing with them. The amount of language used while talking with young children matters greatly.

Qualities of Child-Directed Talk

The quality of the language directed to children becomes of particular importance around age 2, after children have begun acquiring the ability to combine words. Four dimensions of the quality of input that support learning have been identified: 1) syntactic complexity; 2) diversity and frequency of words that a child may not have previously heard; 3) frequency of decontextualized utterances, such as explanations, pretending, storytelling, and exchanges, when the language carries meaning; and 4) adult support for understanding.

Parents' *use of complex syntax* is associated with word learning. The study by Hoff and colleagues (Hoff-Ginsberg, 1991; Hoff & Naigles, 2002) showed that the quantity of input matters and also revealed that children made faster progress when their mothers used longer and more complex sentences. Children who are beginning to use and understand basic syntactic rules hear words in sentences and are able to use syntactic cues to help grasp word meanings. Consider how the variation in the syntax of the following sentences gives nuanced cues to the meaning of *walk*, including signaling that it can be both a noun (sentences 1 and 2) and a verb (sentences 3 and 4).

1. I am going for a walk.

2. We had a good long walk.

3. You are walking very well!

4. I walked to the store with you.

Hearing *walk* in varied syntactic constructions helps children refine their grasp of the word.

Lexical diversity is a second feature of input quality that fosters language growth. Adult use of varied words is especially helpful when some of them are sophisticated words that children are not likely to know. Examination of the videotapes also revealed that lexical diversity contributed to the speed with which children learned words (Hoff & Naigles, 2002).

Rowe (2012) observed children at 18, 30, and 42 months of age whose parents differed in racial and educational background, and she tested for receptive vocabulary knowledge at 30, 42, and 54 months. She found that the complexity of adults' language increased in parallel with children's growth, and parents with more education used more sophisticated words and a greater variety of words. The lexical diversity of mothers' speech when children were 30 months old made unique contributions to the children's development at 42 months, and at 42 months it was also correlated with other features of language that were beneficial.

I (David Dickinson) played a lead role in the Home–School Study of Language Development (HSSLD; Dickinson & Tabors, 2001), a longitudinal study of children from poor and working-class homes. It examined the contributions of language experience in children's homes and classrooms starting at age 3 and followed children through high school. When children were in kindergarten, 53 families recorded mealtime conversations, and we engaged them in tasks designed to elicit language—reading a storybook, reading an informational book, and playing with toys and a set of intriguing magnets (Weizman & Snow, 2001). There was a wide range in how often caregivers used varied words, with mothers' lexical density across the five settings ranging from 2 to 48 words per 1,000 utterances. Lexical density in play settings and mealtimes was associated with children's performance on the standardized assessment of receptive vocabulary at the end of kindergarten. Mothers' ways of using language accounted for nearly one third of the variation in children's language scores in kindergarten and second grade after children's nonverbal IQ and the effects of SES were taken into account (Weizman & Snow, 2001). It is interesting to note that mealtime was the setting that contributed the most to prediction of later outcomes. The quality of teacher–child talk during meals when children eat in the classroom also contribute to language learning (Barnes et al., 2018; Cote, 2001). These findings are highlighted because meals are often overlooked as a site for fostering language learning.

Lexical diversity was also associated with children's vocabulary learning in preschool classrooms. The HSSLD study (Dickinson & Tabors, 2001) observed 4-year-old children in 57 classrooms. When teachers conversed with children during free play and used varied and sophisticated words, children performed better on the end-of-kindergarten and fourth-grade vocabulary and reading tests (Dickinson & Porche, 2011). Another study conducted in preschool classrooms included 52 Head Start classrooms and 489 children, nearly all of whom were African American. We found that teachers' use of many, varied, and sophisticated words was predictive of vocabulary development during preschool (Barnes & Dickinson, 2017). (Note that this book focuses primarily on family support for language; a summary of work on classrooms, written for a practitioner audience, can be found in Grifenhagen et al. [2017]).

Use of *decontextualized language* is a third factor that affects children's language learning. Such language requires children to construct meaning from spoken words rather than relying on contextual information such as pointing, gestures, and shared information. Explanations, pretending, and narratives are examples of decontextualized talk. It can be thought of as the preschool version of academic language; indeed, both constructs have been used to refer to such talk (Dickinson et al., 2014). Rowe (2012) studied development between 18 and 52 months and described parents' use of explaining, pretending, and narratives and studied their association with children's lexical development. The use of narratives was similar among all parents across the ages, but more highly educated parents were more likely to give explanations and engage in pretending. Controlling for the effects of education, Rowe found that variation in decontextualized talk was important among older children. It helped predict growth between 42 and 54 months, with use of narratives and explanations being most important. Note that narratives are an area of special strength among parents with less education and income, so they provide a strength on which programs can build.

Rowe's (2012) results are in line with findings of the HSSLD (Dickinson & Tabors, 2001; Weizman & Snow, 2001). Observations in preschool classrooms found that the extent to which teachers engaged children in analytical conversations during group book reading was predictive of later vocabulary. We predicted considerable variability in language and reading comprehension at the end of fourth grade when we combined book-reading conversation with teachers' use of varied vocabulary during free play (Dickinson & Tabors, 2001). Barnes and Dickinson (2017) used the same theoretical lens and examined book-reading discussions in 52 Head Start classrooms and found that teacher comments and questions that involved defining words, offering explanations, and recalling events were associated with better vocabulary growth. Talk that was most intellectually challenging (e.g., making inferences, classifying, categorizing) was very infrequent and not predictive of growth, either due to its infrequency or because it was beyond the grasp of some of the children.

A fourth feature of the quality of language input is *adult support*. One basic feature of adult support is creating opportunities for sustained engagement. A strategy parents employ with infants is to speak using infant-directed speech (Golinkoff, Can, Soderstrom, & Hirsh-Pasek, 2015). This manner of talking to infants includes considerable variation in pitch, a slower pace, repetition, and expressions of positive affect. Such talk results in heightened activation of language processing areas of the brain, and the manner in which words are pronounced makes it easier for children to analyze words (reviewed in Golinkoff et al., 2015). This language helps establish and sustain back-and-forth exchanges. Because the adult and child are attending to what the other is saying and doing, the child can use all available cues—language, gestures, tone of voice, and eye gaze—to make sense of the activity. These are teachable moments. The child is interested in something; the adult is present and can read the child's mind and use words and gestures to sustain and enrich the interaction. During such exchanges, children can initiate interactions, and these interactions result in more sustained and mature communicative efforts when they successfully engage an adult (Golinkoff et al., 2015).

An example of this construction of joint engagement is shown in a videotape of my (David Dickinson's) granddaughter, Vivian, who was 8 weeks old at the time, and her mother, Liza. (Their interaction is shown in Video 3, which is included in the downloadable materials accompanying this book available at the following link: www.brookespublish ing.com/downloads with [case sensitive] keycode 34ckDaD1k.) Vivian is lying on her back, intently looking at Liza as Liza is speaking to Vinny, her husband, who has the camera while she watches Vivian. After about 4 seconds, Vivian briefly frowns, and Liza immediately says, "What was that? Hi!" quietly and warmly with rising intonation. Liza then says "ah," and Vivian immediately repeats the sound. This exchange is followed by humorous sounds in which each of them echoes the other. This dialogue continues and is punctuated with Liza making comments such as, "Hello! Good morning!" with a high and rising pitch. This highly engaged and humorous duet continues for 2 minutes.

Back-and-forth exchanges are at the core of human interaction as conversational partners take turns contributing to and sustaining the interaction. Because there are two participants, the adult and child need to closely attend to what the other is saying and doing. As previously described, the child who is deeply engaged during teachable moments is using all available cues to make sense of the activity in the presence of an adult who reads the child's mind and sustains the interaction.

An example of the complexity and rich potential for learning that such interactions provide occurred when Vivian was 13 months old and was planting a flower in a planter. Vivian first investigated the dirt. Liza squatted down next to her as they looked at the dirt and held it while Liza made comments. Shortly thereafter, gardening tools captured Vivian's attention as her parents named them and said what a person does with them while watching closely for possible danger. Then Vivian's grandma, father, and mother planted flowers as Vivian watched and commented with sounds and gestures, all of which were responded to immediately by adoring adults.

Extended stretches of mutual engagement, such as this gardening adventure, begin when an adult picks up on something of interest to the child; they include back-and-forth exchanges and an object or shared activity. Sometimes an adult made comments well beyond Vivian's comprehension while planting the flower: "Oh look, a trowel. Grandma uses that to dig in the dirt." Sometimes adults told a running narrative about what is happening: "Now Grandma is going to put the plant in that deep hole we made."

The contributions to language growth that result from multiple ways that parents engage their young children were examined in a study of 60 children who were observed at age 24 months as they played with toys with their primary caregiver (Hirsh-Pasek et al., 2015). All parents were from low-income homes, but they varied in educational background. Children were carefully selected from a much larger pool of children, including those acquiring language quickly, those acquiring language at an average pace, and those making the slowest progress. The quantity of adult–child talk was coded for sensitivity (e.g., nonintrusive, warm, responsive) and sustained. Researchers also coded for the length of time parent and child played with objects and used words or gestures and the cohesiveness and ease with which the interaction flowed between the child and adult. In addition, researchers coded for whether the activity was a routine or ritual (e.g., playing Peekaboo, pretending to eat). Maternal education was related to all of the measures describing the interaction except use of rituals and routines. Language development at 36 months was predicted by all predictors, but the skill in mutually constructing the event and parents' enrichment of it with symbolic meaning through words and gestures was the strongest factor. The researchers concluded their study by saying,

> Our longitudinal findings suggest that interventions must extend beyond focusing on word input per se to encouraging dyads to perform a "conversational duet" that helps build a strong communication foundation that supports word learning. By increasing the potency of language exposure during interactions, such targeted interventions have the potential to help increase language success in at-risk children. (2015, p. 29)

Such fluent duets often do not occur, and duets are undermined when parents issue directives or corrections or redirect their child's activity. Rowe (2008) studied 2 1/2-year-old children as they interacted with their mothers. She found that children whose parents used many directives and corrections heard fewer total words and a less diverse set of words—two features of input that were positive predictors of growth. Other studies found that such comments are associated with slower development (Hoff, 2003) and are conversational moves that change the topic, which interrupts the flow of communication (Peterson et al., 1999).

Thus, children's language growth is nourished by adults from birth. Their responsive, sensitive, and loving exchanges, embellished with language, welcome children into their language-using community. As the child matures, these exchanges become longer, the language used is richer, and the child's role becomes more central and includes more use of language. These interactions also begin to include more and varied adults as the family, teachers, and community members expand the child's circle of conversational partners.

LEARNING A SECOND LANGUAGE

Many children learn more than one language in the years before they enter school. We know less about acquisition among DLLs than those acquiring a first language, and full understanding is difficult because of the influences on dual language learning. There is variability in children's exposure to two or more languages in the home, community, and classroom. For example, older siblings often are learning the language of the dominant country and serve as role models. Society may hold negative attitudes towards the child's first language and children may become aware of them at an early age, especially if older siblings express such views.

Basic Processes

One common concern is that children exposed to two languages may confuse them. This does not seem to be the case. As early as age 4 months, children reliably distinguish between two languages, and once they have learned to speak, they reliably use the language that matches the one used by their conversational partner (reviewed in Hoff, 2015). As children learn the sounds of their languages, they form two separate phonological systems and gain strong ability to recognize all of the sounds of both languages, though the ability to produce the weaker language may be delayed (Hammer et al., 2014). It also seems that children build separate lexicons, or storehouses of words, even when two words refer to the same concept. Because children are acquiring two languages, their progress is slower in each language. However, DLLs acquire vocabulary at a rate that is comparable with monolinguals, when word knowledge is combined across languages to reflect what is called *conceptual vocabulary* (Hoff et al., 2012).

Studies of DLLs' learning examined the effects of the quantity of language input by seeking to determine if there are relationships between children's development of each language and the extent to which a family uses one language or the other. Several studies found a reliable association between the frequency with which parents report using a language and the child's linguistic growth. A groundbreaking study by Pearson and colleagues (Pearson, Fernandez, Lewedeg, & Oller, 1997) followed children from 8 to 30 months of age who were learning two languages at the same time; the study found close correspondence between the children's rate of learning each language and home use of that language. The association between frequency of use and the child's relative strength in a language is very close. Hoff and colleagues (2012) studied children between 1 year, 1 month and 2 years, 6 months of age who were from high SES homes and found that English vocabulary growth was close to that of monolinguals in homes where English was used most of the time. When use was balanced between both languages, English growth was good but less than in homes primarily using English. Spanish language growth was much slower in homes where the languages were balanced than in Spanish-dominant homes, but it slightly outpaced Spanish-language growth in homes using mostly English. Children's Spanish ability flourished when Spanish was used predominantly in the home. An encouraging finding is that there was significant progress in learning English for children growing up in homes where Spanish was the dominant language but some English was used; those children's progress in English began to approach the level of children in balanced bilingual families by the time they were 2 years, 6 months old.

Hoff et al.'s (2012) data come from families in well-educated and relatively affluent homes. Are the same patterns seen among DLLs whose mothers have limited education? The answer is "yes." Marchman and colleagues (2017) had mothers of 3-year-olds wear a sensitive device that records up to 16 hours of talk in the home and community. These mothers had limited education; most had less than a high school education. Mothers also estimated the amount of time they used Spanish and English with their child. Children were tested for their speed of response when shown pictures and given tests of language ability. A moderately strong relationship was found between recorded and reported time.

And the amount of talk children heard in each language was moderately related to language outcomes, just as in more affluent homes.

The quality of input to DLLs has received less attention, but evidence suggests there are some particular and interesting ways that factors related to quality affect learning. Language experience was assessed by Place and Hoff (2011) by asking caregivers to keep diaries of language use. The study included 29 mothers of 2-year-old DLLs who were being reared in homes with both parents and where most had either completed college or had some college education. All families used both languages. Place and Hoff's study replicated the finding that language learning is related to overall exposure, but they also added two important new findings. First, children's acquisition of English vocabulary and grammar were stronger when the input was supplied by a native speaker. Second, vocabulary was fostered when children heard English used by a greater number of different speakers. Children are likely to have more varied conversations about a broader range of topics when they speak with different people, which likely includes use of a broader range of vocabulary.

Development in Preschool and Beyond

Studies that carefully examined the basic process of learning in the homes of DLLs focused on children ages 3 and younger. Two longitudinal studies began to follow children from low-income homes when they were 3 or 4 years old (Hammer, Scarpino, & Davison, 2011; Paez, Tabors, & Lopez, 2007). Each yielded sobering results related to children's levels of language while indicating that center-based Head Start plays a role in supporting English development.

Hammer and colleagues (2011) studied 86 children from low-income homes. The study began when children were 3 years, 6 months old and continued for 2 years until they entered kindergarten. Children who experienced English use in the home started out with better English than those whose parents only spoke Spanish. After 2 years of Head Start, these children gained one third of a standard deviation in scores on the Peabody Picture Vocabulary Test–Fourth Edition (PPVT–IV; Dunn & Dunn, 2007), but they still ended two thirds of a standard deviation below national norms. Those from Spanish-speaking homes had a faster rate of growth in knowledge of English, gaining a full standard deviation. Nonetheless, they entered kindergarten scoring a full standard deviation below national norms. Spanish growth of children in Spanish-dominant homes improved roughly one third of a standard deviation, but was still well below monolingual Spanish age norms. Spanish skill in English-speaking homes was relatively stable, remaining one and one third standard deviations below monolingual norms.

Paez and colleagues (2007) assessed 319 DLLs from low-income homes who varied in the language used at home. Children also made limited progress in acquiring English between fall and spring of their Head Start year, improving less than one third of one standard deviation on vocabulary and language comprehension. More alarmingly, they entered kindergarten two standard deviations below national norms. As they were making slow progress in acquiring English, their Spanish abilities also significantly declined. These studies both indicate that Head Start made some contributions to children's language growth, but children entered school well below their monolingual peers.

Children's knowledge of English at school entry matters greatly. Mancilla-Martinez and Leseaux (2011a) followed the group of children that Paez et al. (2007) studied through sixth grade. They found that early home language use was linked to kindergarten-entry English and Spanish. The amount of exposure was directly related to knowledge of a language, and early differences had effects still perceptible at age 12. All children entered kindergarten well below monolingual children in their knowledge of English, and by Grade 6 those reared in mostly English-speaking homes were still 0.8 standard deviations below national norms, having made up only 0.2 standard deviations of the 1.0 standard deviation gap seen at school entry. Those reared in mostly and only Spanish-speaking homes made much faster growth in English. Both groups had approached the English competence of children from homes where English was the most spoken language, but they were still around one standard deviation below national norms. Spanish acquisition among all three groups was similar and left children three to four standard deviations below Spanish monolingual norms. These differences in children's language at school entry are troubling because DLLs struggle to acquire fluent reading skills in the primary grades. The gaps in knowledge of English present at school entry persist and are associated with weaker reading comprehension in the middle grades (Mancilla-Martinez & Lesaux, 2017).

Early Childhood Classrooms

Typical schooling approaches in classrooms in the United States often fail to provide DLLs from low-income homes the support they need to catch up with their English-speaking peers' language and reading abilities. That need not necessarily be true, however. DLLs benefit when some instruction includes their native language. A study of children who attended state-funded preschool in 11 states found that those who received more instruction in Spanish and whose teachers were more responsive and sensitive made greater growth in reading and math across the preschool year (Burchinal, Field, Lopez, Howes, & Pianta,

2012). Similar results were found for DLLs in kindergarten to second-grade classrooms. Students in classrooms using a mixture of English showed significantly faster growth in English and Spanish than those in English-only classrooms (Collins, 2014). This effect is similar for children from homes that used mostly English to those primarily using Spanish.

The Hammer et al. (2011) and Paez et al. (2007) studies indicated that typical Head Start programs made only very modest contributions to children's English learning, but they may be especially helpful for those who enter with the weakest language skills (Hindman & Wasik, 2015). Well-funded interventions designed specifically to foster language and early literacy have yielded much better results for DLLs at all levels of initial English ability. David Dickinson, Debbie Rowe, and Sandra Wilson engaged in a 4-year, well-funded effort to create language-rich public preschool classrooms. We used a design that allowed them to draw causal conclusions and found that DLLs benefitted significantly, showing effect sizes of between 0.76 and 1.31 standard deviations on two measures of English language growth each of the 3 years for which they had data (Wilson, Dickinson, & Rowe, 2013). The DLLs also reached and even surpassed national norms for early decoding. Han, Vukelich, Buell, and Meacham (2014) drew on the same generous Early Reading First Funding as Dickinson, Rowe, and Wilson and supplied children with preschool experiences that resulted in language and reading that kept pace with national norms through second grade. Promising evidence also shows that interventions delivered at a larger scale can have beneficial effects on instruction and student learning. One such effort is the Nuestros Niños Program (Castro et al., 2017).

Thus, the quantity and quality of English and Spanish that children experience affects their speed of learning, and several studies found that those who have some exposure to both languages derive some benefits. It is likely that these findings also apply to children with hearing other languages in the home. Of particular importance to policy makers are findings that many children have their first concerted exposure to English in classrooms, and knowledge of English at school entry has long-term consequences. Efforts to improve support for those classrooms that focus on and enhance early language development should be a priority.

EFFECTS OF PARENTAL BELIEFS AND ACTIVITY SETTINGS

Provision of supportive language varies with parental income and education, but there are great within-group differences. Many factors affect how language is used. We discuss two that are particularly interesting—parental beliefs and activity settings.

Socioeconomic Status, Parental Beliefs, and Vocabulary

Rowe (2008) videotaped mothers as they played with toys, read books, ate meals, and played with their 2 1/2-year-old children. These 47 children were from diverse racial and economic backgrounds. Rowe coded the interactions, assessed the caregivers' verbal ability, and administered a survey regarding their beliefs about child development. The quantity and variety of words used during the observed time predicted the size of children's vocabulary a year later.

As anticipated, SES predicted vocabulary at age 2½. Yet, Rowe wanted to find if she could identify a factor more specific than income or educational level that accounted for language use. She hypothesized that parents might vary in how much they know about child development and in their beliefs about their role in supporting development. To test that hunch, Rowe also gave parents a questionnaire about their beliefs. She found that the differences that had been linked to SES were gone once she took into account parental knowledge and beliefs. This suggests that parents' knowledge and beliefs may be linked to their education and economic circumstances, and knowledge and beliefs are the active ingredients that help to shape parent–child interactions. Thus, interventions that bolster parental knowledge of development and their role in supporting their children's development may help parents engage in more linguistically enriched interactions with their infants and toddlers.

Conversational Settings

Language use may vary from one activity to the next. This source of variability was studied by Hoff-Ginsberg (1991), who compared conversations between mothers and their children during breakfast, toy play, dressing, and book reading. More highly educated mothers used longer sentences, used more words, more often encouraged children to continue what they were talking about, and used fewer directives. Language use varied by activity setting, which is important for those seeking to help families enrich their language input. All mothers talked the most during book reading. Language use during this activity was the same across different SES groups. Toy play was the setting with the second highest rate of talk for both groups, with middle-class mothers being more talkative. Mealtime levels of talk were less than levels during toy play, and middle-class rates were far higher than those seen among working-class families. Dressing was the final activity setting observed, and middle-class mothers were more likely to talk during that activity.

These results raise several interesting questions for people interested in helping parents increase patterns of language use in the home. First, the disparity in talk during mealtimes is striking, given that the quality of mealtime conversations in working-class homes has been found to be predictive of children's vocabulary in kindergarten and second grade (Weizman & Snow, 2001). Family beliefs about appropriate behavior during meals could partly account for sizable differences in language use during meals. Conversations with a family about the value of talk during mealtimes might encourage parents to recognize that their child might benefit from mealtime conversational norms that encourage more talk. Second, the differential rate of talk during dressing could be because middle-class parents are accustomed to reinforcing actions with words (e.g., "Now I am going to zip up your coat"), whereas working-class parents might simply carry out the action. This too could reflect a standard way of interacting that a parent might decide to change if it were brought to his attention.

Finally, it is fascinating that there were no significant differences between more and less highly educated mothers during book reading. Indeed, working-class mothers used even slightly more language-supporting talk compared with more highly educated mothers. This finding was the same regardless of whether the language of the books was included. Hoff (personal communication, November 19, 2017) noted, however, that the complexity of the book was associated with the level of the language used. This highlights the importance of supplying families with books that contain varied vocabulary and at least some complex syntax and of encouraging them to read often with their child.

Substantial setting-related differences in home language use associated with activities were also found in the home observations of the HSSLD (Weizman & Snow, 2001). When a narrative storybook and informational book were read, the average number of words used per minute was roughly three times greater than what was seen during play with magnets, play with toys, or mealtimes. But the percentage of sophisticated words used was much higher in mealtimes than the other settings. In those mealtime conversations, other adults were present and the topics could vary greatly. This variability could introduce unusual and interesting words. This finding lends support to the value of having conversations in varied locations around one's community. We describe Talk Around Town (Bigelow, Irvin, Turcotte, & Tallmon, 2017), a smartphone app that has been designed to encourage such conversations, when we discuss language support programs in Section II. Also, grocery stores may hold promise for people seeking to encourage enriched mother–child conversations in varied locations. Ridge, Weisberg, Iglaz, Hirsh-Pasek, and Golinkoff (2015) placed signs in grocery stores designed to prompt conversations and found they resulted in increased amounts of conversation.

Book Reading

We have mentioned studies that point to the value of book reading as a means to deepen attachment and build children's understanding of the thoughts and feelings of others. It is also a potent means for nurturing language. Next, we discuss specific ways book reading is connected to children's development of vocabulary, syntax, and narrative skills.

Vocabulary   Because most words are learned in an incremental manner, children benefit from being in language-rich environments that provide multiple exposures to the same words and exposure to different words. Book reading is ideal in this regard. Books are a rich source of varied vocabulary because they have roughly the same density of diverse words found in conversations among college-educated adults (Hayes & Ahrens, 1988). Books have the added advantage of allowing children to hear the same words multiple times. As children hear books reread, they can learn how words are used in sentences, and they can glean information about the words' meaning from the story context and pictures. If they are reading with an adult who engages them in conversations, then they may be given an explicit definition for the word in conversation that deepens their conceptual knowledge. Repetition, discussions about stories, and provision of definitions have repeatedly been found to improve word learning (Biemiller & Boote, 2006; Dickinson & Smith, 1994; Hindman, Wasik, & Snell, 2016; Wasik, Hindman, & Snell, 2016).

A path-breaking study of language use in homes tracked children's activities throughout the day and found that book reading made unique and potent contributions to children's language development (Wells, 1985). Preschool classrooms can also support vocabulary development, and book-reading times have consistently shown beneficial effects. The HSSLD (Dickinson & Tabors, 2001) found that naturally occurring book-reading conversations were related to kindergarten and fourth-grade vocabulary and fourth-grade reading comprehension (Dickinson & Porche, 2011). Scores of intervention studies used book reading to enrich vocabulary, and meta-analyses consistently find they make modest contributions to vocabulary growth (Bus & Van Ijzendoorn, 1995; Bus, Van Ijzendoorn, & Pellegrini, 1995; Marulis & Neuman, 2010; National Early Literacy Panel, 2009).

Books also were found to be a potent means to support DLLs because the same basic content can be provided in both languages. Roberts (2008) supplied parents with books that were in their home language of Spanish, Hmong, or English, and teachers read those books in English in preschool classrooms after the books had been sent home. Children made substantial gains in English vocabulary when books were sent home in English and in the home language; indeed, children who first heard the book in their home language made greater gains than those who heard the book in English in both settings. Strong gains were also found for receptive vocabulary as assessed by the PPVT–IV (Dunn & Dunn, 2007). The home language books were popular with parents, who preferred them over books in English and read them more often than books in English. Dickinson drew on this approach when supporting development of a dual language Arabic–English preschool in Abu Dhabi (Dickinson, Collins, & Pion, 2016). Books were read in the classroom in formal Arabic for 2 days, followed by English readings the next 2 days. Parents, teachers, and external observers evaluating the program for quality were impressed with children's acquisition of both English and formal Arabic.

Syntax   Books provide opportunities for children to hear more complex syntax than what is used in typical conversations. This exposure can facilitate syntactic development. Researchers compared the texts of 20 top-selling children's books with language used in conversations between middle-class mothers and their 5-year-old children (Cameron-Faulkner & Noble, 2013). The study found that books had more complex sentences than conversations and more sentences that followed the canonical order of English: subject–predicate construction. The frequency with which that order occurred in everyday conversations was quite low. Hearing the canonical order of English syntax as books are read may foster syntactic development.

To test the effect of book reading on syntactic development, Vasilyeva, Huttenlocher, and Waterfall (2006) used books to teach children passive sentences. They created two versions of 10 books. One set had a high density of passives ("The ball was kicked by the man"); the other used verbs in active voice constructions ("The man kicked the ball"). Children who heard stories enriched with passives did better on tests of their comprehension and ability to use passives.

Group book reading in classrooms also may support syntactic development. Huttenlocher and colleagues (2002) found that the complexity of teacher language is related to syntactic development, and Vasilyeva et al.'s (2006) experiment demonstrated a causal relationship between book reading and syntactic development. Given those findings, it is interesting that Head Start teachers' language when talking about books tends to be longer and more complex than language they use at other times of the day (Dickinson et al., 2014). The language used in high-quality children's books also provides repeated exposure to syntax that is more complex (Dickinson et al., 2014).

Narrative Development   Book-reading experiences also support students' narrative learning when adults actively draw children into recalling and understanding the book (Lever & Senechal, 2011; Zevenbergen, Whitehurst, & Zevenbergen, 2003). Book reading in these studies involved regular adult–child conversations about stories in which adults asked open-ended questions and then repeated, recast, and expanded on children's utterances. Children developed knowledge about story introductions, orientations, problems or goals, resolutions, and story closings. It may be particularly important that the child is an active participant. A study looked closely at children's roles in book reading and found those who talked more contributed to story evaluations and used more complex vocabulary. They later told stories with more sophisticated language and included more narrative features such as introductions, orientations, resolutions, and endings (Kim, 2011).

THE LANGUAGE-TO-LITERACY CONNECTION

We have repeatedly noted the strong continuity between early and later language ability; children's language ability at school entry plays a central role in determining their later reading comprehension ability. Why is this the case? After all, reading requires one to turn printed symbols into sounds. The print–speech translation process is complicated in English because written English often uses many letter combinations to represent the same phoneme. For example, the long /ā/ sound in *table* can be represented by many letter combinations, including *ay* as in *way, eigh* as in *weigh,* and *ai* as in *wait.* Exactly how does strong early language translate into better reading? The answer is beginning to emerge. It involves an understanding of how early oral language development is linked with decoding and comprehension. Once children have learned to efficiently translate print into words—that is, after they have learned to decode print—reading comprehension is primarily determined by three factors: 1) decoding skill, 2) ability to comprehend connected language, 3) and vocabulary (Cain et al., 2015; Muter et al., 2004; Torgesen et al., 1997; Tunmer & Chapman, 2012b; Vellutino et al., 2007). The approach to understanding the emergence of reading ability is described in detail in Dickinson, Nesbitt, and Hofer (under review). It extends the comprehensive approach to language and literacy development, advanced previously (Dickinson, McCabe, Anastasopoulos, Peisner-Feinberg, & Poe, 2003).

Decoding

The ability to decode draws on three sources—print knowledge, phonological awareness, and language. Children's understanding of print is the most familiar evidence of their progress toward being able to decode. Knowledge of print includes being able to distinguish one letter from the next, associate names and canonical sounds with these letters, and write them. Building this knowledge occurs over a long period. In literate environments, children begin to spontaneously construct that knowledge as early as age 2 (Harste et al., 1984; Rowe & Wilson, 2015).

The second set of abilities that support decoding are those that enable children to attend to the sounds in spoken words apart from their meanings (i.e., phonological awareness). That awareness eventually matures into phonemic awareness, the ability to attend to individual phonemes. Studies that traced the emergence of phonological awareness beginning at ages 2 and 3 found that children with stronger early language are more likely to develop phonological awareness skills more quickly (Chaney, 1992, 1998; Silvén et al., 2007).

The third source of knowledge that supports decoding is language, including knowing the pronunciations and meanings of words and how they are assembled in sentences to convey meaning. A strong vocabulary is at the core of these abilities (Perfetti, 2007; Perfetti & Stafura, 2014). When a beginning reader is trying to decode an unfamiliar word, she may use knowledge of standard letter–sound correspondences to get close enough to the pronunciation of the word to trigger recall of the word that she has stored in her mental lexicon. There is an "aha" moment when the phonological representation of the word is retrieved from memory and the word is pronounced correctly (Tunmer & Chapman, 2012a). Once a word is retrieved from the child's storehouse of words, its syntax and associated concepts are also accessed (Perfetti, 2007). That knowledge enables a child to put words into meaningful phrases. As a child constructs a sentence from print, the words already read limit the likely syntactic categories of the words to come. For example, if you read "The big _____," then you are intuitively aware that the next word will be a noun. That limits the range of possible words one must retrieve. Furthermore, the meanings of words already retrieved help cue readers about the word they might encounter. Evidence supporting this contribution of language comes from longitudinal studies that find children with a strong early vocabulary are more likely to make early progress with decoding (Dickinson et al., under review; Dickinson et al., 2003; Lonigan, Burgess, & Anthony, 2000; Storch & Whitehurst, 2002).

Reading Comprehension

The seeds of later language development are planted in the first 2 years of life and nourished through the toddler and preschool years. Language continues to develop as children enter school, and each phase builds on and extends prior development. The result of this cumulative process is strong continuity in the language ability that supports reading comprehension. When children begin learning to decode fluently, they become able to use letters to retrieve meaning much more efficiently. With practice, separate language-based processes (i.e., vocabulary, syntax, and discourse) become more automatized and tightly integrated. With a lot of practice reading, two parallel strands of abilities emerge—those that support decoding and those that foster comprehension. By the middle grades, many children acquire the ability to decode efficiently. At this point, decoding skill accounts for less variation in reading comprehension, and variation in language ability becomes more central (Cain et al., 2015; Storch & Whitehurst, 2002; Vellutino et al., 2007). Language becomes more important in the later grades because the material children are reading has more complex syntax, requires broader world knowledge, and uses less common vocabulary. An analysis of the vocabulary and related knowledge demands required to answer comprehension questions in third grade compared with fifth grade found a 30% increase with age (Stevens et al., 2015). The analytical thinking abilities children refine as they gain experience using academic language help them construct meaning from ever more complex texts.

BACK TO THE BEGINNINGS

To review the broad range of topics covered so far in this book, let us turn back to our two book-reading vignettes, shown in Videos 1 and 2: Tanya and Eliza, and Janna and Vera. We consider these vignettes through multiple lenses as a way of reviewing the emerging strands of development. Major interwoven strands are depicted in Figure 5.1; just as these major strands are closely intertwined, so too are the more specific competencies associated with each strand. We review book-reading interactions because it is such a potent incubator for the emerging, mutually reinforcing competencies that enable children to be successful later in life.

Attachment and Emotional Nurturance

Deep and lasting bonds of emotional attachment are formed in the first years of life through repeated, predictable, and responsive adult–child

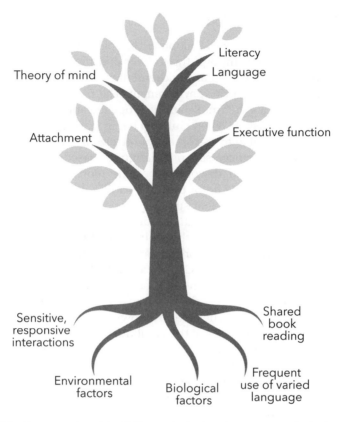

Figure 5.1. How responsive adult–child interaction leads to the emergence of other intertwined strands of development in early childhood: social-emotional development, executive function, language, and ultimately literacy.

interactions. That description aptly characterizes the loving book-reading interactions between Tanya and Eliza and Janna and Vera. The mother and child were snuggled together in each case; they responded to each other and expressed pleasure in each other's comments. The ease and smoothness of the interaction indicate this is a well-practiced routine that benefits from and contributes to the existence of a deep emotional bond. It both reflects and contributes to strong emotional attachment.

Executive Function and Self-Regulation

Children initially acquire the capacity to regulate their own behavior by being supported by adults and then by planning and initiating their own actions. The delicate dance of control between Tanya and

18-month-old Eliza beautifully illustrates this process. Eliza initially held the book and called attention to the cover, and Tanya obligingly followed her lead. Tanya continued to follow and respond to Eliza's initiations until, at one point, she suggested they turn the page. Tanya's responsiveness and the book's appeal helped Eliza sustain attention to specific pictures for several minutes. Similarly, Janna and Vera took turns drawing each other's attention to pictures and remained deeply engaged in the book for several minutes. Also, the child in both cases played a role in selecting the book being read. It was familiar and was a favorite. The familiarity and the child-guided selection reinforce the child's ability to regulate her own behavior.

Joint Attention

In both vignettes, the mothers and children orchestrated events in which they jointly attended to the book. Eliza was adept at drawing her mother's attention to objects of interest and eliciting information about the picture. At the same time, Tanya drew Eliza's attention to pictures as she provided information about them, but she also attempted to draw Eliza's attention to an event from the past. She engaged Eliza in a brief decontextualized interaction: "Remember you and Helly looked for eggs on Easter and put them in your basket [looks at Eliza with slight pause] . . . on Easter?" Janna and Vera's talk was also centered around the book. Janna drew Vera's attention to the thoughts of the chicken:

Janna: What does Minerva Louise think?

 Vera: That water hoses are scarves.

Janna: That's pretty silly, isn't it? Is that a scarf?

Thus, books provide a platform for parents and children to jointly attend first to physically present images and objects and then to mental constructs, such as past events and the thoughts of others.

Theory of Mind

When we considered children's progress in learning to understand the emotions and thoughts of others, we discussed the potency of book reading for supporting that development. The book that Janna and Vera read was filled with opportunities to have fun recognizing that the chicken had an incorrect understanding of the purposes for which various objects are used. Thus, Vera got to enjoy the silliness of a chicken wearing a glove for a hat while recognizing that the book character had thoughts and feelings different from hers. During

Tanya and Eliza's book reading, two passing encounters were relevant to development of theory of mind. First, Tanya used the mental state word *remember* when she asked, "Remember when . . ." The meaning of the word quite likely eluded Eliza, but it provided an early exposure to a sophisticated concept. The issue of differences between appearance and reality briefly surfaced. Eliza referred to an egg as a "ball" and Tanya responded, "Um hmm. It does look like a ball, doesn't it? [Looks at Eliza and pauses.] It's an egg though." This shows how effortlessly such distinctions can be woven into book reading.

Phonology

Eliza provides the best glimpse into how book reading can support phonological development. Eliza approximated the pronunciation of the word *egg* ("eigh"). Tanya immediately picks up on her daughter's attempt and supplies the correct pronunciation. She also repeats it many times during the reading. Later Eliza points to the egg and says "bah," which Tanya interprets as "ball." Once again, Eliza receives feedback about the proper pronunciation of the word.

Vocabulary and Knowledge

Eliza's book reading presents clear examples of explicitly teaching a word, as Tanya corrects Eliza when she calls an egg a ball. More important is the exposure to interesting words in meaningful contexts. Return to this sentence: "Remember you and Helly looked for eggs on Easter and put them in your basket [looks at Eliza with slight pause] . . . on Easter?"

Eliza hears the sophisticated word *remember,* the verb phrase *looked for,* and the clause that uses the verb *put,* along with a relatively uncommon word, *basket.* Eliza has the opportunity to learn a fraction of the meaning of many words in the fleeting moments it took her mother to utter them. Similarly, Janna used words and phrases such as *water hose* and *scarf/scarves* that might be unfamiliar to Vera.

Each of these books likely contributed to the child's knowledge of the world. Eliza was building basic abilities to recognize and name objects. Vera, however, had the opportunity to see illustrations of an old-fashioned farm with hens in nests sitting on their eggs and snow piled high on fence posts and other objects. Some of the objects shown incidentally also might have been new to Vera, depending on her prior knowledge. If Janna had been reading an informational book, it probably would have provided even more opportunities to expand Vera's knowledge of the world.

Syntax

Eliza's book provides her an opportunity to hear language that has the phrasing found in books but not everyday conversations: "Hooray, it's Easter Day. There are eggs to find for everyone." The second sentence is a variant of a passive sentence, with the agent of the action being *everyone*. The book also provides occasions for Tanya to use more complex sentences when she discusses the content with Eliza. Her sentence, "Remember you and Helly looked for eggs on Easter and put them in your basket . . . on Easter?" combines two predicates with the word *and*, and two clauses are combined with *and* in her sentence, "There's a niño . . . and they are looking for eggs."

Decontextualized Talk

Tanya provides explicit support for Eliza to begin to construct a narrative about her own experience when Tanya refers to the event with Helly. Also, her question, "Remember you and Helly . . ." is dense with varied, interesting vocabulary and has complex syntax. The same clustering of complexity occurred as Janna helped prepare Vera to read the book. Note the multiple phrases in Janna's comment:

Vera: I like staying outside. I want to go out all day long and even night.

Janna: You want to play outside in the snow all day and all night? Well, what do you need to do that? Can you just go out with your pajamas on?

Vera used an unusually long 11-word sentence when discussing her typical activities on cold days in the past. Janna replied with an equally long and complex 13-word sentence that includes multiple phrases: "You want to play outside/in the snow/all day and all night." She also pressed Vera to think about this hypothetical situation of going outside in the snow.

Narrative

Narrative ability is supported during book reading by the storyline and the conversations that occur as books are read. Eliza's book had a very basic plot, but Tanya supplied a potent lesson in the construction of personal narrative when she encouraged Eliza to recall her adventure with Helly. Eliza was not able to do so, but such exchanges lay the groundwork for future conversations about past events. The book that Vera heard also had a very basic plot, but Janna asked the type of open-ended questions that foster narrative development. First, she asked an open-ended question, and then she helped Vera to reply by shifting to a yes/no question. In this sequence of questions, Janna scaffolded Vera's ability to think about stories and draw connections between her past experiences and the book.

Janna: You want to play outside in the snow all day and all night? [pause] Well, what do you need to do that? [pause] Can you just go out with your pajamas on?

Good narratives include details about settings, actions, and objects, and those details are supplied by drawing on one's relevant memories in this manner.

SUMMARY: HOW EARLY CHILDHOOD EXPERIENCES FOSTER LANGUAGE AND LITERACY

We have now connected the multiple strands of development that are woven together throughout the preschool years. Each separate strand is nourished by language, and the development of language abilities draws on common interactional sources—repeated loving, responsive, and language-rich interactions with caregivers. Having opportunities to be heard and participate in many conversations, hearing sentences that vary in complexity, and hearing a broad variety of words and related concepts are particularly important to language development. This collection of language-enriching experiences is likely to occur during book reading, when telling and hearing personal narratives, and when caregivers and children engage in pretending as they play. Language enrichment also can occur as caregivers take advantage of routine activities, such as mealtimes, dressing, and bath time, to label objects and actions, recall past events, and engage in flights of fanciful pretending.

6

Enlisting Science
to Support Families

This chapter is written as a bridge between research on development and our descriptions of selected programs. In the preceding five chapters, we have taken you on a whirlwind tour of
children's early development of attachment, executive function, symbolic functioning, theory of mind, language, and literacy. We argued
throughout that language plays a role in supporting all aspects of the
child's development. In this chapter, we begin by summarizing why we
need to view development from a systems perspective (Ford & Lerner,
1992; Nelson, 1996), in which language plays a prominent early role in
organizing cognitive and other affective/behavioral systems that support literacy-related activity (Dickinson, McCabe, & Essex, 2006). This
approach guides us as we discuss the relationship between experience
and neural development, particularly with how stress affects brain
functioning as we discuss the concept of toxic stress (Shonkoff, 2016).

Severe and persistent stress is toxic and can result in lasting effects
on neural functioning. One pathway from experience to behavior is
through epigenetic effects, which are changes in the proteins that govern the activation of DNA. We consider research on social buffering,
which is the way that social supports buffer children from the effects of
stress-inducing experience. We expand our lens from the family to consider the cultural strengths (Gonzalez et al., 1995), linguistic strengths
(Jimenez et al., 2015), and community strengths on which families can
draw (Jutte, Miller, & Erickson, 2015). Family support programs are
one such community resource (Donoghue et al., 2014; Garner, 2013). We
briefly draw on the literature on family support programs, highlighting programs that are profiled in the second section of this book. We
conclude the chapter by identifying program elements, specific strategies, and activities found to foster improved language learning.

A SYSTEMS VIEW OF DEVELOPMENT

We discussed the interconnections among multiple aspects of development and emphasized the place of language for three reasons:

1. Empirical evidence strongly supports its importance.

2. Language is tangible; like a tool, it is something a caregiver can take hold of and use in varied ways to shape less tangible but important competencies, such as attachment, executive function, and theory of mind.

3. With notable exceptions (e.g., Landry, Smith, Swank, & Guttentag, 2008; Landry et al., 2012), discussions of family support programs suggest that many people are not fully aware of its centrality.

Reviews of family support programs pay slight attention to how they affect parents' language use and limited attention to language development (e.g., Filene, Kaminski, Valle, & Cachat, 2013; Howard & Brooks-Gunn, 2009; Kaminski, Valle, Filene, & Boyle, 2008). Our hope is that people who work in family support programs can become more aware of how these programs are already fostering language and consider how they might enhance their effectiveness in fostering parents' and caregivers' language use and track children's language development more consistently. Saying that we take a systems perspective means that we believe that multiple factors work in complex ways, resulting in a combination of forces that shape children's development. This approach means that we need to consider many aspects of a child's life and community and provide a rationale for broad-based efforts that target multiple issues.

Language and Responsive Interactions

Taking a systems view of development leads to the assumption that the opportunity to substantially affect a system is greatest when the system is initially being fashioned into a network. Because language is such an early developing ability and is linked to many other cognitive and affective systems, it can play a role in affecting the function of other emerging systems from a very early age. For example, Dionne and colleagues (2003) studied twins and found that expressive vocabulary was much less affected by genetic factors than the twins' tendency toward aggression, which means that the environment, rather than genetics, affected the rate of language growth. Of importance to us is that twins whose language developed faster were somewhat less likely to display aggression, which suggests that by age 2, language is already beginning to help children regulate feelings and actions that are related to aggression.

In the first 2 years of life, the most potent factor affecting children's development is how their parents interact with them. As discussed in Chapter 1, having a responsive parent is key to developing a strong attachment bond. In the vignettes we have presented, all of the mothers were closely attuned to what their child was doing and saying and responded with actions and words—which is exactly what many studies have found is important. At the same time that these parent–child exchanges contribute to building emotional relationships, they also foster language development because the language children hear during these interactions is particularly well suited to language learning.

Several features of responsive talk help build children's language (Tamis-LeMonda, Kuchirko, & Song, 2014). First, its timing is important. It occurs when children are thinking about an event or object that helps them map their caregiver's talk onto the event. Second, responsive talk is particularly likely to be didactic, or instructive. When children pay attention to something of interest and their mothers respond to the children, mothers are likely to supply information about the object of interest, such as its name: "Yes, that's a doggie!" Third, these exchanges often include gestures and eye gaze, which serve to help the child continue to focus on the object being discussed.

The benefits of such exchanges have been clearly revealed in studies examining the association between mothers' responses to their child and language growth. One study observed mother–child interactions at age 9 and 13 months and then asked mothers to report about their child's different language behaviors until age 19 months (Tamis-LeMonda, Bornstein, & Baumwell, 2001). The researchers found that those children whose mothers were observed responding with specific verbal information immediately after the child's gesture or comment were far more likely to achieve key language milestones, such as the point when the child knew 50 words, began putting words together, and started talking about past events.

Language and Self-Regulation

As mothers engage in responsive, language-rich exchanges with their infants, they also foster the children's developing self-regulatory skills. We discussed contributions of language to executive function development in the preschool years (see Chapter 3). For example, vocabulary, syntax, and self-regulation skills are correlated among 4-year-old Head Start children, and language is a potent predictor of later reading and related academic success (White, Alexander, & Greenfield, 2017). Acquiring good executive function abilities by school entry has lasting consequences. Executive functioning as children are learning to read seems to have particular importance for children's development of phonological awareness and decoding, and these emerging skills, along with executive functioning, have effects on later reading and academic success (Lonigan, Allan, Goodrich, Farrington, & Phillips, 2017; Segers, Damhuis, van de Sande, & Verhoeven, 2016).

A study that followed children from kindergarten through fourth grade found that children with stronger language at the time of school entrance were less likely to display challenging behavior in the upper elementary years (Hooper, Roberts, Zeisel, & Poe, 2003). The capacity to regulate behavior may also affect the children's relationships with teachers. Teachers respond better to children who are positive and cooperative (Pallas, Entwisle, & Cadigan, 1987) and regulate their emotions (Alexander & Entwisle, 1988). The quality of children's relationships with kindergarten teachers has effects still apparent in eighth grade, which indicates the importance of entering school ready to relate well to a teacher (Hamre & Pianta, 2001; Pianta, Hamre, & Stuhlman, 2002).

Language and Literacy

Finally, as discussed in Chapters 4 and 5, in the later preschool years and kindergarten, children's emerging linguistic and print-related abilities are being fashioned into fluent and modularized systems. This may be a particularly sensitive time for literacy development. Early language development makes important contributions to the development of phonological awareness, which matures into phonemic awareness and becomes a cornerstone of later decoding skill. A meta-analysis of phonemic intervention studies found that those done in preschool or kindergarten were twice as effective as those delivered to older children (Ehri et al., 2001). Similarly, children who enter school with strong language ability are on the path toward building the decoding and language comprehension strands of abilities that support reading comprehension.

Thus, viewing development from a systems perspective highlights the potential impact of subtle deviations in early development on later functioning. Think of this in terms of the metaphorical butterfly effect—that is, the notion that very small initial actions can have large effects (e.g., a butterfly flapping its wings in one county can set off a chain of events that weeks later results in a tornado elsewhere).

Adverse Experiences and Toxic Stress

Some infants are born into homes where the parents are unable to provide consistent, supportive parenting, which may subject an infant to prolonged exposure to situations that create stress, and this type of stress has been labeled *toxic stress*. The National Scientific Council on the Developing Child defined *toxic stress* as

strong, frequent, or prolonged activation of the body's stress management system. Stressful events that are chronic, uncontrollable, and/or
experienced without children having access to support from caring
adults tend to provoke these types of toxic stress responses. (2005, p. 2)

(This report provides a readable distillation of the substantial body of
research on this topic. Subsequent articles that have appeared in the
journal *Pediatrics,* authored by Jack Shonkoff and cited later in this
chapter, also provide excellent reviews.)

All children have stressful experiences. For example, a large dog
may bark loudly or a parent may leave the room and not return for
some time. When these experiences are brief and passing, they are
healthy, as they provide occasions for the infant or toddler to learn how
to manage stress. When parents can help a child avoid or control the
stressful situation, the child learns important coping strategies. Stressors become toxic, however, when they are more intense and repeated
and beyond the control of the child. Harmful experiences change
how the brain functions because it is malleable. These changes reflect
humans' evolutionary capacity to adapt in the face of experience, providing a short-term shield from adversity. Unfortunately, short-term
protective measures can have detrimental effects when the stress and
the responses to it are chronic.

The Adverse Childhood Experiences Study as discussed by Blair,
(Blair, 2010) provided a wealth of data documenting the effects of toxic
stress. Since the late 1990s, more than 50 reports of this study of middle-class families have documented effects of early stress on later physical and mental health, including heart disease, obesity, cancer, alco-
holism, and depression (Blair, 2010). One prominent report examined
the association between early stress and later mental health problems
using data from 17,337 adults (Anda et al., 2007). The researchers identified the number of incidents of physical, mental, and sexual abuse
during childhood and determined the rate at which adults were prescribed psychotropic drugs between 1997 and 2004. They found strong
direct associations between the number of early adverse incidents and
psychiatric symptoms in adulthood. This study and others like it con-
vinced people within the medical profession that many adult health
challenges have their origins early in life (Shonkoff, 2016).

Researchers examined effects of three types of maltreatment—
verbal, physical, and sexual—on neural development and activation.
They found different and distinctive patterns associated with each
type of abuse (Teicher, Samson, Anderson, & Ohashi, 2016). For example, exposure to prolonged verbal parental abuse is associated with
reduced density of grey matter and reduced interconnections in areas
of the brain that process language. These changes can be viewed as an
adaptive response that dampens the effects of negative verbal stimuli.

Unfortunately, this response has negative long-term consequences because these changes are associated with reduced language comprehension and verbal ability (Teicher et al., 2016).

Another response to stress is the activation of the hypothalamic-pituitary-adrenal (HPA) axis. Its activation releases hormones that have effects on regions of the brain associated with attention, emotional arousal, memory, and executive functioning. Activation of the HPA leads to the release of cortisol, a hormone that prepares the body for threatening situations (reviewed in Blair, 2002; Blair, 2010). Sustained exposure to cortisol, however, has negative effects on the frontal cortex, which governs planning and other higher cognitive functions. Sustained exposure to cortisol is also associated with shrinkage of the hippocampus (reviewed in McEwen, 2000), an area of the brain associated with memory and behavior regulation. These biological processes set in motion by the body's response to stress may be one explanation for why children who are reared in poverty are at risk of having academic problems (Chatterji, 2006). One way to understand the link between academic success and brain functioning is to administer a battery of tests that tap areas of the brain that vary in their susceptibility to the effects of stress—the frontal cortex and language processing areas. Such research has found that, on average, poverty is associated with reduced performance on measures of language, memory, and executive functioning (Farah et al., 2006; Noble, Norman, & Farah, 2005), which are mental processes associated with areas of the brain susceptible to the effects of stress.

Epigenesis   Another line of research has begun to reveal that stress can affect functioning at the DNA level by regulating the activation of genes. People are each endowed with a unique set of genes that do not change during their lives, but genes may or may not be active. They are like blueprints that are turned on and off by proteins that can attach to them.

Proteins are activated by an experience called an _epigenetic effect_ because the effects are outside the DNA itself. Experience does not alter genes, but it can alter the functioning of proteins that determine when genes are activated. Early experiences can lead to changes in gene activation, and this has effects on later physical and mental development and health. One study found an association between stress in infancy and analyses of DNA at age 15 (Essex et al., 2013). Researchers followed 109 families from mixed SES backgrounds; 17% of the adults had no education after completing high school or had not completed high school. The researchers determined the level of stress children in these families experienced between birth and school entrance (e.g., depression, anger displays within the family, financial stress). DNA was collected from youth at age 15. The researchers found that stress experienced by both mothers and fathers resulted in enduring epigenetic changes in their children. Effects were strongest when mothers experienced severe stress in the first year of the child's life (Essex et al., 2013).

Epigenetic effects may even occur prenatally. Researchers examined DNA samples in the umbilical blood of newborns born to mothers suffering from depression. This blood yielded a molecular measure of fetal exposure to stress. As anticipated, the researchers found proteins that are associated with elevated levels of the hormone cortisol (Gershon & High, 2015). Thus, at birth, some infants had systems already programmed to be particularly responsive to stress.

Social Buffering   It is alarming to think that the challenges expectant mothers face can result in their infants entering the world vulnerable to the harmful effects of those same stressors. A more encouraging picture is emerging from decades of research on animals and humans concerning ways in which supportive child-rearing environments can protect or buffer children from harmful experiences. This protection is called *social buffering* (Hostinar, Sullivan, & Gunnar, 2014). Evidence of social buffering is the finding that people who had frequent recent interactions with others who are supportive are less likely to display elevated levels of cortisol in laboratory-created stress situations. The same protective effects are found among people who have strong self-esteem, optimism, and a sense of psychological control and mastery.

Particularly important for those concerned with children's development is a study of the buffering effects of sensitive parenting in reducing epigenetic effects of maternal depression on infants. Drawing on a large body of research conducted with animals, Conradt and her colleagues (2016) hypothesized that responsive parenting could buffer epigenetic effects on the HPA system that result in elevated levels of cortisol. That is what they found. The mothers participating in this study all had been diagnosed as clinically depressed. They were videotaped while playing with their 4-month-old infants, and researchers coded mother–child interactions for certain types of behaviors. The two most interesting behaviors were responsiveness and touching in a loving manner. Infants whose mothers interacted in that fashion had reduced levels of the stress-inducing proteins. The mothers were still depressed, but some were able to engage in healthy, supportive interactions with their infants, and those interactions had effects on patterns of activation of their child's DNA.

Depression is a common result of stress, and its hallmark is listlessness and lack of desire or ability to engage in social exchanges. Parents who are depressed are less likely to have the emotional energy needed to engage in responsive interactions with their infant. As a result, the child will be deprived of emotional and intellectual nourishment. The most potent form of social buffering for infants is a caregiver who engages in responsive, sensitive interactions. It is through moment-to-moment interactions with parents that infants and toddlers experience, or are protected from, the stresses their parents are experiencing. Given the critical contributions of responsive parenting to language development, a reduction in verbal interaction leads to a dampening of parents' capacities to engage in the kind of responsive interactions that foster language.

SUPPORTING FAMILIES

Toxic stress literature sounds the alarm regarding the urgent need for society to find ways to support families living in poverty; it has led to calls to address societal challenges at the policy and community level (Jutte, Miller, & Erickson, 2015; Shonkoff, Richter, van der Gaag, & Bhutta, 2012). Such efforts are already underway, and evidence indicates that headway is being made. A meta-analysis examining the effects of parent support programs on parenting behaviors found that older programs had stronger effects than more recent ones (Pinquart & Teubert, 2010). The authors speculated that knowledge of effective parenting is more widespread now, resulting in parents beginning from a stronger starting point than in the past. Support for that hypothesis is observational data from one study that compared ratings of mother–child interaction during play with their 3-month-old infants in 2000 with ratings of the same type of mother–child interactions in 1978. The researchers found significantly more evidence of positive interactions in the more recent sample (reviewed in Pinquart & Teubert, 2010).

Improvements in School Readiness: 1998–2010

Since the late 20th century, we have seen national and local efforts to improve children's readiness for school. As the availability of public preschool has increased, the importance of book reading and book ownership has been promoted by public service announcements as well as educational efforts made by libraries, schools, and community groups. The most common message is that book reading will help prepare children for school. This is an easily grasped message that resonates with parents. Indications that these efforts are having an affect come from analyses of a nationally representative data set—the Early Childhood Longitudinal Survey (National Center for Education Statistics; see https://nces.ed.gov/ecls/ for links to many studies done related to this study). Results from 1998 were compared with those from 2010, and several encouraging findings emerged. Between 1998 and 2010, the gap related to SES background in reading skills when children entered kindergarten narrowed by 16%, and the gap in early mathematical knowledge also declined. These results suggest there have been changes in parenting practices related to the value parents place on fostering learning through their interactions with their children.

The data collection in 2010 occurred in the midst of a serious economic depression, reflected in reductions in parents' income and employment levels compared with 1998. At that time there also were widening gaps in the educational levels of those in the lowest and highest income brackets. Despite these trends, there was evidence of positive shifts in parents' child-rearing priorities. Over that 12-year period, the relative number of books owned by the families with the lowest incomes rose faster than the rate of increase found in families with the highest incomes. Also, there was a greater increase in book reading among low-income families, and the differences in library use by high- and low-income families declined by 12% (Bassok, Finch, Lee, Reardon, & Wadfogel, 2016).

Shifts in child rearing are likely partially responsible for a 16% decline in income-related differences in preliteracy skills and 10% decline in this SES-related gap for prenumeracy skills (Bassok & Latham, 2016). These shifts suggest that awareness of the importance of preacademic skills increased across all economic groups. Dramatic evidence of a change in attention to preacademic skills comes from teachers' reports of how many children knew the names of letters at the time of school entrance. In 1998, teachers said that 25% of the children could not name letters and only 15% could do so consistently. In 2010, those figures were reversed: teachers said that 25% of the children could consistently name letters and only 15% were not yet able to do so. Strong gains also were found for early math knowledge. Teachers did not report improvements in oral language ability, however. There was essentially no change in their evaluation of children's ability to interpret stories or understand complex sentences. It may be that societal efforts to encourage adults to help children be ready for school led to increased attention to specific academic skills, but those efforts did not result in the more difficult task of building strong oral language.

Family Support Programs

Efforts to support families have a long history, stretching back to home-visiting programs in England in the 19th century. Family support programs are now widespread in the United States, with programs operating in every state, the District of Columbia, and all five territories serving more than 145,000 parents and children. These programs employ a multitude of models and are operated by many agencies (National Academies of Sciences, 2016b). They have many different goals, including a number that fall outside our purview, such as goals targeting maternal health, abuse prevention, mental health, and parental empowerment. We will focus on programs seeking to enhance parenting skills, help parents prepare their child for school, provide access to books, or specifically encourage enhanced linguistic enrichment.

Meta-analyses have yielded encouraging findings for parent support programs. A review of 142 published reports found significant positive effects on measures of parenting; children's cognitive, social, and motor development; and child and parent mental health (Pinquart & Teubert, 2010). Effects on children were large enough to be practically significant. The effect sizes for the programs studied ranged from very small to small, but even small changes may be important given the potential for early changes to have lasting effects. Encouraging support for that perspective comes from 42 of the studies with follow-up data. Observations—conducted, on average, slightly more than 2 years after the program's conclusion—found most effects were still roughly the same size as at the conclusion of the study. Unfortunately, the long-term effect on cognitive development was only half as large as at the study's conclusion (d = .24 vs. d = .12). This drop-off may mean that as children get older, new parenting methods are needed to support continued intellectual development.

A roughly similar pattern of effects was found in a separate meta-analysis of 77 programs (Kaminski et al., 2008). Even stronger effects were found by an analysis that took a more fine-grained approach to examining the effects on different components of parenting (Filene et al., 2013). It found small- to moderate-sized effects on responsiveness (d = .38 to .74) and promotion of cognitive development (d = .27 to .55). Thus, considerable evidence suggests that parent support programs are contributing to improved outcomes for children.

Although this pattern of results for parent support programs is promising, there is reason for caution when considering these programs' possible effects on language outcomes. Book reading is the most commonly used strategy for fostering language; a widely employed method is dialogic reading. In this approach, parents are encouraged to actively engage children in back-and-forth exchanges about books, similar to the two vignettes discussed earlier. In general, dialogic reading has been found to result in improved outcomes for 2- and 3-year-old children (Mol, Bus, de Jong, & Smeets, 2008). Yet, effects on older preschool-age children, those children most at risk of educational failure, and children from minority backgrounds are weak (Manz, Hughes, Barnabas, Bracaliello, & Ginsburg-Block, 2010; Mol et al., 2008). This variability in the effects of dialogic reading associated with family background has not been explored, but families from different backgrounds vary in their typical approaches to book reading (Manz et al., 2010; van Kleeck, 2006). Programs should be aware of the limitations of a single approach to reading books and be open to investigating varied ways of engaging children in book reading. Also, book reading should not be the only strategy for fostering language growth. For example, our current research is finding that teachers who use games and music that we have created shown growth in vocabulary that is similar to what is seen when teachers read to them (Hopkins et al., 2019).

Effective Approaches to Supporting Families

Programs employ many different approaches to supporting families. It is beyond the scope of this book to go into detail about all of these approaches. We will briefly describe some methods that hold promise. We focus on the strategies that build the competencies discussed throughout this book. The most effective approaches used in family support programs can be briefly summarized as follows:

- Provide parents with practice using interactional strategies.
- Provide feedback.
- Address parents' beliefs.
- Target age-appropriate outcomes.
- Ensure that staff are trained and supported.
- Provide bilingual supports to Dual Language Learners (DLLs).

Introducing these methods serves as a preview of specific programs that Section II discusses in more detail.

Provide Practice Using Interactional Strategies   Two different meta-analyses of family support programs found they are more likely to change parenting and support children's growth when parents are taught specific interactional strategies (Filene et al., 2013; Pinquart & Teubert, 2010). Parents learn to use these methods best when they are able to practice them with their child or in a role-play activity.

Provide Feedback   Parents are more apt to learn and use methods effectively when they receive feedback about what they are doing and about its effects on their child (National Academies of Sciences, 2016b).

It is especially potent when this feedback comes from videotapes of the parents interacting with their child. This approach is used in two of the programs we profile in Section II of this book—the Video Interaction Project (Mendelsohn, Dreyer, Brockmeyer, Berkule-Silberman, & Morrow, 2011a) and Play and Learning Strategies, (Landry, Smith, & Swank, 2006).

Address Parents' Beliefs   Parents have beliefs about children's development and about their own roles as parents. These beliefs shape how they interact with their child. Parents vary in their approach to discipline and their ideas about the extent to which children should be encouraged to be independent. They also vary in their awareness of the need to challenge their children's cognitive abilities. These child-rearing beliefs have an impact on the language they use with their child (Heath, 1983; Rowe, 2008; Rowe, Denmark, Harden, & Stapleton, 2016) and their child's school readiness (Barbarin, Downer, Odom, & Head, 2010; Barbarin et al., 2008; Stephenson, Parrila, Georgiou, & Kirby, 2008).

Most of the programs we profile make an effort to address parents' beliefs about some aspect of parenting. This characteristic is most clearly present in the Home Instruction for Parents of Preschool Youngsters (HIPPY) (Baker, Piotrkowski, & Brooks-Gunn., 1999), which stresses that parents are their child's first teachers. This perspective is novel for many of the low-income parents that HIPPY staff work with because they tend to not to recognize their own competencies and do not view themselves as teachers.

Target Age-Appropriate Outcomes   Between birth and the time of school entrance, children's development is enormous; as a consequence, they benefit most from interactions that are appropriate for their developmental level. Research from parenting programs is consistent with observational studies of parental support that find benefits from increasing attention to 1) supporting cognitive development and 2) supporting development of strong language as children get older. A study of PALS found that in the first year, mothers benefit from help in improving the warmth and nurturance they give their infants (Landry et al., 2008). As their children's language and cognitive abilities improve, they benefit more from assistance meeting children's increasing needs for linguistic and intellectual stimulation (Landry et al., 2008). Similar results come from evaluations of VIP, an intervention delivered in pediatricians' offices during well-baby visits. This intervention helps parents improve their ability to play with children responsively and has beneficial effects on children's development (Mendelsohn et al., 2011a; Weisleder et al., 2016).

Older preschool-age children also can benefit from family literacy programs that are designed to help parents prepare their child for school, with special attention to preliteracy skills (O'Brien et al., 2014). One such program, HIPPY, is widely used and associated with desired changes in parenting and improved school performance (Ellingsen, Myers, & Boone, 2013; Johnson, Martinez-Cantu, Jacobson, & Weir, 2012; Nievar, Jacobson, Chen, Johnson, & Dier, 2011).

Ensure Staff Are Trained and Supported   Programs vary in the educational level they require of their staff who work with families. Staff educational level does not seem to be of critical importance in and of itself. This finding may because some programs that use less highly educated staff, such as HIPPY, have strong training and oversight systems and use structured curricula that guide the home visitors. The benefit of not needing to rely on highly educated staff is that programs can hire people who share the culture and language of those they serve. Although having a highly educated staff may not be critical, it is important that programs have staff who are well trained and supervised (Donoghue et al., 2014; Roberts & Kaiser, 2011).

Provide Bilingual Supports to English Language Learners
Many families in need of support speak a language other than English at home. Home visiting programs often offer their services in the language of the family. Alternative methods have been adopted by family literacy programs. Family literacy programs often serve multilingual families, and many encourage use of both English and the families' native language (e.g., books may be read in both languages) (reviewed in O'Brien et al., 2014; Paez, Bock, & Pizzo, 2011; Paez, Tabors, & Lopez, 2007). One goal of using this bilingual approach is to help parents and children learn English at the same time that the programs encourage maintenance of the native language. Parents benefit from their improved English skills by becoming equipped to advocate for their children when they enter school, and children enter school with a stronger knowledge of English, which is a potent predictor of long-term academic success. Such assistance to families for learning English has been found to have beneficial effects (Taylor, Zubrick, & Christensen, 2016).

Critical Aspects of Parent-Child Interactions

Now we examine the nuances of adult–child interactions that are associated with enhanced language growth. We believe that program effectiveness ultimately hinges on the extent to which parents and children engage in specific kinds of interactions. Think of these as the active ingredients that propel development:

- Responsive interactions that include the use of language

- Frequent exposure to language

- Instructionally useful exposure to varied vocabulary

- Knowledge building

- Extended responsive conversations

Details about these types of interactions are provided next. Programs can vary in how they strive to increase the frequency of such interactions in children's lives.

Responsive Interactions That Include the Use of Language

Responsive interactions are those in which an adult uses language while responding to a child's words or actions. Such language provides additional information about the topic of interest by naming an object or commenting on an event. These comments are often instructive because children hear varied vocabulary used in different contexts that build their knowledge of the words used. Beginning in the 1970s and 1980s, child language researchers found that such exchanges played an important role in early language development (Hoff, 2006b; Snow & Ferguson, 1977). The same kind of interactions are associated with secure attachment (Tamis-LeMonda et al., 2001), and the parallels between development of attachment bonds and language have been explicitly noted by Tamis-Lamonda and colleagues (2014). Experimental studies of parent coaching research provided additional strong evidence of how improving parents' ability to engage in responsive, sensitive parenting has a potent effect on children's language (Landry et al., 2006, 2008). Improving the amount and quality of responsiveness is also important for fostering the language acquisition of children with disabilities such as Down syndrome and ASD (Roberts & Kaiser, 2011). Adults who are verbally responsive are more likely to engage their children in more back-and-forth exchanges. These are the language experiences that predict children's patterns of brain activity that are related to enhanced language development.

Frequent Exposure to Language   The number of times children hear words or syntactic forms contributes to their ability to learn them. The amount of exposure to language helps predict how fast toddlers can link the sound of a word to its meaning, an ability called *lexical access* (Hurtado, Marchman, & Fernald, 2008), and it predicts the speed of early vocabulary development (Hart & Risley, 1995; Huttenlocher,

Haight, Bryk, Seltzer, & Lyons, 1991; Huttenlocher, Waterfall, Vasily-eva, Vevea, & Hedges, 2010). The frequency with which children hear advanced syntactic forms also predicts their rate of acquisition of more complex syntactic structures (Huttenlocher, Vasilyeva, Cymerman, & Levine, 2002; Vasilyeva, Huttenlocher, & Waterfall, 2006). Efforts are now underway that target the amount of language parents use by supplying parents with information about the number of words they use with their child each day. Providence, Rhode Island, has embarked on a large-scale effort to increase language use in this manner. This effort, Providence Talks (http://www.providencetalks.org), is described in Section II of this book. We also describe the Thirty Million Word Project in Chicago, Illinois, that is using similar methods.

Instructionally Useful Exposure to Varied Vocabulary   Children are likely to learn words when adults use them in ways that make their meanings clear (Weizman & Snow, 2001). Adults directly teach word meanings to infants and toddlers by labeling objects and actions; older children benefit from being given definitions of words. The depth of a child's understanding of a word is increased when the child is given additional information about the item. For example, an adult can explain what an object is used for ("This is a saw. It is used to cut things") and tell a child the category a word belongs to ("That is a mosquito. It is a kind of insect"). Vocabulary interventions also often combine use of gestures and pictures with word definitions, and this method is effective (Dickinson et al., in press). The variety of words children hear by age 3 becomes even more important than the total number of words (Dickinson & Porche, 2011; Weizman & Snow, 2001). Children need exposure to increasingly more sophisticated words as they get older because it is the less common words that will be important when they begin reading more complex material in the upper elementary grades.

Knowledge Building   We discussed the powerful association between the size of a child's vocabulary and later reading success. The size of one's vocabulary is also an indication of one's breadth and depth of knowledge about the world. Words are linked to other words and a web of images and associations (see Chapter 4). Going to a novel event or location and engaging the child in conversations is one of the best ways to expose children to new words. For example, grocery stores are replete with opportunities for conversations. One can name the foods and categories they belong to ("Broccoli is a vegetable"), talk about their visual properties, speculate about where they were grown and how they got to the store, and talk about their place in healthy diets. Some parents take advantage of the opportunities for such conversations, but others benefit from prompts. A study found that simply placing signs in stores that prompt such conversations can result in a significant increase in such talk (Ridge et al., 2015). This is a very important insight because parents may benefit from such prompts in other settings as well. For example, Talk Around Town is a GPS-enabled smartphone app designed to prompt parents to draw children into cognitively enriched conversations (Bigelow et al., 2017).

Extended Responsive Conversations   Language is best learned when parent and child are involved in a conversation that extends over multiple turns and enables the child to play a role. Such interactions occur when parents encourage their children to tell personal narratives about their experiences. Studies that encouraged parents to support their child's narratives by prompting them to elaborate and clarify their stories foster vocabulary and narrative skills (Peterson, Jesso, & McCabe, 1999). Simply talking at children is not as effective as taking time to listen and respond in a way that builds on what the child said (Dickinson & Porche, 2011). A phrase we use to encourage such conversations is "strive for five," which means trying to have a sequence of five back-and-forth exchanges with the child.

Promising Settings and Activities

It may seem a bit overwhelming to think about what one needs to do to give children the emotional, linguistic, and intellectual nurturance they need. It is not as complex as it may seem because many of the desirable strategies can be naturally used in the same activity. We discuss several such activities—reading books, building language support into everyday routines, visiting libraries, and supporting language development as children engage with the larger community. In all cases, these activities can be done many times. The most potent effects will occur when these activities become part of a family's routines.

Reading Books   Most parent support programs encourage regular reading, and public service announcements and teachers stress its importance. Book reading can contribute to building strong bonds of affection, and when there is time for back-and-forth conversations, it creates opportunities for discussions that build knowledge, language, and understanding of how others think and feel. When book reading is a familiar routine, it creates a context for deepening bonds of affection. Books often use less familiar words in more sophisticated sentences, so when they are repeatedly read, children have many opportunities to make the language their own. Storybooks with interesting characters facing challenges set the stage for talk about feelings and motivations; informational books can broaden a child's world with pictures and information about animals, places, and events from far and wide.

Reading holds great promise, but it is not magic. Children need to hear good books to reap the benefits we discussed, and adults need to create reading events that are emotionally, linguistically, and cognitively stimulating. Low-income parents often live in neighborhoods that do not have good children's books available and lack convenient libraries (Neuman & Celano, 2001). Simply having access to books can result in improved outcomes (Evans, Kelley, Sikora, & Treiman, 2010; Neuman, 1999). Major efforts around the world are seeking to ensure that children and their families receive high-quality books beginning at birth. In Section II of this book, we profile three such programs— Dolly Parton's Imagination Library (http://www.imaginationlibrary .com), Maktabat al-Fanoos or "Lantern Library" (http://www.al-fanoos .org/english), and Sifriyat Pijama or "Pajama Library" (http://eng.pjis rael.org). We also describe Family Reading Partnership (FRP; http:// www.familyreading.org), which is a multifaceted approach to distributing books and encouraging book reading that has been embraced by the entire city of Ithaca, New York, since the late 1990s.

Books provide powerful opportunities to create rich contexts for interactions, but adults need to draw children into the book and engage them in productive conversations to realize the book's learning potential. Positive effects have repeatedly been found when parents engage children in back-and-forth conversations about books using what are called *dialogic interactions* (Mol, Bus, & de Jong, 2009; Mol et al., 2008). Book distribution programs have greater benefits when they provide parents with some guidance regarding effective reading methods (Dickinson, Griffith, Golinkoff, & Hirsh-Pasek, 2012). The guidance that is often supplied draws on research examining the effects of dialogic reading. Following are few tips that teachers and other early childhood professionals can provide parents that distill the wisdom of many studies of book reading.

- *Select high-quality books* that interest your child; ask a children's librarian or child care providers or teachers for guidance. Take care you do not underestimate the level of language or information your child may enjoy. Sometimes adults select books intended for beginning readers, but these are written using simple words that are easy for a child to read, but they may not stretch your child's spoken language or expand her knowledge.

- *Read different kinds of books,* including storybooks and informational books (e.g., books about animals, machines, and other places in the world).

- *Reread books.* Children enjoy hearing the same book many times, and the repetition gives them many chances to absorb the language of the book. Read high-quality books to increase the usefulness of repeated readings.

- *Make reading an enjoyable routine.* Laugh; respond to your child's interests and comments; and share your own enthusiasm, questions, and enjoyment. Try to read at the same time each day.

- *Engage your child in talk about the book.* Ask questions that stretch your child. These may be about the names for things, but they can also be about why characters are doing things or how they are feeling. Informational books provide rich starting points for talk about the physical world. Respond to your child's questions, and praise him or her for asking questions.

- *Build your child's world knowledge.* Be alert for instances when the time of the book's events take place or the location are unfamiliar. Give the child enough information to understand the story. When reading informational books be especially aware of the need ask questions and respond to your child's questions. These mini-lessons should be brief and can occur at any time during the reading.

- *Build your child's vocabulary.* Watch for words that you think your child may not know and briefly talk about them. When you reread, ask your child if he recalls what the word means, and try to use it at other times of the day.

- *Build your child's comprehension skills* by helping him or her understand the book while remaining alert for questions or signs of confusion. Notice things that might be confusing, and ask your child questions (e.g., "Why do you think he wanted to do that?"). Make connections to your child's life and experiences, and tell him or her information not provided in the book.

Building Language Support Into Everyday Routines   Parents' lives are busy, but every day includes precious moments when conversations can occur. Some are at predictable times, such as mealtimes, bathing, and time spent driving in the car and waiting for appointments. These times can slip away if adults do not make a conscious effort to engage their child in conversations. In contrast, if parents make conscious efforts to take advantage of these times, then their child will benefit, and they will gain delightfully deeper appreciation for their child's interests and thoughts.

Meals can be rich with language that supports vocabulary development (Weizman & Snow, 2001). They also are an ideal time for adults to encourage children to tell about things that happened to them during the day. As we previously noted, children benefit when parents intentionally strive to support their storytelling (Peterson et al., 1999). Bathing is a time when adults need to be with their child and can become a language-rich time. For example, when my (David Dickinson's) daughters were young, I engaged them in many long-running stories about the rubber animals that inhabited the tub and hid in the suds.

Entertainment during car trips is often provided by music, videos, or games. These trips can also be a time for conversation. The quiet of the car provides opportunities for children to initiate conversations and hold extended conversations on a single topic. Waiting rooms are also settings where boredom can be turned into an occasion for reading a favorite book or talking about recent events.

Television is a fact of life in most homes and can help keep children occupied when adults are busy. There is great variability in television programming for children, with proven benefits to encouraging children to watch educational shows such as *Sesame Street* and *Between the Lions* (Kirkorian, Wartella, & Anderson, 2008; Linebarger, Kosanic, Greenwood, & Doku, 2004; Nakamura, 2004). Children are especially likely to benefit from viewing such programs when an adult sits with them and talks about the show.

Visiting Libraries   Most U.S. communities have free public libraries—many with children's librarians who are eager to give advice regarding book selection and programs that include book reading and related activities (e.g., puppet shows, art activities). Low-income parents may use the libraries but may not take time to explore the library's broad range of books and resources with their child (Neuman & Celano, 2006). They may benefit from learning how to maximize the value of their library trips.

Libraries in different countries have programs to encourage parents to come to the library, and they use strategies such as sending library cards to parents of newborns and invitations to visit the library. Libraries often seek to educate parents about the strategies previously introduced, which has enhanced the effectiveness of the programs (Dickinson et al., 2012). Section II profiles Boekstart, one such program in the Netherlands that has been found to have beneficial effects (https://www.boekstart.nl).

Building Language Support Into Interactions With Communities
All communities offer opportunities to engage children in conversations that will expand their horizons. Trips to the grocery store can be transformed from purely pragmatic errands for buying food to

opportunities for broad-ranging conversations. Local celebrations and cultural events are rich with sights, sounds, and experiences that can enrich a child's connection with his or her culture and provide parents, grandparents, aunts, and uncles opportunities to share their experiences and cultural knowledge. Educational settings, such as zoos, museums, botanical gardens, and historical sites, often provide opportunities for a broad range of conversations. Adults can deepen their own knowledge using signs and maps and convey that information to their child.

Caregivers and parents can find many worthy topics if they use excursions around town to engage in conversation with children.

SUMMARY: SUPPORTING FAMILIES IN NURTURING CHILDREN'S DEVELOPMENT

The effects of early experience are potent and can be enduring. Parents' or other caregivers' lives are filled with stress that impedes their abilities to nurture their children in an optimal manner. To fully address these problems, societies must offer access to safe, affordable housing; safe neighborhoods; and employment that pays a living wage. In seeking to achieve these aspirations, we can continue providing families with information and guidance that helps them create emotionally and intellectually nourishing homes. There are many proven methods of achieving these goals, but there is a pressing need to reach more families with strategies that have even more substantial effects. The approaches profiled in Section II may lead to cross-fertilization among programs and development of new exciting initiatives.

II

Programs Supporting Early Literacy

Parent Coaching Programs
   Play and Learning Strategies
   Video Interaction Project
   Thirty Million Words Project
   Home Instruction for Parents of Preschool Youngsters
   Save the Children
Book Giveaway Programs
   Reach Out and Read
   Dolly Parton's Imagination Library
   Bookstart
   Sifriyat Pijama ("Pajama Library") and Maktabat al-Fanoos ("Lantern Library")
   Family Reading Partnership
Emerging Programs
   The Juniper Gardens Children's Project
   Háblame Bebé
   Providence Talks
   Project beELL
   Bridging the Word Gap National Research Network

Children's Learning Institute's Interventions to Support Preschool
Teachers and Parents

The Campaign for Grade-Level Reading

Five Steps to Five

Play and Learning Strategies

After discussing the lesson of the day, the coach videotaped mother and child playing together. This photo shows them reviewing the video on the coach's computer and discussing how Mom implemented these strategies.

Photo courtesy of Ann B. Morse.

SNAPSHOT: **Play and Learning Strategies (PALS)**

When created: 1998-2006

Funding: PALS was developed with support from the National Institute for Child Health and Development (NICHD) (1998-2006) but currently has no source of sustained support. A training team is available, however, to train and certify personnel in interested communities.

Location: United States

Research base (limited, fair, strong, very strong): Strong. Controlled research studies have consistently found PALS to have statistically significant and policy-relevant positive effects on parenting and on children's developing social, language, and academic outcomes.

Who is served: Parents of children age 5-18 months (infant curriculum) and age 18 months-3 years (toddler curriculum) in 30 states.

Web site: https://www.childrenslearninginstitute.org/programs/play-and-learning-strategies-pals

Mission: To strengthen the bond among infants, toddlers, preschoolers, and their parents and enhance young children's language, social, and cognitive growth in order to promote positive developmental outcomes

In brief: PALS originated in Texas as a home-visit program available in English and Spanish and implemented by trained parent educators through 90-minute home visits (10 sessions for the infant curriculum and 12 sessions for the toddler curriculum per year). Some states are adapting the program for implementation in group settings and with more diverse populations. Training includes having parents view and discuss video examples of parent-child interactions and guiding parents in practicing the demonstrated techniques with their own child.

Improving Parent-Child Interactions

We visited one of the 14 PALS groups that meet in 10 locations in Austin, Texas. Classes are offered in either English or Spanish, which reflects the large immigrant population in Austin. This program was employing a group delivery method, partly due to financial constraints and partly because it was responsive to parents' desires to build a social network with other families. Six to eight parents attended an evening group session for 2 hours for 14 weeks. On the evening we visited, all parents met as a group with the coach during the first hour, viewing and responding to the presentation. The lesson was on positive discipline and included simple, illustrated PowerPoint slides. The instructor guided parents in giving children clear, precise instructions; presented strategies to improve behavior; asked questions; and occasionally had parents take turns role playing a typical conflict situation between a parent and child. Their children played in the next room and were supervised by several trained family support specialists who were AmeriCorps volunteers. The parents joined their children during the second hour and practiced what they just learned. The group leader guided and coached two of the parent-child dyads near the end of the second hour, videotaping their interaction (which included the trainer's comments) and reviewing the video and observations with the parent.

When asked for examples of success, a staff person recounted an anecdote from a mother whose teenage daughters had noticed a change in her since she had attended PALS with her infant. They commented that she had been "stern and all business" before PALS, and she has since learned "silliness and having fun" and is more communicative with the teenagers as well as the infant.

The PALS infant curriculum consists of 10 sessions a year and is geared to the parents of children age 5–18 months. The PALS toddler curriculum guides parents of children age 18 months–3 years in 12 sessions a year. In addition to informing parents about age-appropriate typical behaviors, sessions cover the following topics:

- Paying attention to infants' and toddlers' communicative signals
- Responding appropriately to children's positive and negative signals
- Supporting infants' and toddlers' learning by maintaining their interest and attention rather than redirecting or overstimulating
- Introducing toys and activities
- Stimulating language development through labeling and scaffolding
- Encouraging cooperation and responding to misbehavior
- Incorporating these strategies and supportive behaviors throughout the day and during routine activities, such as mealtimes, dressing, and bathing, as well as at playtime

Training techniques include viewing and discussing video examples of mothers and children, which exemplify the concepts the parents being trained are learning. They are then guided in practicing the demonstrated techniques with their own child. In addition to the home-based model typically implemented in Texas, PALS is now implemented in approximately 30 other states, and some are adapting the program for implementation in group settings and with more diverse populations.

The Austin PALS program piloted a model for sustainability in 2017–2018 in which former parent participants are trained as family support specialists and coaches, which further enhances the parents' knowledge of child development and also better positions them for employment opportunities in the community. **PALS** training and certi-fication are provided by Children's Learning Institute (CLI) staff either in Houston, Texas, or locally on site. One requirement for instructor certification is submission of a videotaped training session to CLI PALS staff for review.

RESEARCH HIGHLIGHTS

PALS has been examined in several rigorously controlled longitudi-nal studies. These efforts have been delivered by research teams that achieved a high degree of fidelity to the model. There are no published studies of implementation delivered by local delivery teams function-ing without the benefit of research funding. The controlled research studies have consistently found PALS to have statistically significant and policy-relevant positive effects on parenting and children's devel-oping social, language, and academic outcomes.

An early evaluation included 241 parent–child pairs who com-pleted the 10-session intervention. The sample was divided between infants born with very low birth weight and full-term infants (Gutten-tag, Pedrosa-Josic, Landry, Smith, & Swank, 2006). Across both groups, mothers who received the intervention showed improved skill scaffold-ing their child's attention and using language to label objects, provide explanations, and describe conceptual relationships between objects and actions. Mothers in a comparison group that did not receive the intervention did not demonstrate such improvement. Children's lan-guage growth was greater when they received more input (Landry & Smith, 2006).

A subsequent study randomly assigned parents and 6-month-old infants to 10 sessions of PALS or a control condition. At 24 months of age, these individuals were randomly assigned to receive PALS II, a 10-session program designed for older children, or the control condi-tion. PALS resulted in greater parenting warmth and improved ability to help their child maintain a focus of attention. PALS II was especially effective in supporting mothers' language use and verbal encouragement, and their children displayed stronger language growth than those in the comparison group (Landry et al., 2008). PALS and PALS II interventions resulted in more praise and encouragement, increased verbal facilitation, and more prompting children to participate. PALS II alone enabled mothers to be more responsive. Children benefitted from these improved parenting strategies. They asked more questions, made more comments, and were generally more engaged. The improvements in children's participation were associated with mothers' adoption of supportive behaviors (Landry et al., 2012).

PALS infant curriculum meets the U.S. Department of Health and Human Services criteria for being an evidence-based early childhood home visiting service delivery model for the general population (Sama-Miller et. al., 2018). Delivery in small groups by a community-based group, which is the approach we observed, has not been evaluated, so we are unable to determine the extent to which it retains the potency of the one-to-one coaching method employed in the experimentally controlled studies.

Video Interaction Project

Photo courtesy of Ann B. Morse.

Photo courtesy of Ann B. Morse.

A family plays with a new toy and then reflects on the video of their play session with the interventionist.

SNAPSHOT: Video Interaction Project (VIP)

When created: 1999

Funding: Low-cost program funded by the National Institutes of Health (NIH) research funding, the TIGER Foundation and other foundations, and the New York City Council, primarily City's First Readers.

Location: Originated in New York City at Bellevue Hospital Center, a public hospital affiliated with New York University School of Medicine; since implemented in Brooklyn, New York; Pittsburgh, Pennsylvania; Flint, Michigan; and Children's Aid in Harlem, New York; now becoming more closely aligned with other New York City systems.

Research base (limited, fair, strong, very strong): Very strong

Who is served: Parents of children from birth to age 5 in several areas of New York City as well as Pittsburgh, Pennsylvania and Flint, Michigan. The number of participating families to date is 2,000.

Web site: http://www.videointeractionproject.org

Mission: Empowering parents and providing children from low-income families with an early foundation to succeed

In brief: The VIP originated at Bellevue Hospital Center in New York City and is an intervention delivered in conjunction with 13–15 routine well-child visits between birth and age 5. Parents work with a coach who helps them develop responsive parenting skills by videotaping, viewing, and providing feedback about parent-child interactions during book reading and playing with toys given to the family.

Using Well-Baby Visits to Promote Responsive Parenting

Before going to their 15-month-old's routine pediatrician appointment at Bellevue Hospital in New York City, a young bilingual couple and their child enter the small, crowded room in the VIP offices adjoining the hospital. They have come to VIP in conjunction with every well-baby appointment since their son, Javier, was born to learn how to maximize their input to his development.

They are given a toy or book to share with their child during every visit, and they are videotaped playing with him while the coach enthusiastically and positively comments on their interactions.

At this visit, the coach asks them what Javier has been doing and what he has learned since their last visit. The parents describe how he is communicating more by pointing and using other gestures and sounds. "He's very good at showing us what he wants. He says it in multiple ways." Javier's father also comments on how Javier is responding to the father's English and mother's Spanish utterances and how he is attending to book reading. The adults then move on to discussing motor skills and comment on how he is using his hands to pick up smaller objects and manipulate toys as well as how he is using his body to cruise around furniture and begin to walk. Their coach gives specific positive feedback after each parental comment; for example, when Javier's father states, "You gave us cups for him to stack, and he places them inside each other instead," she responds, "It's good you are allowing him to have opportunities to explore and say 'yes' to what he is doing," and "It's good you let him take the lead."

The coach asks a few more questions and then gives Javier's parents a toy telephone. She asks them for ideas about how they might introduce it to Javier and use it with him, adding a few of her own suggestions. She sets up her small video camera and starts to record the play session. On a mat in the corner of the room, Javier's parents show the young boy the telephone, model talking on it, hand it to him, and continue interacting with him. While filming, the coach makes occasional suggestions, frequently complimenting Javier's parents on their awareness of their child's interests, highlighting his responses, and encouraging their use of language as well as nonverbal interactions with him. The coach reviews the video with the parents after the play session, pointing out and emphasizing the value of specific interactions with Javier, as she continues to positively encourage them. They leave the session with the new toy telephone, the videotape of their session to keep as a record of their son's growth and their own growth as responsive parents, and reconfirmed knowledge that they are their child's first teachers.

———————

VIP was developed in the context of a broadening definition of health and wellness that included parenting, early child development, and school readiness. At the same time, there was increasing recognition that the pediatric primary care setting (i.e., pediatrics, family medicine) was especially well suited to population-level preventive initiatives, given the opportunities for multiple contacts during the critical first 5 years of life, the value of communication through a trusted pediatric provider, and the potential for low-cost services (Cates et al., 2016). Bellevue Hospital Center, a public hospital affiliated with New York University School of Medicine and serving low-income families, was the original home of VIP. In 1999, a team led by Drs. Alan Mendelsohn and Benard Dreyer (recent president of the American

Academy of Pediatrics) and Virginia Flynn, a child life specialist, designed VIP to build on and enhance the benefits of the Reach Out and Read (ROR) program for high-risk families by adding a 25-minute meeting between families and a child life facilitator coach to every well-child appointment. The family is given a developmentally appropriate book or toy at each VIP session, and parents are encouraged to read aloud to their child and encourage talking, teaching, and pretend play. The goal of these sessions is to help parents further develop their parenting skills by observing and interacting with their young children and reflecting with the facilitator on videos of these family interactions. VIP is strengths based because it uses the videos to identify and reinforce positive parent–child interactions and thereby build on parent goals for child development. It was initially designed as a birth-to-3 program, but it expanded in 2009 to serve families with children who are 3–5 years old.

Efforts are underway to expand use of VIP. In 2013, it developed a second clinical site in Brooklyn, New York, and VIP has since been implemented in Pittsburgh, Pennsylvania; Flint, Michigan; and at the Children's Aid Society in Harlem, New York. It also is becoming more closely aligned with other systems in New York City. For example, it has been a partner with City's First Readers since 2014, a New York City Council citywide early literacy initiative that links pediatric primary care parenting programs (ROR and VIP) with programs in the community, including the New York City library system, child care programs, home visiting programs, and preschools. A new effort called Smart Beginnings (funded by NIH/NICHD) integrates universal delivery of VIP in primary care with additional support through home visiting (Family Check Up) for families with additional needs. Additional collaboration with the New York City Department of Health and Mental Hygiene is expected to further support expansion that is possible due to its low cost. The annual cost of VIP at scale was $175–$200 per child in 2017.

RESEARCH HIGHLIGHTS

VIP has been studied using rigorous research designs in which subjects were randomly assigned to VIP or contrasting conditions (Mendelsohn et al., 2011). The delivery system employed is consistent with the approach that will be used when the method is taken to scale, but oversight and assurance of fidelity has been more tightly controlled than is likely to be possible when a fully institutionalized, scaled-up model is employed. Results of all studies have revealed small to moderate positive effects. The first study of VIP randomly assigned 75 children to the intervention and 75 to a treatment-as usual control group, with treatment-as-usual including ROR (Mendelsohn et al., 2007). Parents and children were assessed when children were 21 and 33 months old and after school entry (kindergarten to first grade). Effects on parents' provision of cognitive stimulation were measured with the StimQ (Dreyer, Mendelsohn, & Tamis-LeMonda, 2009), a freely available parent report survey that evaluates multiple ways in which parents enrich their children's learning, including scales that tap reading and teaching activities, verbal interactions, and play with stimulating toys. Parenting stress also was assessed. Parental responsivity was coded from videotaped interactions. Children's cognitive, language, and reading development were assessed, and parents reported on the child's behavior and emotional adjustment. Statistically significant effects on parents were found for their responsiveness and reading support and for reduced levels of stress related to depression and anxiety. At age 21 months, children whose mothers had more than a seventh-grade education also made improvement on measures of cognitive development and expressive language. There was still evidence of a significant effect on selected measures of cognitive development at school entry.

The effects of the first study were further evaluated in an NIH/NICHD-funded follow-up that started with 675 children at birth and randomly assigned them to 1) VIP 0–3, a birth-to-three version of the VIP; 2) treatment as usual that included ROR; or 3) Building Blocks, an alternative intervention that included parenting pamphlets, learning materials, and screening conducted by mail. When the children turned 3, families from the VIP 0–3 and treatment-as-usual groups were rerandomized to either a VIP 3–5 or treatment-as-usual group. This allowed comparison of families receiving VIP early (from birth to age 3, via VIP 0–3), late (at ages 3–5, via VIP 3–5), both early and late, or neither. Children were evaluated at age 14, 24, and 36 months, as well as at 54 months and in early elementary school. Positive findings for VIP have been found concerning its effects on parents and children. Positive effects on parents included increased reading, teaching, talking, and playing when the child was 6 months old (Mendelsohn et al., 2011a), with these changes persisting through age 54 months (Cates et al., 2017). There was less negative parenting, which included reduced screen time (Mendelsohn et al., 2011b) and physical punishment (Canfield et al., 2015). Parents less often reported having maternal depressive symptoms (Berkule et al., 2014) and stress related to parenting (Cates et al., 2017). Beneficial effects were seen on children's social-emotional development because they displayed less disruptive behavior, such as hyperactivity and aggression, from age 14 months to 3 years (Weisleder et al., 2016) and when assessed at 54 months. Children's ability to sustain attention also improved as a result of receiving VIP. There was roughly a doubling of the impact on attention, with a total effect size of about .5 for those who also participated in both VIP 0–3 and VIP 3–5 (Mendelsohn et al., 2018), that suggests children may be more likely to control their behaviors and sustain attention in a manner required to learn in classrooms.

Evidence of the impact of VIP on parents and children is strong when the program is delivered by the team that has developed it. The 0–3 component has been fully manualized, including a training course and protocols and materials to support fidelity, and is positioned for widespread use. The 3–5 component, while also showing evidence, is currently being manualized, and preparations are being made for its implementation.

Thirty Million Words Project

Use every opportunity to introduce new words and engage in conversation with your children and build on their interests.

Photo © iStockphoto/(monkeybusinessimages).

SNAPSHOT: **Thirty Million Words Project (TMW)**

When created: 2013–2018

Funding: Grants from private foundations

Location: United States, based at the University of Chicago

Research base (limited, fair, strong, very strong): Fair

Who is served: Infants and young children from low-income homes and those who are hard of hearing

Web site: http://tmwcenter.uchicago.edu

Mission: Develops and tests language-focused interventions that are being designed for use through different delivery mechanisms, including the medical system and home visiting programs

In brief: TMW is a set of related projects that are working through health-delivery systems to help parents and programs support language development among low-income populations and children with hearing loss.

TMW is based at the University of Chicago and is led by Dana Suskind, Professor of Surgery and Pediatrics and Director of the Pediatric Cochlear Implantation Program. TMW develops and tests language-focused interventions that are being designed for use through different delivery mechanisms, including the medical system and home visiting programs such as HIPPY and Parents as Teachers. Suskind articulated her approach, "There are no silver bullets to impact at a population level . . . our hypothesis is that you need to take a multiple touchpoint approach to really getting this idea and behavior into the groundwater" (personal communication, November 21, 2016).

Suskind and her team plan to embed the TMW suite of evidence-based interventions within the existing health, education, and social service systems of a single medium-size U.S. city. Under the direction of the TMW Center for Early Learning + Public Health, which Suskind now co-leads, the goal is to achieve population-level change in parent and caregiver behavior to optimize their children's foundational brain development.

One strategy the TMW team tested and is using provides caretakers and parents with education about children's cognitive and language development and feedback on their language input using data obtained with the Language ENvironment Analysis (LENA) device (Suskind et al., 2013). This device is a sensitive microphone a person wears that can record conversations for an entire day; the microphone then sends the data to a system that automatically analyzes it to identify which speech is directed to the child, the number of words used, and how conversation partners take turns. Suskind et al. (2013) examined this approach and used it with child care workers who participated in one educational session. They were given language behavior feedback on the amount of their language input and conversational interaction, and they set goals for their future interactions. Significant change in their language input with the children in their care was observed. Developing the Survey of Parent/Provider Expectations and Knowledge (SPEAK), an assessment of parents' knowledge of child development focusing on language and their role in fostering it, is a second thrust of this team's work (Suskind, Leung et al., 2017). It assesses parents' beliefs about their role in supporting their child's development and child-rearing practices that have important implications for language (e.g., use of media). It also assesses parents' attitudes that reflect an orientation toward engaging children in sustained conversations about topics of interest to the child and providing intellectual enrichment. The SPEAK has good psychometric properties, and adults' scores on it correlate with their language ability and their results on a measure of feelings of self-efficacy related to parenting.

The language behavior feedback tool is used to drive behavior change across TMW's suite of curricula, which are aimed at increasing parent–child engagement and promoting children's cognitive, language, and social-emotional development in the first 3 years. TMW curricula are developed in an iterative approach. First, TMW creates a prototype drawing on input from research, key stakeholders, technicians, and pediatricians, and then staff review it with members of the target population to gain feedback to shape the final version (Graf et al., 2017). TMW-Home Visiting, the program's most intensive curriculum, incorporates additional behavior change components beyond language behavior feedback, including video modeling similar to PALS and the VIP, and collaborative goal setting and text nudges (see also Providence Talks, described in Emerging Programs).

Across eight sessions, home visitors introduce families to information about brain development and three core messages, called the *three T's*, that are designed to change behavior—tune in to what the child is saying and doing, talk more, and take turns. The information is conveyed partly through video and computer animations. At each session, parents view videos of themselves as they interact with their child, and they are given LENA feedback about their conversations with their child—the number of words they used, the variety of words used, and the number of speaking turns.

RESEARCH HIGHLIGHTS

The curriculum's effectiveness was initially examined in a pilot randomized controlled trial with 12 intervention families and 11 families in a control group. Results were promising as parents acquired knowledge about child development, which mediated increases in the amount of their talk and the variety of words they used. Children's language use also increased during intervention. The effect sizes at the end of intervention were moderately large, but significant increases in language use and interaction did not sustain at 4 months postintervention (Suskind et al., 2013). Findings from the early study combined with feedback from participants led to program changes. The revised home visiting intervention (12 modules) is now being assessed longitudinally in a 5-year randomized control trial with 206 families in the Chicagoland area. Early results from the longitudinal study reveal that parents who receive the intervention are more knowledgeable about early childhood cognitive and language development, engage in more conversational turn-taking with their child, and utilize more praise, explanations, and open-ended questions but less criticism, physical control, and intrusiveness when interacting with their child (with effect sizes ranging from $\eta 2p = 0.05$ to 0.16; Leung, Hernandez, & Suskind, under review). Future studies will examine the sustainability of caregiver knowledge gain and behavior changes. More important, future research will also investigate the impact of caregiver knowledge gain and behavior changes on young children's cognitive and language outcomes as well as kindergarten readiness.

TMW-Home Visiting was adapted into an initiative called Achieving Superior Parental Involvement for Rehabilitative Excellence (Project ASPIRE) for parents of children with hearing loss and was designed to be implemented through the early intervention program. A small quasi-experimental study examined the effects of this intervention with 32 low-income families and found significant increases in parents' knowledge of child language development and language use with their children, but child effects were not observed (Suskind, Graf et al., 2017). Work is in progress to further develop and assess the effects of this intervention.

TMW has adapted its materials for use with bilingual populations in birthing hospitals and pediatric clinics. TMW-Newborn is used in conjunction with the Universal Newborn Hearing Screening, and TMW-Well Baby is provided during well-baby visits (Suskind, Graf et al., 2017). Other programs include TMW-Let's Talk, being designed for use in group settings, and TMW-Early Childhood Educator, professional development being created for home- and center-based child care providers. All of these foster parents' knowledge of child development and encourage use of the 3T's that are central to TMW curricula.

The TMW Center for Early Learning + Public Health is currently reviewing request for proposal applications and planning the crucial next steps in their effort to select the first TMW community. Through this process, the TMW Center for Early Learning + Public Health hopes to partner with a medium-size U.S. city to deliver its message to all parents and caregivers through varied channels in ways that are tailored to the family's needs and interest.

Home Instruction for Parents of Preschool Youngsters

Mother was once a HIPPY coaching recipient, but now she has advanced to being a HIPPY instructor—empowerment!

Photo courtesy of Ann B. Morse.

SNAPSHOT: **Home Instruction for Parents of Preschool Youngsters (HIPPY)**

When created: 1969

Funding: Diverse public and private sources at state, local, and national levels

Location: International; serving families in 33 countries, including the United States, New Zealand, Australia, Germany, South Africa, Austria, Italy, and Canada

Research base (limited, fair, strong, very strong): Fair

Who is served: Parents of children age 3–5. HIPPY served more than 15,000 children and families in 139 programs across 23 states and Washington, D.C. in 2017.

Web site: http://www.hippyusa.org

Mission: To help vulnerable children achieve long-term academic success, improve parent–child relationships, and increase parent involvement in their children's schools and communities

In brief: HIPPY is a long-standing home visiting program focused on families of children age 3–5 that is highly scripted and has a clear academic focus. It has a widespread presence in the United States and is available in several other countries around the world. Its research base includes studies conducted in Texas, New York, and Arkansas, and the U.S. Department of Health and Human Services evaluated it as being an evidence-based early childhood home visiting service delivery model for the general population (Sama-Miller et. al., 2018).

Empowering Parents to Be Children's First Educators

The home visitor and her guests pull into a housing development in Fairfax County, Virginia, and are greeted at the apartment door by a mother in a bright yellow shirt and blue comfy shoes. The home visitor—a tall, handsome woman dressed in black with a long, colorful, striped scarf—exchanges warm smiles with the mother. Then, as they do for an hour every week, they enter the living room and proceed to role-play and practice the curriculum the mother will be teaching her 4-year-old son. This visit relates to the Week 6 curriculum, which includes different activities tapping literacy, math, science, language, motor, and alphabet skills.

In sharp contrast with other programs, the parent is the immediate focus of attention in HIPPY and the child is nowhere in sight. This allows the parent to gain the skills to be her own child's teacher. The home visitor and parent take turns in the role of parent and child. The home visitor initially assumes the role of the parent, engaging in the first activity with the child, who is played by the mother. This role play permits the mother to predict how her child might react to the activities and demonstrates techniques to encourage positive child engagement. Immediately afterward, the mother takes the role of the teaching parent and presents the next activity to her home visitor, now playing the role of the child. The home visitor alternately cooperates with and gently challenges the mother, allowing her to practice how she might best engage her child effectively during their 15- to 20-minute daily one-to-one sessions during the week.

A great range of activities is presented for this week—reading a book and teaching new book-related vocabulary (literacy), discussing how the main character in the book is feeling and relating those feelings to the child's own life (social-emotional development), making playdough (science) and cutting it into multiple pieces (math and fine motor skills), guessing and predicting how materials react to gravity (science), and throwing beanbags into holes of different shapes in a target (eye–hand coordination). The session ends with celebratory moving and dancing to upbeat music.

After the session, the mother offered that her parent–child bond with her son, who participates in HIPPY, is different than her bond with her older daughter, who did not participate in the program. He sees her as a primary educator. "HIPPY teaches him to find what he has learned in his everyday habitat," she says, and, "He brings back themes they have worked on together." For example, a month after exploring the shape of a six-sided hexagon, he said, "You still haven't shown me an octagon." She feels the knowledge learned through HIPPY empowers him to help her as well, as evidenced by his statement, "Mommy, it's a red light—you supposed to stop!" The mother adds, "HIPPY taught him to be detailed, inquisitive, thoughtful . . . He is now getting differentiated activities at school because he is so advanced."

The mother also reported that the HIPPY program has strengthened her knowledge. When she meets with her son's teacher, she is confident in her understanding of educational vocabulary, and that helps her feel empowered and not intimidated. The program has encouraged her to go out in the community, work with other parents, and tell them "to embrace your role as your child's first educator!"

———————

At the Fairfax County Public Schools HIPPY program office, the program leaders, trained instructors, and members of the on-site parent group were eager to express their pride in, and enthusiasm for, the program and its positive effects on diverse families. Many of the home visitors are mothers who previously participated in the program with their children, and they are delighted to be employed by the organization.

According to Donna Kirkwood, former National Program Director of HIPPY USA, "HIPPY partners with parents to help them prepare their children for success in school." If at all possible, instructors are peer models for the parents in the program because they come from the same communities or background as the parents, which increases the probability that they will be welcome into the parents' homes. The Fairfax County program, for example, strives to pair families with home visitors who are peers from the community—a challenging proposition within a program that in 2016 served 272 children from 33 countries who communicated in 19 languages, including sign language.

In addition to home visits, HIPPY offers biweekly group meetings where parents can learn from each other in the community, review and prepare curriculum activities, and experience enrichment activities geared toward helping them become better advocates for their children and more confident members of their communities.

HIPPY is a long-standing program that is free to families. It started in Israel in 1969 with a mission to enable immigrant children to keep up with their peers and was developed by the National Council of Jewish Women Research Institute for Innovation in Education at Hebrew University, Jerusalem. It grew to be an international program, adopted in the United States in 1984 when Governor Bill Clinton and Hillary Clinton introduced it in Arkansas. In 2017, HIPPY served more than 15,000 children and families in 139 programs in 23 states and Washington, D.C. It is also available in New Zealand, Australia, Germany, South Africa, Austria, Italy, and Canada.

HIPPY USA trains people within the programs but does not fund the programs themselves, so sustainable funding is a major challenge. Programs across the country have received support from diverse sources—private and public early childhood resources at state, local, and national levels (e.g., federal Maternal, Infant and Early Childhood Home Visiting Programs, or MIECHVs; Head Start; Even Start; Title I). Some states have state-funded programs, including Alabama, Florida, and Texas. Other programs are funded through school districts, public housing initiatives, job-training programs, early intervention and prevention programs, civic organizations, and foundations. The programs are intended to serve families most at risk due to poverty, limited English proficiency, and limited parental education. The funders specify income eligibility requirements.

All U.S. HIPPY programs are licensed by HIPPY USA, which requires them to comply with its training and organizational structure.

Training is built in at all levels. New program coordinators receive 4 days of preservice training, and on-site training and technical assistance for new programs is available from HIPPY USA.

The very structured HIPPY curriculum is provided by home visitors from the communities they serve. Each week the home visitors deliver the next set of the 30 scripted, developmentally appropriate curriculum units to the families of the 3- or 4-year-old children in their caseloads. They provide families of 5-year-old children with 15 biweekly units that supplement kindergarten learning. In addition to the weekly curriculum packets, families also receive 26 storybooks and sets of shapes.

RESEARCH HIGHLIGHTS

Because of its long history, HIPPY has been examined in various ways by different research teams. The U.S. Department of Health and Human Services (2018) reviewed the data on HIPPY and determined that it qualifies as an "evidence-based early childhood home visiting service delivery model" for the general population. The program has been evaluated while being delivered by local teams with support by the national HIPPY organization. Most studies found positive and lasting effects on children's academic performance and school adjustment, but there has been variability in findings, which may reflect the difficulty of ensuring consistent, high-quality delivery and continued participation by families who are contending with multiple stressful conditions.

One study randomly assigned participants to enrollment in an existing, locally delivered program or to a no-treatment condition upon entry to a preschool program (Baker, Piotrkowski, & Brookes-Gunn, 1999). The program was delivered in New York for 2 years, with 30 sessions being provided each year. Two cohorts were enrolled. For the first cohort, there were encouraging results at the end of the program and at the end of first grade, 1 year after the program's conclusion. There were moderate to strong positive effects ($d = .28$ to .75) on assessments of children's cognitive skills, reading, math, and teacher ratings of classroom adjustment. These results were not replicated in the second cohort.

A study conducted in Arkansas by the same research team used a matched control group instead of random assignment, and children were not enrolled in preschool during the year prior to kindergarten. At the end of that program, there was evidence of small but not statistically significant effects on reading, math, and school readiness in kindergarten but not at the end of first grade.

Two samples of Latino participants were studied in Texas (Nievar et al., 2011). One analysis compared randomly selected participating families with a randomly selected group from the waiting list. The HIPPY curriculum consisted of 30 sessions delivered 1 year prior to kindergarten. Program participation significantly predicted the quality of home support for learning, taking parental stress and depression into account. The second study examined mathematics scores on a state test given at the end of third grade. Families who had participated in HIPPY were compared with nonparticipants who were eligible for the program. After controlling for income, the comparison showed that HIPPY helped predict mathematics achievement. A similarly designed study also found evidence of positive effects of HIPPY on Latino children's math and reading assessments at the end of third grade (Garcia, 2006, summarized by Ellingsen, Myers, & Boone, 2013).

It was not possible to determine factors accounting for the variability in effects found in the New York and Arkansas studies. Possible causes include differential attrition, subject involvement, quality of program delivery, and differences in the cultural and racial backgrounds of participants. The Arkansas families were nearly all African American, whereas the New York sample was roughly equally divided among African American, Latino, and Caucasian families, with a substantial number of other groups represented. Positive results from Texas were for Latino families. HIPPY uses home visitors from the community, but there may be variability in how different communities respond to the HIPPY approach.

Save the Children

The parent coach guides Mother in using books to promote conversations with her child.

SNAPSHOT: **Save the Children**

When created: 1919

Funding: Charitable organization; funded by individual supporters, collaborations with corporate partners and foundation partners around the world, and other organized philanthropic efforts

Location: International

Research base (limited, fair, strong, very strong): Strong

Who is served: Save the Children serves more than 50 million children in 120 countries, including the United States, prioritizing those who are the most deprived and marginalized. Of these, the Early Childhood and Development (ECD) programs target children from birth to age 6.

Web site: https://www.savethechildren.net

See also *Global Strategy: Ambition for Children 2030* available at https://www.save thechildren.net/sites/default/files/Global%20Strategy%20-%20Ambition%20for%20 Children%202030.pdf

Mission: To provide services related to health and nutrition, education, child protection, and child poverty and protecting rights of children; Save the Children's statement of vision for 2030 states that it will achieve its goals through evidence-based innovation, giving a voice to children as it advocates for improved practices and policies, building partnerships in communities and countries, and achieving results at scale

In brief: Save the Children was established after World War I and now serves children in 120 countries, focusing on the most deprived and marginalized and addressing five broad areas of need—health and nutrition, education, child protection, child poverty, and protecting the rights of children. Literacy and child development outcomes are integral to its focus.

Glimpses From Nepal

It is March 2017. We have traveled to Nepal to meet with the leaders of Save the Children's work there. Afterward, we climb into a van and drive 2 hours outside of Katmandu. We are accompanied by Chhabi Chalagain, the local

director and Binod Davrota, the man responsible for other program staff, data collection, and analysis. When we arrive, they proudly lead us into their new two-room schoolhouse, alive with activity. In one room of this newly painted cement-block building, the teacher is surrounded by eager 4- and 5-year-old children listening to a story being told with great animation. After it ends, they break into small groups and move to the corners of the room where hands-on activities are laid out. One group clusters around a bowl with brightly colored plastic pieces, which the children are encouraged to arrange into patterns of alternating colors. Others are playing a game with small cards that have words written on them, and others are in a book area. The teacher and two aides move among the groups, guiding the children in these activities that have been planned using the Early Literacy and Math (ELM) curriculum that guides preschool teachers in Nepal and other countries served by Save the Children.

A parent educator and the director are waiting in the adjoining room for the mother of one of the children who is participating in the preschool class to arrive and be tutored in parenting skills. The trainer greets her when she arrives, and they sit on the floor at a low table and discuss a picture that depicts a mother dressed in traditional attire, talking with her son as she is doing household work. The trainer engages the preschool student's mother in a conversation about what is happening in the picture and explains the importance of talk and communication. They discuss how she communicates with her child at home and together consider how she might find time to talk with her child. She takes the card home at the end of the lesson and uses it as a reminder. This lesson addressed one of eight central messages, each depicted on a card that is the focus for discussion each week. Other messages include the importance of love and affection, play and games, positive discipline, and health and hygiene. Each one has been carefully developed using guidance from the World Health Organization.

This vignette is a glimpse of two of Save the Children's early childhood programs. Save the Children was founded in 1919 by Eglantyne Jebb to help cope with the devastation wrought by World War I. It now serves more than 50 million deprived and marginalized children in 120 countries, including the United States. It initially focused on nutrition and health-related issues but more recently expanded its focus and now organizes its services around five themes—health and nutrition, education, child protection, child poverty, and protecting rights of children. Its statement of vision for 2030 includes a theory of change that it will achieve its goals by implementing evidence-based innovation, giving a voice to children as it advocates for improved practices and policies, building partnerships in communities and countries, and achieving results at scale. (*Global Strategy: Ambition for Children 2030*, its vision for the future, is available through Save the Children's web site.)

The program we observed reflects several key ingredients of Save the Children's early childhood initiatives. It draws on the local community because it has a local director and a social mobilizer to inform families about the service and recruit volunteers. Coherence and quality are ensured by supplying the teachers and parent educators with material carefully designed to capture essential elements of each activity. Materials are created that the users can understand (e.g., pictures are key to the parenting program because many parents cannot read). We observed two programs being delivered in the same building; this reflects Save the Children's efforts to link its services with others supplied by the government or other agencies. The programs we saw addressed multiple areas of child development through direct service to children and by having parents as mediators. Data are also regularly collected to track program delivery and impact.

RESEARCH HIGHLIGHTS

Multiple rigorous studies have examined the impact of Save the Children's early childhood programs on children and families. Researchers in Bangladesh conducted a study of a version of the early childhood stimulation program that we saw being delivered to the mother (Chinen & Bos, 2016). That program was paired with a nutrition program. Researchers used a randomized control approach in 78 communities in which some families received only the nutrition program and others received the nutrition intervention combined with the parenting program. After families had participated in the program for 18 months, the evaluators found some evidence that parents were providing more stimulating learning in home environments. More important, the study found improved child outcomes in indicators of health, cognition, and social-emotional development. Effects on cognition and social-emotional functioning were small because there were logistical problems delivering the intervention, but the evaluators examined the impact on those who actually received the program as intended. The effect size nearly doubled when only that subgroup was examined, bringing it to a level on par with the impacts seen for more expensive programs. The enhanced health outcome was of special interest because there had been concern that adding the early childhood stimulation program to the nutritional program would detract from the effectiveness of that effort.

Save the Children has developed an open source tool called the *International Development and Early Learning Assessment* (IDELA) that assesses early social, language, attention regulation, and cognitive development (Pisani, Borisvoa, & Dowd, 2015). It has been used to assess early childhood interventions around the world (e.g., Afghanistan, Bhutan, Cambodia, Ethiopia, Vietnam, Rwanda). A summary of findings measured using the IDELA shows these efforts are resulting in quantifiable effects on child development (Save the Children, 2017). In Ethiopia and Rwanda, a version of the ELM that we observed being used in classrooms was delivered in homes over eight sessions. Hands-on activities were provided, along with picture cards to remind parents about the activity. Children whose parents received the materials made stronger gains on the IDELA than those who only went to an early childhood classroom, and they made larger learning gains than their peers who did not receive any early childhood support. Furthermore, children whose families received the parenting programs had skills similar to those of children who had been enrolled in standard early childhood learning centers.

The potential long-term impact of these intervention efforts is signaled by a study conducted in Jamaica. In 1986 and 1987, children between the ages of 9 and 24 months who were identified as having stunted growth were randomly assigned to different experimental conditions, two of which included encouraging parents to increase the quantity and quality of their interactions with their infant (Gertler et al., 2014). A group of children whose growth was not stunted was also identified. When participants and control group children were located 20 years later, those who received intellectual and social stimulation had higher IQs, were more likely to have completed school, and were less likely to be depressed or violent (Walker, Chang, Vera-Hernandez, & Grantham-McGregor, 2011). These benefits translated into the ability to participate in the work force, which was indicated by the fact that they were more likely to hold full-time jobs and other jobs than control group children and were more likely to catch up with the performance of the group of children whose growth was not stunted.

Save the Children has shown itself to be capable of delivering early intervention services throughout the world using diverse systems of delivery that are aligned with local circumstances. Rigorous evaluation studies demonstrate that children and families who are living in poverty, are poorly educated, and are facing serious financial and health-related challenges can benefit from early interventions that promote cognitive and linguistic development. The impact of these early interventions has the potential to translate into substantial long-term benefits.

Reach Out and Read

Good medicine! The pediatrician prescribes reading regularly to children.

Photograph courtesy of Reach Out and Read National Center.

SNAPSHOT: **Reach Out and Read (ROR)**

When created: 1989

Funding: Funding sources vary; the specific medical practice site is responsible for coordinating activities and funding books

Location: International; available in all 50 states and eight other countries. In addition, ROR has inspired replication and supplied technical assistance to 12 other countries, including Brazil, Swaziland, and Haiti.

Research base (limited, fair, strong, very strong): Strong

Who is served: Families of children from birth until kindergarten entry. The program currently serves 4.7 million children and their families at more than 5,800 sites in the United States as well as eight other countries.

Web site: http://www.reachoutandread.org

Mission: To promote language and literacy development in early childhood by having pediatricians work with families during well-baby/well-child visits

In brief: ROR works with pediatricians to make literacy a part of each well-baby/well-child visit. During a doctor's visit, the pediatrician gives a new book to the child and prescribes that the parents regularly read aloud to their infants and young children. The pediatrician models this process as needed to enhance parent–child language interaction and help promote the child's brain development.

Making Literacy Part of Every Checkup

Four-year-old Kamryn is sitting on an examining table holding her new book Don't Let the Pigeon Drive the Bus *(Willems, 2003), which she received upon arrival at the pediatric clinic of Vanderbilt University's Children's Hospital. After the usual check-up procedures, Dr. Pespisa, her pediatrician, reads her the book as her mother looks on. As he reads, he comments on pictures and asks some questions, and Kamryn's mother chimes in with some questions and comments of her own. The pediatrician's comments are designed to model effective reading for the parent while engaging the child. Such interactions*

around books also have been used to help the doctor assess the child's devel-
opmental level at every well-baby visit since Kamryn was 6 months old, and
they will continue until she enters kindergarten.

This interaction was possible because of Jo's Reach Out and Read Book Club, an affiliate of ROR in Nashville, Tennessee. This affiliate was founded by Dr. Rebecca Swan and her husband in memory of their daughter, Johanna. ROR, however, originated in Boston.

In 1989, two pediatricians—Barry Zuckerman and Robert Needleman—and three early childhood educators—Kathleen Mclean, Jean Nigro, and Kathleen Fitzgerald-Rice—developed ROR at Boston City Hospital. Aware that medical practitioners, including medical doctors, nurse practitioners, physician's assistants, and osteopaths, had the unique opportunity to regularly interact with young children and their families, they decided to seize the opportunity to promote the children's overall development as well as physical health. Their idea was that the pediatrician would give a new book to the child during each well-baby/well-child visit and prescribe that the parents regularly read aloud to their infants and young children as a way to enhance parent–child language interaction and help promote the child's brain development. Ideally, the doctor would incorporate exposure to the age-appropriate book during the examination and model for the parents how best to read aloud to a child of that age.

The model became so popular that the program expanded to all 50 states within 12 years, distributing about 1.6 million books per year at about 1,500 sites. By 2017, ROR had become a national organization serving 4.7 million children and their families through more than 5,800 sites in the United States, as well as serving children in eight other countries. The program has inspired replication and supplied technical assistance to 12 other countries, including Brazil, Swaziland, and Haiti. ROR's vision is to incorporate these practices in all well-child visits. When the program is implemented in an optimal fashion, the waiting room is decorated with colorful posters and handouts that encourage reading, contains books for children of different ages, and provides volunteers to model book-reading methods. See the ROR training video "Throughout the Clinic" (https://www.youtube.com/watch?v=nffi-n_HR7o&t=29s) to see the ROR program in action in such an optimally functioning office (located at the Pediatric Primary Care Center at Boston Medical Center).

In order to become an official ROR site, the staff at a given medical practice need to identify a Medical Consultant to provide oversight and a Program Coordinator to deal with administrative tasks. They also need to find a funding source for the books, submit letters of commitment, fill out the ROR application, and participate in online training.

RESEARCH HIGHLIGHTS

Numerous studies examined the impact of ROR on parents and children using varying methodologies. We provide a brief overview here; see "Reach Out and Read: The Evidence," available through the ROR web site (http://www.reachoutandread.org/our-impact/reach-out-and-read-the-evidence), to gain access to all the supporting research.

Randomly assigning children to the program on alternating days of the week is one approach used in research on ROR. Other studies have compared families and children who are receiving the service in one clinic with those who use a clinic that is not offering the service. Nearly every study has found some evidence of beneficial effects. Eight studies found that parents reported increased frequency of reading and more positive orientations to reading (Needleman, Klass, & Zuckerman, 2006). For example, one study was conducted in a clinic that served mostly Hispanic families. On alternating days, 65 children between ages 5 and 11 months were enrolled and received books; 70 children were not enrolled. At the end of the study, those who were enrolled were three times more likely to list book reading as a favorite activity (Golova, Alario, Vivier, Rodriguez, & High, 1999). The frequency with which parents report reading to their child is also associated with participation. Seven of the nine studies that included this as an outcome found the ROR participants were more likely to report increased frequency of reading. For example, at the end of the study by Golova and colleagues, 64% of participating families reported reading three or more times a week compared with only 24% of nonparticipating families. It is noteworthy that nearly all of these studies were carried out in clinics that served low-income families, many of whom were from racial or ethnic minority groups or learning English as a new language.

ROR is also associated with stronger early language development. In the prospective studies that assigned children to the experimental (ROR) condition on alternating days, parents were asked to report what words children knew, using a well-validated parent report tool (Golova et al., 1999; High, LaGasse, Becker, Ahlgren, & Gardner, 2000). High et al.'s study found small but statistically significant evidence of program impact among children older than 18 months. The strongest evidence comes from a study that compared 4-year-old children in two clinics that served similar populations of African American and Latino families. One clinic had just begun to use the program, whereas the other one had participated for 3 years. Those at the clinic with the estab-

lished intervention reported receiving four books and having conversations with their pediatrician about reading on three occasions compared with the families in the comparison group, who reported being
encouraged to read an average of 1.7 times and had rarely received
a book (an average of .5 books). Children's receptive and expressive
vocabularies were assessed, and the intervention group was found to
have a 6-month advantage on receptive language ability and a 3-month
expressive vocabulary advantage (Mendelsohn et al., 2001).

Evidence consistently indicates this intervention that takes less
than 3 minutes of a pediatrician's time can have a beneficial impact
on children and home child rearing. These studies have strong ecological validity because all have been conducted in settings where the
approach is being used in a real-world manner, rather than in a carefully controlled effort carried out by researchers, and many studies
have appeared in peer-reviewed journals. True random control studies
have not been done, however, and studies have not directly observed
home interactions.

Dolly Parton's Imagination Library

Mom and daughter get cozy to read their new monthly book from Dolly Parton's Imagination Library.

Photo courtesy of Ann B. Morse.

SNAPSHOT: **Dolly Parton's Imagination Library**

When created: 1995

Funding: Mixed public and private sources, including state grants, privately raised funds at the local level, and local affiliates with nonprofit status

Location: International. Dolly Parton's Imagination Library is based in Tennessee, but partnerships have now been created in parts of all 50 states; the program has also expanded to parts of Canada, the United Kingdom, and Australia.

Research base (limited, fair, strong, very strong): Limited

Who is served: Families of children from birth to age 5. Dolly Parton's Imagination Library originated in Tennessee and now serves 68% of the age-eligible children in Tennessee, including (since 2011) all age-eligible children in the Tennessee foster care system. The program is now available to children from birth to age 5 in all U.S. communities that have collaborating local nonprofit partners. Program access varies widely.

Web site: http://www.imaginationlibrary.com

Mission: To inspire a love of books and reading in preschool-age children by ensuring that they have their very own, age-appropriate library of books at home

In brief: Dolly Parton's Imagination Library coordinates the process of ensuring that every enrolled child, regardless of income level, receive a free, new, developmentally appropriate book monthly, from birth to their fifth birthday. Its goal is to inspire a love of books and reading in preschool-age children by ensuring that they have their very own age-appropriate library of books. In 2014, Dolly Parton's Imagination Library earned a Best Practice Award from the U.S. Library of Congress for addressing social barriers to literacy.

Instilling a Love of Reading

Looking out the window, 3½-year-old Hope sees the mailman put a small packet in their mailbox. She calls out excitedly to her mother, "Mommy, Dolly Parton sent me another book in the mail!" Delighted that the book is addressed to her, the child helps unwrap the book, saying, "Mama, read it to me!" Then, as she cuddles up in her mother's lap, they read the new treasure several times. When they are done, Hope puts it on her bookshelf, which

includes 42 books from Dolly Parton's Imagination Library, received one at a
time during each month of Hope's life. Hope has received these books courte-
sy of Governor's Books from Birth Foundation (GBBF), the entity that supports
and sustains Tennessee's partnership with Dolly Parton's Imagination Library.

Hope's mother, Carolyn, says, "It is so special to see, as she gets older,
her excitement at getting a book, seeing her understand it's all for her. It really
has encouraged her to read. We don't always get new books, you know, so
getting a new book is exciting for her." Each book comes with a guide on the
book flap: "It tells you what to do before you start reading, while reading, and
then after you read . . . with hands-on things you can do later, like using action
figures to reenact the story."

Dolly Parton, whose father never learned to read or write, started Dolly
Parton's Imagination Library in her home county in the hills of east
Tennessee in 1995. Her intention was to provide a new book (including her favorite, *The Little Engine That Could*; Piper, 1991) to all of the
children in this rural, low-income area every month between birth and
their fifth birthday. She hoped to instill a love of books and reading in
the children and families. But that was only the beginning of "the little
program that could."

With Tennessee Governor Bredesen's support, Governor's Books
from Birth Foundation (GBBF) was created in 2004 to expand Dolly Parton's Imagination Library statewide, the first state to do so. GBBF's vision
is "a Tennessee where all preschool children have books in their homes,
develop a love of reading and learning, and begin school prepared to
succeed," according to its web site (http://www.governorsfoundation.
org). How was this possible? According to Theresa Carl, president of
GBBF, it creates a unique funding model in which half the cost of purchasing and mailing the books is covered by a state grant and the other
half by privately raised funds at the local level. The GBBF partnered
with local affiliates with nonprofit status to expand access to the Dolly
Parton's Imagination Library to children in every county in Tennessee.
Every enrolled child, regardless of his or her family's income level, is eligible to receive a free, new, developmentally appropriate book monthly
from birth to age 5 (all books are Penguin Young Readers). More than 14
years since the program's inception, all counties have maintained their
investment in the program, despite the challenges involved in raising
local funds for the books. By February 2018, more than 32 million books
had been mailed to more than 68% of the age-eligible children in Tennessee, including those in the Tennessee foster care system (since 2011).

Expanding beyond the state of Tennessee, the opportunity to
receive monthly books is now available to children from birth to age 5
in all U.S. communities that have collaborating local nonprofit partners.

This diverse group of organizations most frequently includes, but is not limited to, United Way, Rotary Club and other service clubs, library foundations, family foundations, and local government or school districts. According to Jeff Conyers, Executive Director of the Dollywood Foundation, Dolly Parton's Imagination Library partnerships had been created in parts of all 50 states by 2018. Access varied widely. Tennessee and North Carolina provide universal access to enrolled children (Tennessee has done so since 2004; North Carolina launched this in 2018). Access in other states is limited to children enrolled in specific participating counties, cities, districts, or even specified zip codes. Other states with robust enrollment in 2017 include Ohio (85,000), Michigan (about 60,000), Minnesota (about 38,000), and South Carolina (about 37,000), as well as Washington, D.C. (27,000).

How does this complex enterprise work? Who organizes this massive distribution, and who pays for the books and mailing? It is a unique and well-coordinated public–private partnership. Dolly Parton's Imagination Library, a program of the Dollywood Foundation, covers overhead and administrative expenses, selects the developmentally appropriate books, and coordinates ordering and fulfillment of the special-imprint Penguin Young Readers book orders at reduced cost. The community partners and local nonprofit organizations—in the U.S., 501(c)(3)s who are entitled to cheaper, bulk-mailing costs—promote the program and creatively market it. They raise money to cover half the cost of each book and mailing, and they recruit and enroll local children, forwarding that information to Dolly Parton's Imagination Library. For every 1,000 children, the total cost for purchasing and sending 12 books is about $25.00. For example, in Tennessee GBBF covers half the cost of each book ($2.10 in 2017) through an annual state grant, and each county affiliate matches that cost. In addition to managing the state grant, GBBF recruits corporate partners and donors and provides support to affiliates. In addition, GBBF and each affiliate mount local fundraising events, such as social media campaigns.

Dolly Parton's Imagination Library continues its tremendous growth. It has expanded to parts of Canada (2006), the United Kingdom (2007), and Australia (2014), adapting book selection to include some more country-specific books. In 2017, Dolly Parton's Imagination Library mailed more than 232,000 books to Canada, almost 410,000 books to the United Kingdom, and more than 57,000 books to Australia. Executive Director Jeff Conyers indicates that the Dollywood Foundation was mailing an astounding 1,150,000 books per month and more than 13,140,000 books annually by 2017. By March 2018, they reached the milestone of mailing more than 100 million books since the program's inception—one third of those to children in one state: Tennessee.

Dolly Parton's Imagination Library web site provides information to help visitors determine where the program is currently available and how to enroll a child. Given that the people involved in running this program have an interest in expanding it further, clear guidance is presented for groups and organizations that would like to learn how to replicate the program in their area.

RESEARCH HIGHLIGHTS

Dolly Parton's Imagination Library has tracked its success in delivering books on a monthly and annual basis, and it monitors total book distribution efforts using qualitative data, interviews, focus groups, and surveys of parents and community partners. Many studies have examined book distribution and participants' responses and sought to determine the impact of the program on families and children (https://imagination library.com/news-resources/research). Although different reports vary in their specific findings, there is general consistency related to two patterns of results:

1. Family members appreciate the program and view it as having positive effects on their children's interest in books and home patterns of reading.

2. Dolly Parton's Imagination Library partners, along with preschool and kindergarten teachers, believe it has a positive impact on book ownership and home literacy practices.

Because of the program's widespread and long-standing use in Tennessee, several studies conducted there give a sense of the findings that have been reported about Dolly Parton's Imagination Library in general. In Shelby County, Tennessee, an evaluation was conducted in 2015–2016 that included 19,000 children who received books between birth and the time of school entry (The Urban Child Institute, 2017). These children were matched to all fourth graders in 2013–2015. Participating children had statistically significantly better scores on assessments of reading, math, and phonics, and those who had participated in the program longer had the strongest results. Participants also had better school attendance records and fewer suspensions.

In Memphis, Tennessee, 389 kindergarten children who had participated were matched with nonparticipants. The method for identifying control families was not reported; nor were characteristics of participating and nonparticipating families. The school readiness of all children was evaluated by teachers, and parents supplied information about reading practices and family income (Seeding Success, 2017; Sell, Imig, & Shahin, 2014). When income, age, reading habits, and preschool attendance were controlled, participating children scored roughly 10% higher on the reading readiness measure than nonparticipants. Participating families also reported more use of the library. The effects of participating in the program were strongest among families who reported owning the fewest books. A second-grade follow-up study found no group differences in SES or gender and used statistical controls to adjust for differences in participation by race, first language, and pre-K experience (Sell et al., 2014). Participants were significantly more likely than nonparticipants to be in the highest performance level on a computer-delivered reading test, with statistically significant better performance on the vocabulary and reading comprehension scales. No differences between groups were found for student mobility or attendance.

A similar study was conducted in Knox County, Tennessee. It drew on kindergarten entry data from a sample of 8,377 children (Satter, 2014) and found that 70% of the eligible children in the county had signed up for the program. Researchers compared these children's test results with test results of nonparticipating children. Participants were more likely than nonparticipants to be reading on grade level at the end of kindergarten, and they displayed small but statistically significant better performance on print and language-related measures at school entry. Results controlled for gender, ethnicity, and economic status. These effects were not found for ELLs or children with special needs.

One of the evaluations found that participation rates among African American families and families for whom English is not the home language were lower than for other groups. To address this challenge, Governor's Books from Birth is seeking to increase enrollment through collaboration with community organizations such as the Tennessee Department of Human Services, the Tennessee Department of Education, the Appalachian Regional Commission, and 19 birthing hospitals.

Although the results are promising, it is important to note that all of the studies use correlational data that cannot demonstrate a causal association between participation in Dolly Parton's Imagination Library and outcomes. The potential complicating factor is that families who participated might have been more effective in supporting their children's development in many ways, including using these books effectively.

Bookstart

At the library, parents and librarians read books to children with colorful pictures, and librarians actively engage children in book reading before they take the books home.

SNAPSHOT: **Bookstart**

When created: 1992

Funding: Funding varies widely across different countries. In the Netherlands, each municipality supports the program.

Location: Bookstart originated in Birmingham, England. It later spread to Wales, Scotland, Portugal, Italy, Belgium, Germany, and the Netherlands—where it is widely implemented as BoekStart—and outside of Europe to Australia, Canada, Colombia, Jamaica, Japan, Korea, New Zealand, and Thailand.

Research base (limited, fair, strong, very strong): Strong

Who is served: Parents of children from birth to age 4 in multiple European countries and several countries outside of Europe. The program is widespread in the Netherlands, where all parents of newborns are invited to participate; as of 2015, the program was delivered throughout the country in 99% of libraries.

Web site: https://www.boekstartpro.nl/home.html

Mission: Bookstart is a program that aims to promote reading with very young children and allow parents with young children to enjoy books

In brief: Bookstart programs work to encourage parents of newborns to read to their infants. The programs operate through local libraries and supply parents with a broad selection of books and information about new books. Tips for reading to children are provided through print and online materials as well as in-person meetings.

A Glimpse From Holland: Inge and Ton Visit Their Local Library

We enter an inviting local library in Leiden, Holland, and are met by the librar-ian who is responsible for the delivery of the BoekStart. She greets Inge, who has been coming to the library on a monthly basis since her son Ton was an infant. (This information is based on a questionnaire that surveyed parents [A. Bus, personal communication, February 25, 2018].) Their initial visit was in response to an invitation they received from their municipality. Ton was 4 months old when they first visited, and Inge was given a small plastic suitcase containing books, a CD with songs, and information about reading aloud. Today, the librarian accompanies Inge and Ton to the comfortable corner that has a rocking chair, a rug, pictures and posters, and a large collection of infant books made possible by BoekStart funds. Inge and Ton browse the books. The librarian chats with them as they select a book and then spend a few minutes reading it before checking it out. The books need to be clean because they are read and actively used by many infants and toddlers; therefore, books are cleaned between uses, and many libraries have washing machines for books made of cloth and other washable material. As mother and child are getting ready to leave, the librarian asks Inge if she has any questions. She tells Inge about an upcoming meeting for parents about reading and about storytimes that recently have been given in Polish and Turkish to accommodate the linguistically diverse local population.

The goal of BoekStart is to encourage parents to begin reading to their infant, preferably on a daily basis. In addition to supplying a broad selection of books, the program informs parents about new books and gives tips for reading, provided through a web site, printed material, and meetings for parents and children. Libraries' budgets include time for the person who supports the program. The BoekStart effort is reinforced by the national health care system. At the 7-month visit to the health clinic, parents are asked whether they have picked up the BoekStart case at their local library and if they have started to read to their young child. There is currently a study to determine the value of having BoekStart coaches present at the health clinic to talk with parents about reading in the waiting room.

This effort has spread rapidly across the Netherlands as increasing numbers of municipalities have adopted it. In 2011, 61% of parents of newborns who were surveyed in participating municipalities had received an invitation to participate, and that number had risen to 88% by 2013. In 2011, 25% of the parents of newborns joined and received the starter kit suitcase; this had risen to 30% by 2013, with about 54,000 families participating. An evaluation conducted in 2013 determined that most libraries (91%) incorporated BoekStart into their standard operations, allocating space and employee effort that enabled libraries to hold an average of 3.7 parent meetings a year. By 2015, the program was delivered throughout the country in 99% of the libraries. BoekStart has a web site that provides parents guidance for selecting books and lists other programs that support early literacy development.

BoekStart is the outgrowth of Bookstart, which began in Birmingham, England, in 1992. Similar programs are now functioning in

Wales, Scotland, Portugal, Italy, Belgium, and Germany and in many countries outside Europe, including Australia, Canada, Colombia, Jamaica, Japan, Korea, New Zealand, and Thailand. In 2000, EURead was founded (https://www.euread.com). It is a consortium of programs that foster early literacy, including book distribution programs throughout the European Union. In England, every child is entitled to a free Bookstart pack at birth to 12 months and again at 3–4 years. Each year, there is a National Bookstart week with a theme with events celebrating the sharing of books, stories, and rhymes. (Visit the following link at the BookTrust web site for more information about Bookstart in the United Kingdom: https://www.booktrust.org.uk/supporting-you/families/our-programmes/bookstart.)

RESEARCH HIGHLIGHTS

One way that Bookstart programs have been evaluated is by tracking the number of books distributed and the spread of the programs. This approach has been widely adopted and is built into the operations of libraries and communities across several countries in Europe. In England, health visitors, librarians, and nursery workers personally give packets of books to families in addition to their regular work responsibilities; this personalized gifting is most common when infant packets are given.

Several studies examined the impact of these programs. A study conducted in the Netherlands found causal evidence of a small but significant effect of BoekStart participation on children's language at age 15 and 22 months, with this effect being carried by parental reports of home verbal interactions with children (Van den Berg, 2015). The effects were especially noteworthy for reactive children; that is, for children who were rated by parents as relatively irritable. It may be that parents of such children tend to shy away from engaging in verbal interactions, but when they are encouraged to do so, children respond particularly well, resulting in a positive cycle of improved interactions (Van den Berg & Bus, 2014).

A follow-up study of 5- and 6-year-old children compared children who participate in BoekStart with a control group from the Home Literacy Environment (Bus & De Bondt, 2017). Books have been available in most families, and children have had access to many books; almost all have received books as a present, have seen their parent reading, and have been read to daily. Interestingly, children's attitude toward reading seems to be associated with participation in The Netherlands version of the program (BoekStart). The study found that children who had participated were more likely to initiate book reading, read independently for a longer period, and visit reading sessions in the library or bookstores. Their parents seem to be better informed about books because they scored significantly higher on a measure of knowledge of children's books.

A randomized control trial study of the effects of the program on families of 2-year-olds found that nearly half (48%) said they were aware of the benefits but receiving the Bookstart+ pack had encouraged them to read more frequently. There was a statistically significant but small positive effect on parents' attitudes toward reading (O'Hare & Connolly, 2010). A second British study found evidence that children who participated in Bookstart were ahead of others in reading when they entered school (reviewed in Dickinson et al., 2012). Other research examining the effects of library-based programs that distribute books in the United States found evidence that showing parents how to read to their children can change patterns of interaction during book reading up to at least 4 months after parents received this guidance. Those who received such training also reported reduced levels of parental stress (reviewed in Dickinson et al., 2012).

In sum, library-based efforts in several western countries have yielded small positive effects on parenting and children's language and early reading. Because true random assignment methodology has not been used, we cannot conclude that these programs cause the observed group level differences because families might initially have had different orientations toward literacy and child development. What is clear is that these programs are popular with parents and libraries and enrich the literacy experiences of countless families.

Sifriyat Pijama and Maktabat al-Fanoos

After teachers introduce the new book in school, children get their own copy to take home.

SNAPSHOT: **Sifriyat Pijama ("Pajama Library")** (for families in Israel who speak Hebrew)

Maktabat al-Fanoos ("Lantern Library") (for families in Israel who speak Arabic)

When created: 2009 (Sifriyat Pijama); 2014 (Maktabat al-Fanoos)

Funding: Multiple sources; the Ministry of Education funds about 60% of costs for the books and distribution, whereas philanthropic sources fund the rest

Location: Israel

Research base (limited, fair, strong, very strong): Fair

Who is served: Hebrew- and Arabic-speaking children in Israel from birth through second grade. Sifriyat Pijama serves about 250,000 preschool children. As of 2016, more than 80,000 first- and second-graders in poorer communities have been served. Maktabat al-Fanoos serves more than 90,000 Arab Israeli children attending public Arabic kindergarten and pre-K schools. As of January 2018, all 80,000 children in first and second grade attending public Arabic schools have been served.

Website: Sifriyat Pijama: http://eng.pjisrael.org
Maktabat al-Fanoos: http://www.al-fanoos.org/english

Mission: To promote early literacy and cultural values through book distribution in schools

In brief: Sifriyat Pijama and Maktabat al-Fanoos are nationwide, parallel programs in Israel promoting reading among Hebrew- and Arabic-speaking families, respectively. Books are delivered to teachers for the children and classroom, along with supporting lesson plans.

Israel has implemented two ambitious book distribution programs designed for both Hebrew- and Arabic-speaking families thanks to collaboration among the Ministry of Education and concerned philanthropic organizations. These programs are the outgrowth of the Harold Grinspoon Foundation's initiative to distribute free, Jewish-themed books to children around the world.

In 2005, Harold Grinspoon, a Massachusetts philanthropist who was inspired by Dolly Parton's Imagination Library program, launched PJ Library, a program that sends out free, Jewish-themed books and music to children age 6 months to 8 years old. The books promote values such as friendship, cooperation, curiosity, creativity, inclusion, kindness to animals, honoring parents and elders, and respecting teachers. Because the Grinspoon Foundation was interested in providing books to as many Jewish children as possible, it established PJ Library programs in Australia, Mexico, and Russia and also developed PJ Library in Spanish for families in several Latin American countries: Costa Rica, El Salvador, Guatemala, Panama, and Uruguay. Subsequently, it launched Sifriyat Pijama (Hebrew for "Pajama Library"), which is designed to support early literacy and Jewish values in Hebrew-speaking Israeli children. The more recently established parallel program, Maktabat al-Fanoos (Arabic for "Lantern Library"), is geared toward non-Jewish, Arabic-speaking children in Israel's Arab communities. It provides culturally appropriate books for the Arab population with plots that explore the values, ethical issues, and emotions that influence children's lives. The books are distributed in partnership with the Ministry of Education, and together, the programs serve about half a million children a year.

Unlike other book distribution programs, these efforts deliver the books to teachers and provide lesson plans for their use. Teachers are given two copies for the classroom library and then distribute a copy to each family. Children in pre-K and kindergarten are each given eight books a year, which is in addition to the eight books they may have already received in their child care programs. Four more books are provided in first and second grade. The books each contain a section in the back with suggestions to parents about book-related activities and conversations. This strategy helps ensure the children have conversations about the books in the classroom and in the home. By distributing the same book to thousands of teachers and hundreds of thousands of children, these efforts create shared points of reference and reinforce widely shared values.

SIFRIYAT PIJAMA

The Sifriyat Pijama program currently provides Hebrew-language books each month to about 250,000 preschool children in more than 8,000 preschools—more than 80% of government preschools in Jewish communities throughout the country. Most books are provided by the Ministry of Education at no cost to the municipality. The program expanded in 2016 to reach more than 80,000 first- and second-graders in poorer communities.

Teachers in participating schools receive training through the ministry and via a monthly newsletter from Sifriyat Pijama. Sifriyat Pijama's annual evaluation consistently reveals that more than 80% of teachers are "very" or "highly" satisfied with the books, and teachers nearly always read them at least once. A strong majority of the teachers read the books two to five times every year, nearly all plan an activity linked to at least one book, and most make such connections for most books. A more extensive evaluation was conducted by the Ministry of Education in 2013–2014 after the program had been operating for 5 years, with many classrooms using it multiple years. There were widespread, very positive perceptions of the program, with 95% or more of the teachers and 96% of the parents expressing satisfaction with it. Teachers had integrated it into their standard classroom routines, and 96% believed it should be mandatory in all classrooms. Teachers consistently said they found it easier to implement in subsequent years and reported slightly stronger approval the longer they used it. Given the importance of religious schools in Israel, it was noteworthy that religious and secular teachers and parents were equally supportive of the program.

Teachers' positive responses reflected the fact that they saw many positive effects on children and home reading practices. In the Ministry of Education evaluation and others, teachers reported that children were increasing their interest in hearing and reading books and acquiring Jewish vocabulary and moral values. They reported that the program fostered stronger bonds with parents, who also read to their children more.

MAKTABAT AL-FANOOS

Maktabat al-Fanoos (Arabic for "Lantern Library") was launched in 2014, and it serves more than 90,000 Arab Israeli children attending public Arabic pre-K and kindergarten schools in Israel. In January 2018, it also began delivery to all 80,000 children in first and second grades. Its goals are well articulated on the home page of its web site (http://www.al-fanoos.org/english): Maktabat al-Fanoos empowers teachers and parents to help children develop learning and mother-tongue language skills, to create a tradition of reading stories together, to enhance children's emotional awareness, and to celebrate the richness of Arab culture.

This program also supplies books to classroom teachers and families, and the books that are sent home are often the only picture books in the children's home. Children receive eight books a year while in preschool and four books a year in first and second grade. The preschool program was evaluated by the Israel Ministry of Education in 2015–2016, its second year of operation, when it served 2,500 classrooms. This evaluation found that nearly all teachers (96%) and parents (93%) were very positive about the program, and nearly all read the books at least once. Evidence of a significant impact on classroom practices includes the findings that 60% of the teachers read the books five or more times, and 93% did a book-related activity. Teachers and parents reported that the program resulted in more regular reading in the classroom and home as well as stimulating discussions about books and the values reflected in them. Teachers often worked with children in small groups, and parents and teachers reported that children were using vocabulary and expressions from the books.

These programs have an admirable record of efficiently delivering millions of books per year that have been well received by parents and integrated into classroom instruction. Data supporting the programs' effectiveness come from surveys that have a good response rate, interviews, and an active Facebook page of teachers' and parents' photographs of book-related art projects, theater productions, and other activities. There have been no formal efforts to study the programs' impact on classrooms or homes, and there are no published studies reporting the programs' effectiveness. The wealth of findings reported in this book regarding the importance of books and book-related conversations, however, supports the value of such an effort. By providing the same books and guidance for instruction to classrooms and homes through the country, each of the Israeli programs is providing shared frames of reference for teachers, children, and parents. Thus, while seeking to enhance early literacy, the programs also strive to improve social cohesion and reinforce cultural values among two different but closely intertwined cultures.

Family Reading Partnership

A highlight of a trip to Wegmans grocery store is getting a free book from the Bright Red Bookshelf (BRB)!

Photo courtesy of Ann B. Morse.

SNAPSHOT: **Family Reading Partnership (FRP)**

When created: 1997

Funding: Nonprofit agency; receives funding from local foundation grants, donations, and sponsorships and relies heavily on volunteers

Location: Tompkins County, New York

Research base (limited, fair, strong, very strong): Limited, but specific program components such as book giveaways have been proven effective in other settings

Who is served: Families of children from birth to 5, starting when the mother is pregnant.

Web site: http://www.familyreading.org

Mission: To create a culture of literacy in which all children have early, frequent, and pleasurable experience with books, together with a loved one, as a special part of everyday family life, right from the start

In brief: FRP coordinates a variety of experiences to encourage literacy in children from birth to age 5. Its flagship program is Books to Grow On, which works in partnership with pediatric offices, hospitals, and the school system to distribute new books to families with young children, starting during the mother's pregnancy and continuing until the child is 5.

CREATING A CULTURE OF LITERACY

Imagine, if you would, taking your 3-year-old child to her pediatrician for an ideal well-child visit. On the way to the doctor's office, you see billboard-size banners posted with child-friendly illustrations and the slogan, "Read to Me, Any Time, Any Place" on the walls outside Wegmans Food Markets, the Salvation Army, the YMCA, and many other businesses. As you enter the doctor's waiting room, you drop off a board book that your child no longer reads into a bin marked, "Donate gently used children's books here." Then your child runs over to the BRB and selects a book to keep that she heard while cuddled in the lap of a Traveling Books volunteer reader at her child care program. The pediatrician gives your child a carefully selected, age-appropriate new book to keep and incorporates the book in assessment of your child's skills. For example, the pediatrician may observe how well your child turns the pages and at what distance she holds the book from her eyes. At the end of the appointment, you and your child go home with the one or two new books, which you place in the library corner of your child's bedroom to read at bedtime. Using well-child visits to facilitate early reading is part of the FRP's (2017) efforts in "creating a culture of literacy one book, one child, one family, and one community at a time."

These are only a small selection of the myriad of literacy-encouraging experiences coordinated by FRP that are available to all children from before birth to age 5 in Tompkins County, New York. In 2015, the Library of Congress Literacy Awards Program identified 14 organizations in the world that use evidence-based practice to enhance the promotion of literacy and reading, and FRP received honorable mention for demonstrating best practices in "creating a community of literacy" (Davis, 2015).

FRP was created in 1997 as the brainchild of founder Brigid Hubberman and its mission was to create a culture of literacy in which all children have early, frequent, and pleasurable experience with books, together with a loved one, as a special part of everyday family life, right from the start. The initial effort focused on providing free, gently used books to children of all economic backgrounds in Ithaca and the rest of Tompkins County, New York. Hubberman reflects 20 years later, "Together we truly changed the very culture of a community, with children's books and family reading reminders becoming embedded enough to feel like this is who we are, and what we do here" (personal communication, 12/16/2016).

Throughout its history, FRP's BRB has been central to the program. It relies on the efforts of hundreds of community volunteers who donate the books individually or through book drives and those who clean, repair, label, and distribute books. They stock the books in BRBs located in schools, child care centers, supermarkets, food pantries, farmer's markets, camps, doctor's offices, courts, the WIC office, and other locations all around the county.

Books to Grow On is the FRP's main program. It partners with pediatric offices, hospitals, and the school system to distribute new books to families, starting before children are born and continuing until the children are age 5. Starting in the last trimester of pregnancy, the obstetrician-gynecologist gives the mother a book and tips for reading aloud to the infant. The infant is given the book *The Very Hungry*

Caterpillar (Carle, 1994) at the hospital when he or she is born. FRP further collaborates with community resources to infuse a culture of book reading in the community by providing a series of books to medical care providers, who give a specific, developmentally appropriate book to all children, regardless of the family's income, along with a prescription for parents to read and tips for reading aloud to the child at eight well-baby and well-child visits: at 2 months, 4, months, 6 months, 12 months, 18 months, 2 years, 3 years, and 4 years of age. The child receives another book when he or she enters kindergarten or when the child enrolls in an Ithaca City School District kindergarten program. Because all of the children in the county are given the same 11 Books to Grow On by kindergarten entrance, they have the common bond of a shared book experience and cultural literacy, which is inclusive across all economic levels in the community.

In addition to receiving the books given to all children, low-income and low-literacy families are eligible for extra benefits designed to encourage book reading, talking, and singing during the infant's first year. Some of these families are eligible for or enrolled in the Maternal Obstetrics Medicaid Services (MOMS) program. Through the Tompkins County Health Department, home visiting nurses give these expectant families *Read-Along Songs,* a colorful bag filled with five books, an accompanying CD, and other resources designed to invite and support talking, reading, singing, and playing with infants right from the start.

Currently managed by Interim Executive Director Amber Smith and advised by Aly Evans, who served as Executive Director from 2016 to 2018, the organization also employs Dorothy Lovelace, Program and Outreach Coordinator, and Jeff Wilkinson, Operations and Program Assistant. Together with their multidisciplinary board, FRP is looking at innovative ways to fund the partnership as it moves forward. FRP's message to value books and read aloud with children has permeated the community and rallied teams of volunteers and collaborations with community partners. The organization provides resources for families on their web site.

RESEARCH HIGHLIGHTS

FRP's success and scope of activities have been impressive, given that there are only three paid staff since 2017, and they are currently receiving neither state nor federal money—only local foundation grants, donations, and sponsorships. FRP now collaborates with more than 150 community agencies with whom families are already engaged, such as schools, child care centers, social services, WIC programs, Head Start and pre-K programs, MOMS programs, local businesses, and more than 35 pediatricians and obstetricians. Through nine pediatric clinics at well-child visits (at 2, 4, 6, 12, 18, 24, 36, and 48 months), it delivered roughly 800 books to each age cohort each year between 2015 and 2018. Two hundred and forty low-income families were provided *Read-Along Songs* books and CDs during their 28th-week visit.

The BRB continues to be the most visible and widely distributed FRP program. There are currently 53 bookshelves and 56 sites where books are given away. Between 2015 and 2016, FRP collected 26,000 books and distributed 23,000 of them. A solid core of volunteers is the engine that keeps the program running; 74% of the volunteers have been with the program for 3 or more years.

This effort has not been subjected to rigorous scientific research due to its grassroots origins, so data regarding its impact on children and families are not currently available. However, thanks to a grant from a local foundation, in 2016–2017 the most complete study of FRP's operations was conducted. Program staff are moving to enhance their collection of implementation data into their routine systems as they position themselves for possible funding from federal, state, or national foundations, which could provide long-term financial security for the organization.

Promising Emerging Programs

Courtesy of Melissa Baralt.

We are not able to include extended descriptions of many of the exciting efforts that are designed to help parents foster their child's language and learning. This section provides an annotated list of a few varied, interesting projects. Further information is available through the web resources provided in the following list.

TECHNOLOGY-BASED PROJECTS

The Juniper Gardens Children's Project at the University of Kansas:
https://jgcp.ku.edu

Researchers at the Juniper Gardens Children's Project have developed the following interventions, observation systems, and apps.

Promoting Communication Strategies (PC TALK): http://www.talk.ku.edu

Promoting Communication Strategies Observation System (PCObs): http://www.talk.ku.edu/pcobs

Project Engage: Using Text Messaging to Build Parents' Capacity to Improve Child Language Learning: http://projectengage.ku.edu

Talk Around Town: A Mobile App: http://TAT.weegoapp.org

Háblame Bebé: A Phone App to Reduce the Word Gap and Promote Bilingualism:
http://www.talkwithmebaby.org/en_espanol

Providence Talks: http://www.providencetalks.org

Project beELL (beELL-NYC): http://beell.org

NATIONAL COALITIONS AND LOCAL PROJECTS

Bridging the Word Gap National Research Network:
http://www.bwgresnet.res.ku.edu

Children's Learning Institute's (CLI's) Interventions to Support Preschool Teachers and Parents: https://www.childrenslearninginstitute.org/contact-us

The Campaign for Grade-Level Reading: http://gradelevelreading.net

Five Steps to Five: https://www.5stepstofive.org

TECHNOLOGY-BASED PROJECTS

The following projects aim to use technology to promote language, communication, and literacy in early childhood. Technologies such as language-encouraging phone apps and text message prompts on mobile phones provide a handy platform for encouraging parents to stimulate their baby's language.

The Juniper Gardens Children's Project at the University of Kansas

The Juniper Gardens Children's Project has developed and studied a variety of naturalistic communication interventions for parents and early interventionists. They include the following interventions:

- PC TALK

- PCObs

- Project Engage: Using Text Messaging to Build Parents' Capacity to Improve Child Language Learning

- Talk Around Town: A Mobile App

Promoting Communication Strategies   PC TALK is described in *Strategies for Promoting Communication and Language of Infants and Toddlers* (Walker & Bigelow, 2012). This manual, which is available in Spanish, describes how strategies can be used across early education and home routines (e.g., meals, play, reading, daily care) to build on child communication from infancy through preschool and make communication goals more intentional. The intervention strategies were designed to be delivered in any language, as long as the speakers delivering the intervention and children speak the same language; therefore, the strategies are appropriate for DLLs.

Promoting Communication Strategies Observation System This tool (PCObs) was developed by Walker, Bigelow, Turcotte, Reynolds, and Muehe (2015). PCObs uses that system in an application that was developed for Android mobile devices. It provides a frequency count and printed graph and report for each language promoting strategy and corresponding child communication. The criterion validity correlation between the adult's use of communication strategies measured by the app and measured by the Infant–Toddler Environment Rating Scale (Harms, Clifford, & Cryer, 1998) was $r = .42$, and the criterion validity correlations to the Preschool

Language Scale, Fifth Edition (Zimmerman, Steiner, & Pond, 2011), were r = .47–.53. Interobserver agreement reported is satisfactory.

Project Engage: Using Text Messaging to Build Parents' Capacity to Improve Child Language Learning Project Engage is developing and studying the effectiveness of using cell phone text messaging in home visiting programs to increase parental engagement and involvement in the program and help home visitors promote parents' use of language-promoting strategies with children in naturalistic settings.

Talk Around Town: A Mobile App Talk Around Town is a mobile app that uses the GPS in a smartphone to provide location-specific tips to parents to stimulate conversations with their children during community outings (e.g., grocery stores, parks) (Bigelow et al., 2017). It was a finalist in the Phase 2 Bridging the Word Gap Challenge. This application consists of two primary components—a mobile application for parents and an online web portal for coaches (e.g., home visitors, speech-language pathologists). The mobile application and web portal interact with each other as coaches select and individualize the prompts directed toward each parent on the mobile app.

Háblame Bebé: A Phone App to Reduce the Word Gap and Promote Bilingualism

The Háblame Bebe phone app, geared to low-income Hispanic mothers, encourages communication in the mother's first language as well as bilingual acquisition. It suggests language to use within the context of daily routines (e.g., dressing, feeding, diaper changing), tracking baby's words in Spanish and English as well as informing parents about language development through videos and weekly text messages. This application was the grand-prize winner of the Health Resources and Services Administration Word Gap Challenge.

Providence Talks

Providence Talks is an effort led by Mayor Jorge Elorza and was the grand-prize winner of the Bloomberg Philanthropies' 2013 Mayors Challenge. Providence Talks is designed to increase the frequency of parent–child conversations. Parents work with a coach who explains the importance of language, discusses strategies for increasing communication, and gives the family a Language ENvironment Analysis (LENA) device that tracks the parent–child interaction. Parents get the feedback and discuss it with their coach.

Project beELL

Project beELL is based at New York University. This program's web site states that it is "harnessing Behavioral Economic insights to build positive parenting habits and optimize the impact of early childhood interventions; recognizing that Early interactions are the cornerstones of child success; and that Language and Literacy activities stimulate children's brains . . . from birth."

Project beELL infuses behavioral economics design elements with early childhood interventions and delivery systems to empower parents and improve children's developmental outcomes. One program that includes 20 community agencies is using texting to encourage parents to read, sing, and talk to their infants. In another project, the beELL-GRS (Getting Ready for School), it is using behavioral economics strategies in an effort to increase parent and family engagement in a play-based early childhood curriculum for preschoolers.

The beELL-DUET program, a collaboration with Temple University, is for expectant low-income mothers. It is striving to gain understanding of expectant low-income parents' knowledge of, and beliefs about, early childhood development, adapt an existing DUET curriculum for use with expecting families, and use behavioral economic principles to encourage uptake and use of the curriculum.

NATIONAL COALITIONS AND LOCAL PROJECTS

Noteworthy national coalitions and local projects that aim to improve early childhood language and literacy include Bridging the Word Gap National Research Network, CLI's Interventions to Support Preschool Teachers and Parents, Campaign for Grade-Level Reading, and Five Steps to Five.

Bridging the Word Gap National Research Network

This research network is composed of researchers, policy makers, practitioners, and funders who collaborate to create and promote a coordinated national research agenda that addresses the word gap (Carta, Greenwood, & Walker, 2014). The Practice-Based Research Collaborative consists of partnerships between researchers and community groups working to develop and test research projects intended to help close the word gap. It is a vibrant and growing group. Several of the projects we have reviewed are part of this effort (e.g., The Juniper Gardens Children's Project, The Thirty Million Words Project at the University of Chicago, Providence Talks).

Children's Learning Institute's Interventions to Support Preschool Teachers and Parents

The CLI has developed a suite of tools and programs designed to improve practice in preschools and child care settings. Many are free to programs based in Texas. They have been developed as part of the highly successful program of research and intervention led by Susan Landry.

The Campaign for Grade-Level Reading

This is a coalition of foundations, nonprofit partners, business leaders, government agencies, states, and communities across the nation designed to enable more children from low-income families to read at grade level by third grade. It includes many initiatives, with nine major early childhood organizations focusing on school readiness.

Five Steps to Five

This is an example of a small grassroots program that was created by two retired businessmen and an experienced group social worker, with input from an early childhood educator. During the school year, on the weekends, the program offers 90-minute early childhood classroom experiences to infants through preschool and employs Head Start staff. Parent education is included and is delivered in English and Spanish. The enthusiasm of families is reflected by the fact that average attendance in 2017 was 16 sessions, and more than 150 families attended three or more times in 2017.

III

Putting It
All Together

7

The Economics of Providing
Support in the Early Years

Children's success in life is fundamentally important to their families and a major concern to society. The chances that a child will grow into a self-sufficient, well-adjusted, and contributing member of society depend on interconnected strands of development that we have discussed—language, conceptual knowledge, executive functioning, and social adjustment. Out of the multitude of experiences and abilities that help shape a child's later development, we focused on language and the experiences that support its emergence. As language develops, it contributes to and benefits from the child's emerging intellectual and social-emotional capabilities.

Families and caregivers play a central role in nourishing the development of these competencies that contribute to early success in school. Children's chances of long-term success are enhanced when they enter school with strong language, broad knowledge of the world, and good self-regulatory ability. Whether a child will ultimately experience success in school is also heavily determined by broader forces associated with schools, peer groups, and the community (Snow et al., 2007), but families and caregivers have the greatest ability to nurture linguistic, intellectual, and social-emotional growth in the years prior to formal schooling. This investment of love, time, and finances can pay long-term dividends because children who are successful in school are more likely to be healthy, live satisfying lives, and contribute to the economic and political life of their communities. Reading is the academic ability that is most directly shaped by children's early language experiences, and early reading is a good predictor of later reading and associated academic success (Dickinson & Tabors, 2001; Duncan et al., 2007; National Early Literacy Panel, 2009; Storch & Whitehurst, 2002).

READING, LANGUAGE, AND ACADEMIC SUCCESS

Cities, states, and countries invest heavily in schools to prepare children to acquire the skills needed by their society. Countries use standardized tools that evaluate their students' academic skills, and these data enable comparisons of students within countries over time and among students in different nations. The following sections discuss trends in student performance data in recent decades within the United States and abroad.

Trends in the United States

The United States tracks the success of its schools by assessing student performance using the National Assessment of Educational Progress (NAEP), otherwise known as our Nation's Report Card (National Center for Education Statistics, 2013c). Since 1971, the U.S. National Center for Education Sciences has tracked the reading abilities of 9-, 13- and 17-year-olds. The NAEP is scored on a scale ranging from 0 to 500, with scoring bands classified as "basic," "proficient," or "advanced" (see Table 7.1, which provides scoring bands for 9-year-olds). At Level 150, basic reading, children can follow brief written directions and match phrases and sentences to pictures. Readers are proficient by the time they reach Level 200 and can understand sequential information, locate facts in paragraphs, and make inferences when reading simple passages. Advanced readers, those scoring above 250, are able to make generalizations, comprehend longer passages, and identify main ideas. Between 1971 and 2012, the gap between the average performance of White and Black children decreased by 21 points, nearly half a score band. The gap between White and Hispanic students decreased by 13 points.

Overall reading skills of students have improved more slowly (National Center for Education Statistics, 2013a). Fourth-grade results

Table 7.1. National Assessment for Educational Progress scoring bands for 9-year-old children

Basic (150–200)	Proficient (201–250)	Advanced (251–296)
153 Recognize an explicit detail in a poem	201 Connect explicit details to a main idea	255 Recognize the main idea of instructions
177 Recognize explicit information	221 Make an inference based on explicit information in a biographical sketch	271 Interpret story details to recognize what happened
198 Recognize an explicitly stated sequence		289 Generalize from details to recognize the meaning of a description
	244 Locate and recognize a fact in an expository paragraph	

Source: National Center for Educational Statistics (2013b).

from 1992 revealed that 62% of fourth graders were reading at the Basic level or above, compared to 68% in 2013. In 1992, only 28% were rated at the Proficient or Advanced levels that are required to integrate and interpret text. In 2013, those higher levels of skill were achieved by 35% of all fourth graders. A study in the state of Tennessee revealed an even more alarming picture (Tennessee Department of Education's Office of Research and Strategy, 2016). In 2013, 43% of third graders were judged to be Proficient or Advanced, but more than three fourths had failed to keep pace with the increasing reading demands of fifth grade, dropping one or more levels (e.g., from Proficient to Basic, from Advanced to Proficient). This is an ominous trend because students who fail to acquire Proficient reading skills by fourth grade are at risk of failing to complete high school (Hernandez, 2012).

Why are students failing to master higher reading levels? Why are some students losing ground in the upper elementary grades? Instructional quality may be one answer, but another explanation has to do with the nature of reading challenges students face as they move through the grades. As children move beyond the initial struggles of learning how to read, they start reading to learn, and the complexity of reading material increases. They encounter more varied and complex vocabulary, sentence, and discourse structures, which require analytic thinking and integration of ideas across long passages (Stevens et al., 2015). After they master the basic mechanics of translating print into language, students' ability to comprehend what they read is increasingly dictated by how well they understand the kind of language used in academic settings. Those with strong skills advance, whereas others encounter problems.

Evidence of the failure to achieve advanced levels of reading comes from an NAEP assessment launched in 2009 that evaluated vocabulary knowledge (National Center for Education Statistics, 2013b). Vocabulary results from 2009 and 2013 for fourth, eighth, and 12th graders and students' reading comprehension are closely related. When reading comprehension and vocabulary scores are compared by quartiles, the stepwise improvement seen in one outcome is mirrored in the other (see Figure 7.1). For example, fourth-grade students in the bottom quartile on their vocabulary assessment were reading at a level of 177 (Basic), whereas those in the top quartile averaged 255 (Advanced). Similar disparities were found at each age.

These are correlations, so it could be that the reading scores account for the vocabulary results just as well as the reverse. Improving reading may partially account for these associations, but early language skills measured very early in life are strongly predictive of later language, which is a good predictor of reading comprehension in the primary grades.

Grade 4

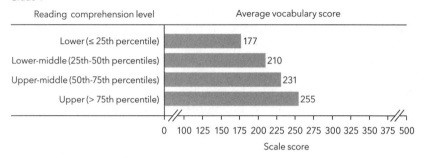

Grade 8

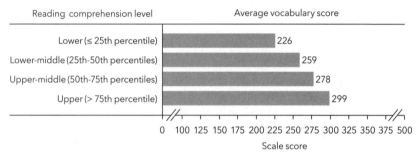

Grade 12

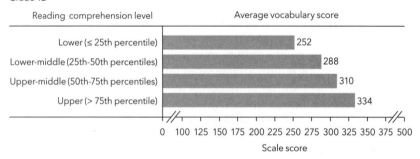

Figure 7.1. Comparison of National Assessment of Educational Progress (NAEP) reading comprehension and vocabulary scores by quartiles. (*Note:* The results for Grades 4 and 8 are from the 2011 reading assessment, and the results for Grade 12 are from the 2009 assessment.) (From National Center for Education Statistics. [2013b]. *The Nation's Report Card: Vocabulary results from the 2009 and 2011 NAEP reading assessments* [NCES 2013 452] [p. 5]. Washington, DC: U.S. Department of Education, Institute for Educational Sciences. Retrieved from http://nces.ed.gov/nationsreportcard/pdf/main2011/2013452.pdf)

International Trends

Countries around the world face the same challenges as the United States. The Organization for Economic Cooperation and Development (OECD) is a collaboration among 34 democracies and more than 70 nonmember economies that conducts studies of education and its impact on economic development. The OECD (2016b) conducted a study in 33 countries of the adults' skills and the degree to which they are prepared to participate in the work force. Adults of all ages were given reading tests, and results were placed into five bands, from basic, low-level literacy (1) to advanced proficiency comprehending complex passages (4, 5). A finding of major significance to this book is that there are very few totally illiterate adults. Although most adults have a good knowledge of basic print skills, many struggle to understand complex text, just as in the United States. The OECD (2016b) report found that poor readers had trouble understanding complex passages. The challenge is to ensure that adults can read complex material with understanding because stronger reading skills are required for skilled jobs that command higher salaries.

The tight link among income, educational background, and educational achievement is similar across all the countries included in the OECD (2016b) study. Low achievement in reading skills was strongly associated with being raised in a home in which neither parent had completed secondary education. Adults from families in which one or both parents had completed college scored 40 points higher on a 500-point assessment scale with an OECD average of 263 than those whose parents had not completed secondary school. A 40-point difference equates to a difference in an entire skill band and would distinguish between reading at band 2 (the level that includes the OECD average) and reading at skill band 1. Skill band 2 tasks require respondents to make matches between the text and information and may require paraphrasing or low-level inferences. Skill band 1 reading tasks simply ask the respondent to read relatively short digital or print statements to locate a single piece of information that is identical to or synonymous with the information given in the question.

ECONOMIC BENEFITS ASSOCIATED WITH EDUCATION

Economic arguments are a major factor driving efforts to improve education, for good reason. *Knowledge economy* refers to workers needing to know far more than facts and doing more than mechanical, repetitive tasks. Rather, those in growing sectors of the economy must understand complex concepts, apply their knowledge, analyze and evaluate information, and communicate effectively (OECD, 2015). According to a report issued by the United Nations Educational, Scientific and Cultural Organization (UNESCO; 2014), the economic impact of improving education is potent, and an OECD (2015) report concluded that by 2030 the gross domestic product could show gains of 1.6% in high-income economies if the country is able to bring all current students up to the basic literacy level required for a knowledge economy.

The Annie E. Casey Foundation launched a campaign in the United States to ensure that children are successful readers by third grade by releasing *Early Warning* (Fiester & Smith, 2010). That report included this startling conclusion: "Every student who fails to complete high school [in the United States] costs society $260,000 in lost earnings, taxes, and productivity" (Fiester & Smith, 2010, p. 5). It also reported that the U.S. economy could have been between $1.31 and $2.3 trillion dollars larger in 2006 if the country had met educational achievement levels of higher performing countries between 1983 and 1998. Similarly, states and cities recognize the vital role of schools in ensuring that businesses have access to the type of educated work force they require.

Economic concerns also drive efforts to improve education worldwide. UNESCO is championing the use of education as a means to achieve sustainable development (UNESCO, 2014). It views education as a primary means of reducing worldwide poverty. The benefits of education are far reaching, and it is a major force for economic growth. For instance, UNESCO used Guatemala as an example in its call for improvements in education. Educational levels in Guatemala only improved 2.3 years between 1965 and 2005, the second lowest increase in that region of the world. If Guatemala had matched the regional average, then its average annual income growth between 2005 and 2010 could have been twice as large—3.6% instead of 1.7%. That is equivalent to an additional $500 per person.

School success has a powerful effect on individuals as well. Workers in the United States who did not complete high school had, on average, an annual salary of $9,161 in 2013 (U.S. Department of Health and Human Services, 2016), which is below the poverty line for a family of one ($11,490) (Hernandez, 2012). Completing high school is also critical to economic success around the world. The OECD's (2016a) annual report stated that citizens who lack high school education were 19% less likely to be employed. Those with college degrees earned 55% more than others who only had a secondary degree. Adults who received scores in skill band 4 or 5 had an average median hourly wage 65% higher than those scoring at or below band 1. Advanced literacy and numeracy skills are clearly needed for jobs that require technological expertise—the growing sector in the economies of all countries.

It has become clear in recent years that a student's likelihood of reaping the benefits of a high school education is heavily determined by the student's early success in school. If students are not reading proficiently by third grade, then they are four times more likely to fail to complete high school as proficient readers (Hernandez, 2012). The odds against students increase as they face additional challenges. Although

16% of all third-grade readers fail to complete high school on time, chances of this occurring rise to 26% among students from low-income families and to 35% among students from low-income families who live in urban communities. The economic benefits that accrue to people who receive a good education are not equally available to all.

EDUCATION, HEALTH, AND WELL-BEING

Education and literacy in particular are also national priorities in many countries because of their association with improved health and well-being. These benefits are tied to economic factors; healthy, well-adjusted citizens are better able to participate in society, and those who have satisfying jobs that pay a living wage are more likely to be healthy and well adjusted. The fact that the United States funds research on reading through the NIH demonstrates recognition of the connection between literacy and health. This association between health and literacy was examined by a team of investigators that reviewed more than 3,000 studies conducted between 1980 and 2003 (DeWalt, Berkman, Sheridan, Lohr, & Pignone, 2004). Higher literacy levels were related to reduced hospitalization, consistency in taking medications, and the ability of parents to control their children's diabetes. Women with little education were more subject to depression. Moreover, youth from low-income families who were 2 years or more behind in reading were at risk for other adverse outcomes as well. They were more likely to carry a weapon, miss school, and be in a fight that required medical treatment. The authors concluded, "People who read at lower levels are generally 1.5 to 3 times more likely to have an adverse outcome as people who read at higher levels" (DeWalt et al., 2004).

If a lack of education is associated with adverse outcomes, then the converse is also true—increased levels of education are associated with better outcomes in health and other aspects of life. In 1970, 50% of adults over age 15 in less well-developed countries had never attended school. That number had dropped to 34% in 2000 (Levine, Levine, Schnell-Anzola, Rowe, & Dexter, 2012). These increases in education have had a broad range of beneficial effects. In addition to boosting the income of individuals and communities, educational improvements have reduced inequality, improved nutrition and health among children, and led to greater gender equality and lower fertility levels (UNESCO, 2014).

Anthropologists have offered varying explanations for the often-noticed association between increased education and reduced fertility and child mortality. An effort to understand this relationship was launched in 1983 by Sarah and Robert Levine (Levine et al., 2012). They

Table 7.2. Effects of girls' learning academic language patterns of discourse as students on the health and educational outcomes of their children later in life

Teacher-pupil role	
Health outcomes	Educational outcomes
Internalize pupil role; follow expert verbal instructions	Internalize teacher role; give verbal advice and ask questions
Attend to and understand expert advice given in the clinic and through the media; effectively communicate health history and concerns	Adopt pedagogical mother practices; talk to infants and toddlers; respond to their interests and questions
Use health services including prenatal care, immunization, emergency care and adopt domestic hygiene and health practices	Child learns vocabulary and orientation toward using language to communicate
Reduce infant and child mortality and disease	Child's school performance and reading abilities are stronger

From Levine, R. A., Levine, S., Schnell-Anzola, B., Rowe, M. L., & Dexter, E. (2012). *Literacy and mothering: How women's schooling changes the lives of the world's children.* New York, NY: Oxford; reprinted by permission.

carried out investigations in Mexico, Zambia, Nepal, and Venezuela over the next 15 years that included observational research and testing using a battery of assessments of mothers' language and literacy skills. Steady decreases in infant mortality and fertility rates, accompanied by increases in the number of adults being educated, occurred between 1970 and 2000. Their findings are surprising and remarkable. Schooling helped mothers learn to read, but it also taught them ways of using language associated with schooling—academic language. Surprisingly, Levine et al.'s analyses led them to conclude that that most important factor accounting for improved outcomes was not improvement in reading skill. What mattered most was learning to use academic language and internalizing the ways of interacting used by teachers as they relate to pupils in traditional schools. As students, girls were in the role of learners, but they became familiar with the adult role. Later, as mothers, they knew how to exchange information with authority figures such as doctors and were more likely to adopt the tutorial and supportive role of teachers with their children. Levine et al. summarized the pathway leading from schooling to beneficial outcomes in Table 7.2.

The findings of this study show the subtle ways that patterns of language use can shape parenting practices. This study highlights that girls learned more than the information being taught in school; they also learned patterns of back-and-forth dialogue used to teach information and display knowledge. These ways of using language shaped how they related to public health officials and how they interacted with their own children. Also, mothers who attended school across societies tended to adopt ways of interacting that were different from those typically found in their culture. The shift in their approach was not directly taught in school; rather, it was the result of having learned new ways of interacting that later proved to be adaptive. Ways of rearing and interacting with young children in the 21st century vary across national, cultural, racial, economic, and ethnic groups. This variability affects how language is used in the home and the nature of language that children acquire. Ways of using language highlighted in Chapter 6 are especially well aligned with the uses of language valued by schools in technological societies.

FACTORS LINKED TO READING ACHIEVEMENT

Education levels are correlated with economic benefits as well as positive outcomes for health and overall well-being. It is important to examine factors linked to long-term reading achievement, including children's home background, their performance at the time of school entry, and the ways that schools respond to the educational needs of young children, given that educational success is so dependent on success in reading.

Reading Achievement and Home Background

Countries around the world face the uncomfortable fact that success in learning to read is strongly related to race, income, and home language background. Historical trends in reading scores in the United States, traced back to 1971, show persistent achievement gaps by race and ethnicity (National Center for Education Statistics, 2013a) . Nine-year-old children classified as Black have consistently lagged behind those classified as White (see Figure 7.2); so have 9-year-old children classified as Hispanic (see Figure 7.3). On average, Whites scored in the middle of the Proficient range in 2015, whereas students from minority backgrounds were just beginning to display Proficient reading skills. Race and ethnicity are strongly correlated with income and parental education, both of which are also associated with achievement. Performance differences were noted between fourth-grade students who did not qualify for free or reduced lunch (i.e., those from richer families) and those who did qualify (i.e., those from poorer families). Children from more affluent homes scored 29 points higher than those from less affluent homes, a gap that was larger than the race/ethnicity gap (National Center for Education Statistics, 2015). DLLs showed a similar

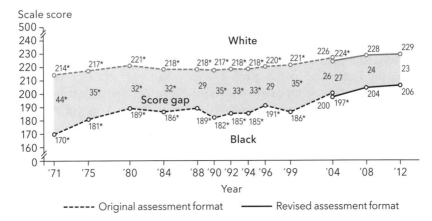

Figure 7.2. Trend in National Assessment of Educational Progress (NAEP) reading average scores and score gaps for White and Black 9-year-old students. (*Note:* Black includes African American. Race categories exclude Hispanic origin. Score gaps are calculated based on differences between unrounded average scores.) (From National Center for Education Statistics. [2013c]. *The Nation's Report Card: Trends in academic progress 2012* [NCES 2013-456] [p. 16]. Washington, DC: U.S. Department of Education, Institute of Education Sciences. Retrieved from https://nces.ed.gov/nationsreportcard/subject/publications/main2012/pdf/2013456.pdf)

level of disadvantage relative to native English speakers (25 points). Parental education data were collected in 12th grade. Students with college-educated parents showed an advantage of 25 points relative to those whose parents did not finish high school. The NAEP vocabulary assessment revealed the same pattern of associations between vocabu-

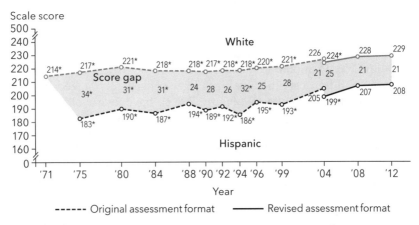

Figure 7.3. Trend in National Assessment of Educational Progress (NAEP) reading average scores and score gaps for White and Hispanic 9-year-old students. (*Note:* White excludes students of Hispanic origin. Hispanic includes Latino. Results are not available for Hispanic students in 1971 because Hispanic was not reported as a separate category at that time. Score gaps are calculated based on differences between unrounded average scores.) (From National Center for Education Statistics. [2013c]. *The Nation's Report Card: Trends in academic progress 2012* [NCES 2013-456] [p. 16]. Washington, DC: U.S. Department of Education, Institute of Education Sciences. Retrieved from https://nces.ed.gov/nationsreportcard/subject/publications/main2012/pdf/2013456.pdf)

lary scores and demographic factors (National Center for Education Statistics, 2013b). For example, in each grade, far more White than Black or Hispanic students scored in the top quartile, and students from low-income homes were three times more likely to score in the bottom quartile.

School Entry Performance Levels

Many of the major studies that track student performance begin to collect data after children have been in school several years. This raises an important question. When do the gaps associated with home factors, which are seen in third and fourth grade, start to appear? If these gaps grow between kindergarten and fourth grade, then schools must shoulder major responsibility for the growing discrepancies. If significant gaps are evident at school entry, however, then child-rearing experiences prior to school are implicated. Of course, one can still fault schools for failing to reduce gaps, but if the gaps are present when children enter school, then they are the product of years of development and may require special efforts to overcome. It is sobering to know that gaps in achievement are present when children enter kindergarten, and gaps seen when children enter school do not disappear over time. Indeed, they are highly predictive of later achievement levels.

All children make considerable growth in academic skills from kindergarten through the grades that follow. The problem is that differential performance levels seen at school entry remain essentially unchanged. Duncan and colleagues (Duncan et al., 2007) combined data from six large longitudinal studies conducted in the United States, Canada, and Britain to identify factors at school entrance that predict later academic success. Reading at school entry was the best predictor of later reading; mathematical skill, language, and attentional skills were also important. Reardon and Portilla (2016) used a similar approach and combined results of five U.S. major studies that assessed children's school readiness and tracked development between 1998 and 2010. In 1998, they found a large gap of 1.25 standard deviations between the performance of children in the top 90th percentile and those in the bottom 10th percentile. To give a sense of the magnitude of a gap of 1.25 standard deviations, consider age equivalences on a widely used standardized assessment tool—the PPVT–IV (Dunn & Dunn, 2007). Suppose a 6-year-old child scored 1.25 standard deviations below the average score of peers in the 90th percentile. That would mean the 6-year-old scored at the level that would be average for a child at 4 years, 2 months. This is a lot of ground to make up, especially considering that the breadth of one's vocabulary is an indicator of one's general knowledge of concepts and facts that are important for school success.

The Role of Schools

We have focused on children's development because families play the dominant role in fostering early development. That comes with a risk. When we link children's home supports for language to later academic outcomes, we risk supporting negative stereotypes based on race or economic status. This is particularly concerning because language is not only of pivotal importance to the competencies we have explored, but it is also central to how people enact and construct their social and cultural identities (Gee, 2005, 2008). Our focus has been strictly on ways of using language that equip children for school success; different sets of competencies are needed for success with peers and in one's community. Patterns of language use vary across cultures and socioeconomic backgrounds in ways that we are just beginning to understand. Available evidence suggests that the ways of using language found in many well-educated middle-class homes mesh well with the demands of schooling (Heath, 1982; Leseman & De Jong, 1998; Leseman & van Tuijl, 2006). Frequent back-and-forth, child-focused conversations and discussions about varied topics during conversations and while reading books support acquisition of broad vocabulary and knowledge. Such interactions also tend to call for use of complex syntax. Furthermore, children become familiar with conversations that encourage them to analyze the characters' motivations and intentions. Homes in which such conversations occur lay the groundwork for children to engage in academic discourse in schools (Scheele, Leseman, Mayo, & Elbers, 2012). Children in other homes spend relatively more time relating to peers, telling and enacting stories, and using language as part of social exchanges.

Different patterns of using language manifest themselves in how children tell stories (Heath, 1983; McCabe & Bliss, 2003; Miller, Cho, & Bracey, 2005) and in the topics about which they are knowledgeable. Their ways of using language and the vocabulary and knowledge they bring with them to school are less well aligned with the routinized, teacher-dominated world of many classrooms and with the expected ways of using language. Patterns of language use tend to correspond to families' socioeconomic backgrounds, but there is considerable variability among those from the same economic and racial background in uses of language that align with schools (see Chapter 5) (Rowe, 2008; Sperry, Sperry, & Miller, 2018; Weizman & Snow, 2001). Those working with families from varied races, cultures, and income levels need to be cognizant of that school-linked variability and aware of culturally linked strengths that children and their families may have. We have mentioned the vibrant storytelling traditions in many cultures.

When I (David Dickinson) was teaching fifth grade in a working-class African American community, I became aware of the amazing poetry written by elementary children from a low-income, African American community in Philadelphia who were taught by Gloria Bush, a gifted teacher. Based on her success, I did a unit encouraging poetic uses of language, including metaphor, and found that my students responded with remarkable eloquence. Such verbal abilities need to be noted and used to support children from all backgrounds.

The strong correlations between standardized assessments of school-entry ability and later schooling success can be viewed as evidence of inadequacies in the home—parents have not prepared children for school. But one can equally conclude that schools are failing to respond to the needs of children. Schools can be faulted for failing to identify and build on the competencies that children have and miss opportunities to celebrate the rich and diverse cultural, linguistic, and ethnic heritages of families (Jimenez et al., 2015; Moje et al., 2004; Rowe & Fain, 2013). At the same time, schools cannot overlook the cold, hard fact that to be academically successful, some children have farther to go than others in acquiring the skills and knowledge required. The differences in their home-rearing experiences place them at a disadvantage relative to demands placed on them by schools. Schools, researchers, and publishers have spent considerable effort developing instructional regimes that teach basic decoding skills (e.g., phonemic awareness, phonics, decoding). Far less attention has been given to building children's oral language and world knowledge; yet, that is where great variability is found in early home support for development, and the resulting differences in children's starting points when they enter school matter greatly. Society can help parents recognize the language, conceptual, and social competencies that will pay dividends when their child arrives in school, but it is the schools' task to recognize and celebrate the abilities that children bring with them and to work intensively to ensure that all children have the opportunity to acquire the competencies they need for a technological society.

CAUSE FOR HOPE: POSITIVE TRENDS

Achievement gaps associated with demographic factors are concerning, but certain positive trends are a reason to be hopeful. African American and Hispanic children have made substantial gains in reading skill since the late 1980s. Reardon (Reardon, 2011) analyzed data from 19 longitudinal surveys that included SES information between 1940 and 2001 and found that the disparity between achievement levels of Black students compared with White students declined by approximately 40% (Reardon, 2014). African American and Hispanic students' average scores have improved between 1971 and 2010, moving from scores reflecting basic reading skills, such as simply identifying facts in a paragraph, to beginning-level proficiency abilities, such as connecting facts to the main ideas in a paragraph (Reardon, 2011). Unfortunately, as achievement gaps related to racial background have declined, those associated with income have grown. Income is now two to three times more powerful than race as a predictor of achievement.

The increased impact of economic factors is of great interest to our focus on the role of parents in supporting development. Reardon (2011) suggested that as the gaps in families' wealth and income have grown over the past decades, parents who have more money are increasingly investing in their children's well-being. Enrollment of 3- and 4-year-olds in pre-K has been one form of this investment. Although this trend would seem to increase the educational gap between children from different socioeconomic backgrounds, other trends may be reducing this gap.

A separate study used information from more than 20,000 families collected between 1998 and 2010 and analyzed results of kindergarten entrance examinations, studying children's performance on readiness tests (Bassok et al., 2016). The differences in children's performance associated with family income decreased by 16% over the 12-year period. Teacher reports of students' readiness skills reflected a similar reduction of the impact of income on skills at school entrance.

To understand why children from less advantaged homes were entering school relatively better prepared, Bassok et al. (2016) examined parents' reported child-rearing practices. When they compared the most affluent parents with the least affluent (the top 10% vs. the bottom 10%), they found heartening evidence that the least affluent parents increased more than the top 10% with respect to engaging in several activities that contribute to children's language, knowledge acquisition, and school readiness skills. There was a dramatic reduction in income-linked differences concerning participation in enrichment activities such as book reading, trips to the library, parent involvement in arts and crafts activities, playing games, and opportunities to talk about nature and do science projects. These shifts in parents' practices may be having far-reaching effects on children's developing language and knowledge of the world.

The shifts in parenting behaviors were paralleled by changing beliefs. Parents' responses reflected the increased value they place on readiness skills such as counting and knowing letters. Yet, a change in the value placed on the ability to verbally communicate was not evident, which suggests that parents are coming to recognize the importance of basic skills that are stressed in school, such as the ability to count, name letters, and name colors. These skills are important and easily observed. They also are skills that kindergarten and first-grade teachers are relatively adept at teaching, however. If parents are to prepare children for the type of reading required for success in the technological world, then teachers and policy makers must attend more fully to the importance of language-related skills that support analytical thinking, understanding complex texts, and acquiring a broad and deep vocabulary that is associated with world knowledge.

It is encouraging that families with limited income are gaining in their awareness of and engagement in activities that support their children's learning. Income is very unequally distributed in society (Burton, Mattingly, Pedroza, & Welsh, 2017) and these disparities are likely to last a long time. But parents, early educators, and local, state, and national policy initiatives can help those at the lower end of the socioeconomic ladder better ensure that their children enter school prepared to engage in the demands of academic learning. Income need not determine educational outcomes. The OECD Programme for International Student Assessment found that countries around the world differ greatly in the extent to which students' SES influences their learning outcomes. Countries can foster equitable systems that reduce the impact of socioeconomic background on performance and outcomes. The United States has historically been among those in which income carries the most weight. Programs such as those we have profiled in this book are one way society can continue its progress in leveling the academic playing field for children from all backgrounds.

SUMMARY: IMPLICATIONS FOR POLICY MAKERS

We have been able to draw on decades of rigorous research that has examined many facets of early development with unparalleled rigor. Several core insights have become clear as we traced varied strands of development. First, beginning in the first days of life, sensitive, responsive, and loving parents and caregivers begin to shape their child's development, helping them form strong bonds of attachment while fostering the growth of language and executive functioning. Second, these emerging strands of development are interdependent and nourished by similar types of parent–child interaction. Third, when children enter formal schooling, their ways of using language, coping with their emotions and managing their attention, and relating to others, as well as the breadth and depth of their knowledge, help determine their ability to benefit from school. Fourth, powerful cultural, economic, and historical forces converge and limit the chances that some children will be successful in school. Their struggles can have devastating effects on their lives and communities and negative economic consequences for their communities.

The years between birth and school entry are of pivotal importance for acquiring the competencies required for success in 21st-century societies. We have focused on factors that foster healthy development of children. We have limited the attention paid to the darker picture of the early years that is being painted by those who examine the damaging effects of poverty on both short- and long-term development. Millions of families are raising children while they struggle to earn enough to feed themselves, struggle to find affordable housing as they cope with stresses associated with living in dangerous neighborhoods, and experience subtle and blatant expressions of hostility born of racism and ethnocentrism. There is a robust literature describing the toxic effects of these harmful experiences on children's early and long-term development (Cameron, Eagleson, Fox, Hensch, & Levitt, 2017; Gershon & High, 2015; Jutte, Miller, & Erickson, 2015; Shonkoff & Garner, 2012). Evidence indicates that intervention programs designed for families can play an important role in addressing these problems, especially when delivered in the first 3 years of a child's life, but these initiatives alone are not enough (Shonkoff, 2016). Major societal changes are needed to reverse the systemic problems faced by many families, but these require political will born of broad recognition of the need to create a world that supports families as they engage in the vital task of raising healthy children. A willingness to reverse the growing gap between the haves and have-nots and to share wealth in a more equitable manner is needed for that to occur (Reardon, 2014). Given the political and economic realities, the societal transformation required to create these conditions conducive to rearing young children is in the distant future. Meanwhile, children and families are in need of assistance now, and there are effective strategies.

Organizations around the world are working diligently to help parents and caregivers engage their children in linguistically and intellectually stimulating interactions. Book distribution programs in many countries reach millions of children, setting the stage for parents to read and talk with their children. In Europe, these efforts seek to draw parents to their local libraries; in Israel, they provide a point of connection between preschools and families while spreading coherent messages regarding ethical behavior to all of the country's citizens. Pediatricians around the world give families books, along with advice and a prescription to read. Varied programs use coaching strategies to supply personalized support that is particularly valuable to families with acute needs. Technology is now being used in creative ways to assist parents and programs. These are powerful forces at work today around the world.

A multitude of approaches help parents engage in emotionally, linguistically, and intellectually nurturing interactions with their infants, toddlers, and preschool-age children. What is lacking in the United States, in particular, is coordination of efforts and funding at local, regional, and national levels. Each program must struggle to secure and retain its own funding. Individual pediatricians, clinics, and counties raise funds to buy books; coaching programs depend on hard-to-obtain local or federal grants or limited-time contracts; and individual hospitals and libraries prioritize a program and allocate scarce resources to ensure delivery.

Coordination can occur at a local level. For more than 20 years, the Family Reading Partnership in Ithaca, New York, has encouraged book reading through multiple related initiatives involving clinics, preschools, and volunteers, as it has promoted the importance of reading. Yet, it also struggles to maintain its funding year to year. Although there is political gridlock at the national level, there is broad support for initiatives that benefit young children among communities and states, book distribution programs are widely popular, and health clinics and libraries are eager to deliver programs that benefit all and are particularly eager to serve the most vulnerable citizens. Yet, coordinated delivery of services to promote responsive, nurturing parenting is lacking, so it is not known which models are most likely to be effective. Also, there is a lack of understanding about which approaches are most likely to work with specific segments of society. Immigrants needing to learn English are different from marginalized African American communities that have experienced poverty and racism for generations. People in those communities are distinct from those who are poor and live in isolated communities with few resources such as clinics and libraries. Initiatives to develop models of coordinated delivery systems are needed that work for different communities and systematically study their effects.

There are decades of empirical evidence to build on. A coherent vision of what is possible and strong leadership that includes multiple organizations and sustained funding for program delivery and research is needed. This is a daunting challenge, but it is one that is worth tackling for the sake of generations of children.

References

Abboub, N., Nazzi, T., & Gervain, J. (2016). Prosodic grouping at birth. *Brain and Language, 162*, 46–59. doi:10.1016/j.bandl.2016.08.002

Aber, L., Morris, P., & Raver, C. (2012). *Social policy report: Children, families and poverty: Definitions, trends, emerging science and implications for policy.* Washington, DC: Society for Research in Child Development.

Adamson, L. B., & Bakeman, R. (1991). The development of shared attention during infancy. *Annals of Child Development, 8*, 1–41.

Adger, C. T., Wolfram, W., & Christian, D. (2007). *Dialects in schools and communities.* Mahwah, NJ: Lawrence Erlbaum Associates.

Adrian, J. E., Clemente, R. A., Villanueva, L., & Rieffe, C. (2005). Parent-child picture-book reading, mothers' mental state language and children's theory of mind. *Journal of Child Language, 32*(3), 673–686. doi:10.1017/s0305000905006963

Ainsworth, M. D. S. (1979). Infant-mother attachment. *American Psychologist, 34*(10), 932–937. doi:10.1037//0003-066x.34.10.932

Ainsworth, M. D. S. (1989). Attachments beyond infancy. *American Psychologist, 44*(4), 709–716. doi:10.1037//0003-066x.44.4.709

Alexander, K. L., & Entwistle, D. R. (1988). Achievement in the first 2 years of school: Patterns and processes. *Monographs of the Society for Research in Child Development, 53*(2), 157.

Anda, R. F., Brown, D. W., Felitti, V. J., Bremner, J. D., Dube, S. R., & Giles, W. H. (2007). Adverse childhood experiences and prescribed psychotropic medications in adults. *American Journal of Preventive Medicine, 32*(5), 389–394. doi:10.1016/j.amepre.2007.01.005

Anthony, J. L., Lonigan, C. J., Burgess, S. R., Driscoll, K., Phillips, B. M., & Cantor, B. G. (2002). Structure of preschool phonological sensitivity: Overlapping sensitivity to rhyme, words, syllables, and phonemes. *Journal of Experimental Child Psychology, 82*(1), 65–92. doi:10.1006/jecp.2002.2677

Anthony, J. L., Lonigan, C. J., Driscoll, K., Phillips, B. M., & Burgess, S. R. (2003). Phonological sensitivity: A quasi-parallel progression of word structure units and cognitive operations. *Reading Research Quarterly, 38*(4), 470–487. doi:10.1598/rrq.38.4.3

Arriaga, R. I., Fenson, L., Cronan, T., & Pethick, S. J. (1998). Scores on the Macarthur Communicative Development Inventory of children from low- and middle-income families. *Applied Psycholinguistics, 19*(2), 209–223. doi:10.1017/s0142716400010043

Ayoub, C., Vallotton, C. D., & Mastergeorge, A. M. (2011). Developmental pathways to integrated social skills: The roles of parenting and early intervention. *Child Development, 82*(2), 583–600. doi:10.1111/j.1467-8624.2010.01549.x

Baker, A. J. L., Piotrkowski, C. S., & Brookes-Gunn, J. (1999). The Home Instruction Program for Preschool Youngsters (HIPPY). *The Future of Children, 9*(1), 116–133.

Barbarin, O. A., Downer, J., Odom, E., & Head, D. (2010). Home–school differences in beliefs, support, and control during public pre-kindergarten and their link to children's kindergarten readiness. *Early Childhood Research Quarterly, 25*(3), 358–372. doi:10.1016/j.ecresq.2010.02.003

Barbarin, O. A., Early, D., Clifford, R., Bryant, D., Frome, P., Burchinal, M., . . . Pianta, R. (2008). Parental conceptions of school readiness: Relation to ethnicity, socioeconomic status, and children's skills. *Early Education and Development, 19*(5), 671–701. doi:10.1080/10409280802375257

Barnes, E. M., & Dickinson, D. K. (2017). The relationship of Head Start teachers' academic language use and children's receptive vocabulary. *Early Education and Development, 28*(7): 794-809. doi:10.1080/10409289.2017.1340069

Barnes, E. M., Dickinson, D. K., & Grifenhagen, J. B. (2016). The role of teachers' comments during book reading in children's vocabulary growth. *Journal of Educational Research, 110*(5): 515-527. doi:10.1080/00220671.2015.1134422

Barnes, E. M., Grifenhagen, J. F., & Dickinson, D. K. (2016). Academic language in early childhood classrooms. *The Reading Teacher, 70*(1), 39–48. doi:10.1002/trtr.1463

Barnes, E., et al. (2018, under review). *Mealtimes in Head Start Pre-K classrooms: Examining language-promoting opportunities in a hybrid space.*

Bassok, D., Finch, J. E., Lee, R., Reardon, S. F., & Wadfogel, J. (2016). Socioeconomic gaps in early childhood experiences: 1998 to 2010. *AERA Open, 2*(3), 1–22. doi:10.1177/2332858416653924

Bassok, D., & Latham, S. (2016). *Kids today: Changes in school-readiness in an early childhood era.* Charlottesville, VA: University of Virginia.

beELL. (n.d.). *Home page.* Retrieved from http://beell.org

Belsky, J., & Fearon, R. M. P. (2002). Infant–mother attachment security, contextual risk, and early development: A moderational analysis. *Development and Psychopathology, 14*(2), 293–310.

Berk, L. E., & Spuhl, S. T. (1995). Maternal interaction, private speech, and task-performance in preschool-children. *Early Childhood Research Quarterly, 10*(2), 145–169. doi:10.1016/0885-2006(95)90001-2

Berkule S. B., Cates, C. B., Dreyer, B. P., Huberman, H. S., Arevalo, J., Burtchen, N., . . . Mendelsohn A. L. (2014). Reducing maternal depressive symptoms through promotion of parenting in pediatric primary care. *Clinical Pediatrics, 53*, .460–469.

Bernier, A., Beauchamp, M. H., Carlson, S. M., & Lalonde, G. (2015). A secure base from which to regulate: Attachment security in toddlerhood as a predictor of executive functioning at school entry. *Developmental Psychology, 51*(9), 1177–1189. doi:10.1037/dev0000032

Bernier, A., Carlson, S. M., Deschenes, M., & Matte-Gagne, C. (2012). Social factors in the development of early executive functioning: A closer look at the caregiving environment. *Developmental Science, 15*(1), 12–24. doi:10.1111/j.1467-7687.2011.01093.x

Bernier, A., Carlson, S. M., & Whipple, N. (2010). From external regulation to self-regulation: Early parenting precursors of young children's executive functioning. *Child Development, 81*(1), 326–339.

Biemiller, A., & Boote, C. (2006). An effective method for building meaning vocabulary in primary grades. *Journal of Educational Psychology, 98*(1), 44–62. doi:10.1037/0022-0663.98.1.44

Biemiller, A., & Slonim, N. (2001). Estimating root word vocabulary growth in normative and advantaged populations: Evidence for a common sequence of vocabulary acquisition. *Journal of Educational Psychology, 93*(3), 498–520.

Bigelow, K. M., Irvin, D. W., Turcotte, A., & Tallmon, N. (2017). *Talk Around Town: A mobile app to bridge the word gap.* Paper presented at Bridging the Word Gap Demo Day 2016, Washington, D.C.

Bigelow, K., Walker, D., Turcotte, A., Jia, F., & Irvin, D. (n.d.). *Project Engage: Using text messaging to build parents' capacity to improve child language-learning opportunities.* Retrieved from http://www.bwgresnet.res.ku.edu/wp-content/uploads/2017/04/Bigelow-et-al..pdf.

Binder, J. R., Desai, R. H., Graves, W. W., & Conant, L. L. (2009). Where is the semantic system? A critical review and meta-analysis of 120 functional neuroimaging studies. *Cerebral Cortex, 19*(12), 2767–2796.

Bindman, S. W., Hindman, A. H., Bowles, R. P., & Morrison, F. J. (2013). The contributions of parental management language to executive function in preschool children. *Early Childhood Research Quarterly, 28*(3), 529–539. doi:10.1016/j.ecresq.2013.03.003

Bivens, J. A., & Berk, L. E. (1990). A longitudinal study of the development of elementary school children's private speech. *Merrill-Palmer Quarterly Journal of Developmental Psychology, 36*(4), 443–463.

Blair, C. (2002). School readiness: Integrating cognition and emotion in a neurobiological conceptualization of children's functioning at school entry. *American Psychologist, 57*(2), 111–127. doi:10.1037//0003-066x.57.2.111

Blair, C. (2010). Stress and the development of self-regulation in context. *Child Development Perspectives, 4*(3), 181–188. doi:10.1111/j.1750-8606.2010.00145.x

Bloom, P. (2002). *How children learn the meanings of words.* Cambridge, MA: The MIT Press.

Bohlmann, N. L., Maier, M. F., & Palacios, N. (2015). Bidirectionality in self-regulation and expressive vocabulary: Comparisons between monolingual and dual language learners in preschool. *Child Development, 86*(4), 1094–1111. doi:10.1111/cdev.12375

Bowlby, J. (1969). *Attachment and loss: Vol. 1. Attachment.* New York, NY: Basic Books.

Bretherton, I. (1992). The origins of attachment theory: John Bowlby and Mary Ainsworth. *Developmental Psychology, 28,* 759–775.

Brock, L. L., Rimm-Kaufman, S. E., Nathanson, L., & Grimm, K. J. (2009). The contributions of 'hot' and 'cool' executive function to children's academic achievement, learning-related behaviors, and engagement in kindergarten. *Early Childhood Research Quarterly, 24*(3), 337–349. doi:10.1016/j.ecresq.2009.06.001

Brooks, R., & Meltzoff, A. N. (2008). Infant gaze following and pointing predict accelerated vocabulary growth through two years of age: A longitudinal, growth curve modeling study. *Journal of Child Language, 35*(1), 207–220. doi:10.1017/s030500090700829x

Brown, P., & Levinson, S. C. (1987). Universals in language usage: Politeness phenomena. In E. Goody (Ed.), *Questions and politeness* (pp. 56-289). New York, NY: Cambridge University Press.

Burchinal, M., Field, S., Lopez, M. L., Howes, C., & Pianta, R. (2012). Instruction in Spanish in pre-kindergarten classrooms and child outcomes for English language learners. *Early Childhood Research Quarterly, 27*(2), 188–197. doi:10.1016/j.ecresq.2011.11.003

Burgess, S. R., Hecht, S. A., & Lonigan, C. J. (2002). Relations of the home literacy environment (HLE) to the development of reading-related abilities: A one-year longitudinal study. *Reading Research Quarterly, 37*(4), 408–426.

Burton, L. M., Mattingly, M., Pedroza, J., & Welsh, W. (2017). Poverty. *Pathways, Special Issue: State of the Union—The Poverty and Inequality Report*, 9–12.

Bus, A., & De Bondt, M. (2017, July). *Long-term effects of BookStart on the home literacy environment.* Paper presented at the annual meeting for the Society for Scientific Studies in Reading, Halifax, Canada.

Bus, A. G., & Van Ijzendoorn, M. H. (1988). Mother–child interactions, attachment, and emergent literacy: A cross-sectional study. *Child Development, 59*(5), 1262–1272. doi:10.2307/1130489

Bus, A. G., & Van Ijzendoorn, M. H. (1995). Mothers reading to their 3-year-olds: The role of mother–child attachment security in becoming literate. *Reading Research Quarterly, 30*(4), 998–1015. doi:10.2307/748207

Bus, A. G., Van Ijzendoorn, M. H., & Pellegrini, A. D. (1995). Joint book reading makes for success in learning to read: A meta-analysis on intergenerational transmission of literacy. *Review of Educational Research, 65*(1), 1–21.

Byrne, B., Wadsworth, S., Corley, R., Samuelsson, S., Quain, P., DeFries, J. C., . . . Olson, R. K. (2005). Longitudinal twin study of early literacy development: Preschool and kindergarten phases. *Scientific Studies of Reading, 9*(3), 219–235. doi:10.1207/s1532799xssr0903_3

Cain, K., Catts, H., Hogan, T., Lomax, R., Justice, L. M., Lomax, R., . . . Language and Reading Research Consortium (2015). Learning to read: Should we keep things simple? *Reading Research Quarterly, 50*(2), 151–169. doi:10.1002/rrq.99

Cain, K., & Oakhill, J. (2006). Profiles of children with specific reading comprehension difficulties. *British Journal of Educational Psychology, 76*, 683–696. doi:10.1348/0007099056x67610

Callaghan, T. C., Rochat, P., & Corbit, J. (2012). Young children's knowledge of the representational function of pictorial symbols: Development across the preschool years in three cultures. *Journal of Cognition and Development, 13*(3), 320–353. doi:10.1080/15248372.2011.587853

Cameron, J. L., Eagleson, K. L., Fox, N. A., Hensch, T. K., & Levitt, P. (2017). Social origins of developmental risk for mental and physical illness. *Journal of Neuroscience, 37*(45), 10783–10791. doi:10.1523/jneurosci.1822-17.2017

Cameron-Faulkner, T., & Noble, C. (2013). A comparison of book text and child directed speech. *First Language, 33*(3), 268–279. doi:10.1177/0142723713487613

Canfield, C., Weisleder, A., Cates, C. B., Huberman, H., Dreyer, B. P., Legano, L., . . . Mendelsohn, A. L. (2015). Primary care parenting intervention effects on use of corporal punishment among low-income parents of toddlers: VIP 0–3 impacts on reduced physical punishment. *Journal of Developmental and Behavioral Pediatrics, 36*(8), 586–593.

Carle, E. (1994). *The very hungry caterpillar.* New York, NY: Philomel Books/Penguin.

Carey, S. (1978). The child as word learner. In M. Halle, J. Bresnan, & A. Miller (Eds.), *Linguistic theory and psychological reality* (pp. 264–293). Cambridge, MA: The MIT Press.

Carlson, S. M., Mandell, D. J., & Williams, L. (2004). Executive function and theory of mind: Stability and prediction from ages 2 to 3. *Developmental Psychology, 40*(6), 1105–1122. doi:10.1037/0012-1649.40.6.1105

Carlson, S. M., & Wang, T. S. (2007). Inhibitory control and emotion regulation in preschool children. *Cognitive Development, 22*(4), 489–510. doi:10.1016/j.cogdev.2007.08.002

Carta, J., Greenwood, C., & Walker, D. (2014). *Bridging the Word Gap Research Network.* Retrieved from http://www.bwgresnet.res.ku.edu/

Castro, D. C., Gillanders, C., Franco, X., Bryant, D. M., Zepeda, M., Willoughby, M. T., & Mendez, L. I. (2017). Early education of dual language learners: An efficacy study of the Nuestros Niños School Readiness professional development program. *Early Childhood Research Quarterly, 40,* 188–203. doi:10.1016/j .ecresq.2017.03.002

Cates, C. B., Weisleder, A., Berkule Johnson, S., Seery, A. M., Canfield, C. F., Matalon, M., . . . Mendelsohn, A. L. (2017). *Enhancing early development through promotion of parenting in pediatric healthcare: A factorial rct of the video interaction project.* Paper presented at the Society for Research in Child Development, Austin, TX.

Cates, C. B., Weisleder, A., Dreyer, B. P., Berkule Johnson, S., Vlahovicova, K., Ledesma, J., & Mendelsohn, A. L. (2016). Leveraging healthcare to promote responsive parenting: Impacts of the Video Interaction Project on parenting stress. Journal of Child and Family Studies, 25(3), 827–835. https://doi .org/10.1007/s10826-015-0267-7

Catts, H. W., Adolf, S. M., & Weismer, S. E. (2006). Language deficits in poor comprehenders: A case for the simple view of reading. *Journal of Speech, Language, and Hearing Research, 49*(2), 278–293.

Catts, H. W., Fey, M. E., Tomblin, J. B., & Zhang, X. (2002). A longitudinal investigation of reading outcomes in children with language impairments. *Journal of Speech, Language, and Hearing Research, 45*(6), 1142–1157.

Champion, T., & McCabe, A. (2015). Narrative structures of African American children: Commonalities and differences. In S. Lanehart (Ed.), *Oxford handbook of African American language* (pp. 492–511). New York, NY: Oxford.

Chaney, C. (1992). Language development, metalinguistic skills, and print awareness in 3-year-old children. *Applied Psycholinguistics, 13*(4), 485–514. doi:10.1017/s0142716400005774

Chaney, C. (1998). Preschool language and metalinguistic skills are links to reading success. *Applied Psycholinguistics, 19*(3), 433–446. doi:10.1017/ s0142716400010250

Chatterji, M. (2006). Reading achievement gaps, correlates, and moderators of early reading achievement: Evidence from the Early Childhood Longitudinal Study (ECLS) kindergarten to first grade sample. *Journal of Educational Psychology, 98*(3), 489–507. doi:10.1037/0022-0663.98.3.489

Chinen, M., & Bos, J. M. (2016). Final report for the impact evaluation of the Save the Children Early Childhood Stimulation Program in Bangladesh. Washington, DC: American Institutes for Research.

Christiansen, M. H., & Kirby, S. (2003). Language evolution: Consensus and controversies. *Trends in Cognitive Sciences, 7*(7), 300–307. doi:10.1016/ s1364-6613(03)00136-0

Collins, B. A. (2014). Dual language development of Latino children: Effect of instructional program type and the home and school language environment. *Early Childhood Research Quarterly, 29*(3), 389–397. doi:10.1016/j .ecresq.2014.04.009

Conradt, E., Hawes, K., Guerin, D., Armstrong, D. A., Marsit, C. J., Tronick, E., & Lester, B. M. (2016). The contributions of maternal sensitivity and maternal depressive symptoms to epigenetic processes and neuroendocrine functioning. *Child Development, 87*(1), 73–85. doi:10.1111/cdev.12483

Cote, L. (2001). Language opportunities during mealtimes in preschool classrooms. Beginning literacy with language. In D. K. Dickinson & P. O. Tabors

(Eds.), *Beginning literacy with language: Young children learning at home and school* (pp. 205–222). Baltimore, MD: Paul H. Brookes Publishing Co.

Craig, H. K., Connor, C. M., & Washington, J. A. (2003). Early positive predictors of later reading comprehension for African American students: A preliminary investigation. *Language, Speech, and Hearing Services in Schools, 34*(1), 31–43. doi:10.1044/0161-1461(2003/004)

Cunningham, A. E., & Stanovich, K. E. (1997). Early reading acquisition and its relation to reading experience and ability 10 years later. *Developmental Psychology, 33*(6), 934–945. doi:10.1037/0012-1649.33.6.934

Dansky, J. L. (1980). Cognitive consequences of sociodramatic play and exploration training for economically disadvantaged preschoolers. *Journal of Child Psychology and Psychiatry and Allied Disciplines, 21*(1), 47–58. doi:10.1111/j.1469-7610.1980.tb00015.x

Davis, J. (2015). *Library of Congress literacy awards: Best practices.* Library of Congress, Washington, DC. Read.gov/LiteracyAwards

de Villiers, J. G., & Pyers, J. E. (2002). Complements to cognition: A longitudinal study of the relationship between complex syntax and false-belief-understanding. *Cognitive Development, 17*(1), 1037–1060. doi:10.1016/s0885-2014(02)00073-4

Decasper, A. J., & Fifer, W. P. (1980). Of human bonding: Newborns prefer their mothers' voices. *Science, 208*(4448), 1174–1176. doi:10.1126/science.7375928

Decasper, A. J., & Spence, M. J. (1986). Prenatal maternal speech influences newborns' perception of speech sounds. *Infant Behavior and Development, 9*(2), 133–150. doi:10.1016/0163-6383(86)90025-1

DeLoache, J. S. (2004). Becoming symbol-minded. *Trends in Cognitive Sciences, 8*(2), 66–70. doi:10.1016/j.tics.2003.12.004

Demir, O. E., Rowe, M. L., Heller, G., Goldin-Meadow, S., & Levine, S. C. (2015). Vocabulary, syntax, and narrative development in typically developing children and children with early unilateral brain injury: Early parental talk about the "there-and-then" matters. *Developmental Psychology, 51*(2), 161–175. doi:10.1037/a0038476

DeWalt, D. A., Berkman, N. D., Sheridan, S., Lohr, K. N., & Pignone, M. P. (2004). Literacy and health outcomes: A systematic review of the literature. *Journal of General Internal Medicine, 19*(12), 1228–1239. doi:10.1111/j.1525-1497.2004.40153.x

Di Santo, A., Timmons, K., & Pelletier, J. (2016). Mommy that's the exit: Empowering homeless mothers to support their children's daily literacy experiences. *Journal of Early Childhood Literacy, 16*(2), 145–170. doi:10.1177/1468798415577872

Dickinson, D. K. (2001). Large-group and free-play times: Conversational settings supporting language and literacy development. In D. K. Dickinson & P. O. Tabors (Eds.), *Beginning literacy with language: Young children learning at home and school* (pp. 223–255). Baltimore, MD: Paul H. Brookes Publishing Co.

Dickinson, D. K., Collins, M. F., Nesbitt, K. T., Toub, T. S., Hassinger-Das, B., Hadlely, E. B., . . . Golinkoff, R. M. (in press). Effects of teacher-delivered book reading and play on vocabulary learning among low-income preschool children. *Journal of Cognition and Development.*

Dickinson, D. K., Collins, M. F., & Pion, G. (2016, December). *English–Arabic dual language instruction in an Abu Dhabi preschool.* Paper presented at the Annual Convention of the Literacy Research Association, Nashville, TN.

Dickinson, D. K., Darrow, C. L., & Tinubu, T. A. (2008). Patterns of teacher–child conversations in Head Start classrooms: Implications for an empirically grounded approach to professional development. *Early Education and Development, 19*(3), 396–429. doi:10.1080/10409280802065403

Dickinson, D. K., Griffith, J. A., Golinkoff, R. M., & Hirsh-Pasek, K. (2012). How reading books fosters language development around the world. *Child Development, Research,* Article ID 602807, 15 pagesdoi:10.1155/2012/602807

Dickinson, D. K., Hofer, K. G., Barnes, E. M., & Grifenhagen, J. B. (2014). Examining teachers' language in Head Start classrooms from a systemic linguistics approach. *Early Childhood Research Quarterly, 29,* 231–244.

Dickinson, D. K., McCabe, A., Anastasopoulos, L., Peisner-Feinberg, E., & Poe, M. D. (2003). The comprehensive language approach to early literacy: The interrelationships among vocabulary, phonological sensitivity, and print knowledge among preschool-aged children. *Journal of Educational Psychology, 95*(3), 465–481. doi:10.1037/0022-0663.95.3.465

Dickinson, D. K., McCabe, A., & Essex, M. A. (2006). A window of opportunity we must open to all: The case for high-quality support for language and literacy. In D. K. Dickinson & S. B. Neuman (Eds.), *Handbook of early literacy research* (Vol. II, pp. 11–28). New York, NY: Guilford Press.

Dickinson, D. K., Nesbitt, K. T., & Hofer, K. G. (under review). *Contributions of multiple language competencies to early literacy development.*

Dickinson, D. K., & Porche, M. V. (2011). Relation between language experiences in preschool classrooms and children's kindergarten and fourth-grade language and reading abilities. *Child Development, 82*(3), 870–886. doi:10.1111/j.1467-8624.2011.01576.x

Dickinson, D. K., & Smith, M. W. (1994). Long-term effects of preschool teachers' book readings on low-income children's vocabulary and story comprehension. *Reading Research Quarterly, 29*(2), 105–122.

Dickinson, D. K., & Snow, C. E. (1987). Interrelationships among prereading and oral language skills in kindergartners from two social classes. *Early Childhood Research Quarterly, 2*(1), 1–25. doi:10.1016/0885-2006(87)90010-x

Dickinson, D. K., & Tabors, P. O. (2001). *Beginning literacy with language: Young children learning at home and school.* Baltimore, MD: Paul H. Brookes Publishing Co.

Dionne, G., Tremblay, R., Boivin, M., Laplante, D., & Perusse, D. (2003). Physical aggression and expressive vocabulary in 19-month-old twins. *Developmental Psychology, 39*(2), 261–273.

Donoghue, E., Glassy, D., DelConte, B., Earls, M., Lieser, D., McFadden, T., . . . Council Early, C. (2014). Literacy promotion: An essential component of primary care pediatric practice. *Pediatrics, 134*(2), 404–409. doi:10.1542/peds .2014-1384

Dreyer, B. P., Mendelsohn, A. L., & Tamis-LeMonda, C. S. (2009). *StimQ cognitive home environment.* Retrieved from https://med.nyu.edu/pediatrics/ developmental/research/belle-project/stimq-cognitive-home-environment

Duncan, G. J., Dowsett, C. J., Claessens, A., Magnuson, K., Huston, A. C., Klebanov, P., . . . Japel, C. (2007). School readiness and later achievement. *Developmental Psychology, 43*(6), 1428–1446.

Dunn, L. M., & Dunn, D. M. (2007). *Peabody Picture Vocabulary Test–Fourth Edition (PPVT-IV).* Minneapolis, MN: NCS Pearson.

Dunn, C. C., Walker, E. A., Oleson, J., Kenworthy, M., Van Voorst, T., Tomblin, J. B., . . . Gantz, B. J. (2014). Longitudinal speech perception and language performance in pediatric cochlear implant users: The effect of age at implantation. *Ear and Hearing, 35*(2), 148–160. doi:10.1097/AUD.0b013e3182a4a8f0

Durham, R. E., Farkas, G., Hammer, C. S., Tomblin, J. B., & Catts, H. W. (2007). Kindergarten oral language skill: A key variable in the intergenerational transmission of socioeconomic status. *Research in Social Stratification and Mobility, 25*(4), 294–305. doi:https://doi.org/10.1016/j.rssm.2007.03.001

Dyer, J. R., Shatz, M., & Wellman, H. M. (2000). Young children's storybooks as a source of mental state information. *Cognitive Development, 15*(1), 17–37. doi:10.1016/s0885-2014(00)00017-4

Ehri, L. C., Nunes, S. R., Willows, D. M., Schuster, B. V., Yaghoub-Zadeh, Z., & Shanahan, T. (2001). Phonemic awareness instruction helps children learn to read: Evidence from the National Reading Panel's meta-analysis. *Reading Research Quarterly, 36*(3), 250–287. doi:10.1598/rrq.36.3.2

Eilers, R. E., & Oller, D. K. (1994). Infant vocalizations and the early diagnosis of severe hearing impairment. *Journal of Pediatrics, 124*(2), 199–203. doi:10.1016/s0022-3476(94)70303-5

Ellingsen, K., Myers, L., & Boone, D. (2013). *Summary of Home Instruction for Parents of Preschool Youngsters (HIPPY) child outcome research* [Press release].

Ertel, K. A., Rich-Edwards, J. W., & Koenen, K. C. (2011). Maternal depression in the United States: Nationally representative rates and risks. *Journal of Women's Health, 20*(11), 1609–1617. doi:10.1089/jwh.2010.2657

Essex, M. J., Boyce, W. T., Hertzman, C., Lam, L. L., Armstrong, J. M., Neumann, S. M. A., & Kobor, M. S. (2013). Epigenetic vestiges of early developmental adversity: Childhood stress exposure and DNA methylation in adolescence. *Child Development, 84*(1), 58–75. doi:10.1111/j.1467-8624.2011.01641.x

Evans, M. D. R., Kelley, J., Sikora, J., & Treiman, D. J. (2010). Family scholarly culture and educational success: Books and schooling in 27 nations. *Research in Social Stratification and Mobility, 28*(2), 171–197. doi:10.1016/j.rssm.2010.01.002

Family Reading Partnership. (2017). *Home page.* Retrieved from http://www.familyreading.org

Farah, M. J., Shera, D. M., Savage, J. H., Betancourt, L., Giannetta, J. M., Brodsky, N. L., . . . Hurt, H. (2006). Childhood poverty: Specific associations with neurocognitive development. *Brain Research, 1110,* 166–174. doi:10.1016/j.brainres.2006.06.072

Farkas, G., & Beron, K. (2004). The detailed age trajectory of oral vocabulary knowledge: Differences by class and race. *Social Science Research, 33*(3), 464–497. doi:10.1016/j.ssresearch.2003.08.001

Farroni, T., Chiarelli, A. M., Lloyd-Fox, S., Massaccesi, S., Merla, A., Di Gangi, V., . . . Johnson, M. H. (2013). Infant cortex responds to other humans from shortly after birth. *Scientific Reports, 3,* Article #2851 doi:10.1038/srep02851

Fearon, R. P., Bakermans-Kranenburg, M. J., van Ijzendoorn, M. H., Lapsley, A. M., & Roisman, G. I. (2010). The significance of insecure attachment and disorganization in the development of children's externalizing behavior: A meta-analytic study. *Child Development, 81*(2), 435–456.

Fenson, L., Marchman, V. A., Thal, D. J., Dale, P. S., Reznick, J. S., & Bates, E. (2006). *Macarthur-Bates Communicative Development Inventories: User's guide and technical manual* (2nd ed.). Baltimore, MD: Paul H. Brookes Publishing Co.

Fernald, A., Perfors, A., & Marchman, V. A. (2006). Picking up speed in understanding: Speech processing efficiency and vocabulary growth across the 2nd year. *Developmental Psychology, 42*(1), 98–116. doi:10.1037/0012-1649.42.1.98

Fernald, A., Thorpe, K., & Marchman, V. A. (2010). Blue car, red car: Developing efficiency in online interpretation of adjective–noun phrases. *Cognitive Psychology, 60*(3), 190–217. doi:10.1016/j.cogpsych.2009.12.002

Fernyhough, C., & Fradley, E. (2005). Private speech on an executive task: Relations with task difficulty and task performance. *Cognitive Development, 20*(1), 103–120. doi:10.1016/j.cogdev.2004.11.002

Fiester, L., & Smith, R. (2010). *Early warning! Why reading by the end of third grade matters.* Annie E. Casey Foundation, Baltimore, MD.

Filene, J. H., Kaminski, J. W., Valle, L. A., & Cachat, P. (2013). Components associated with home visiting program outcomes: A meta-analysis. *Pediatrics, 132*, S100–S109. doi:10.1542/peds.2013-1021H

Fitch, W. T. (2005). The evolution of music in comparative perspective. In G. Avanzini, S. Koelsch, L. Lopez, & M. Majno (Eds.), *Annals of the New York Academy of Sciences: Vol. 1060. The Neurosciences and music II: From perception to performance* (pp. 29–49). New York, NY: New York Academy of Sciences.

Fivush, R., & Fromhoff, F. A. (1988). Style and structure in mother–child conversations about the past. *Discourse Processes, 11*(3), 337–355.

Fivush, R., Habermas, T., Waters, T. E. A., & Zaman, W. (2011). The making of autobiographical memory: Intersections of culture, narratives and identity. *International Journal of Psychology, 46*(5), 321–345. doi:10.1080/00207594.2011.5 96541

Flavell, J. H. (2004). Theory-of-mind development: Retrospect and prospect. *Merrill-Palmer Quarterly, 50*(3), 274–290. doi:10.1353/mpq.2004.0018

Ford, D. H., & Lerner, R. M. (1992). *Developmental systems theory: An integrative approach.* Thousand Oaks, CA: Sage Publications.

Fox, S. E., Levitt, P., & Nelson, C. A. (2010). How the timing and quality of early experiences influence the development of brain architecture. *Child Development, 81*(1), 28–40.

Fraley, R. C. (2002). Attachment stability from infancy to adulthood: Meta-analysis and dynamic modeling of developmental mechanisms. *Personality and Social Psychology Review, 6*(2), 123–151. doi:10.1207/s15327957pspr0602_03

Friederici, A. D. (2006). The neural basis of language development and its impairment. *Neuron, 52*(6), 941–952. doi:10.1016/j.neuron.2006.12.002

Fuentes, A. (2015). Integrative anthropology and the human niche: Toward a contemporary approach to human evolution. *American Anthropologist, 117*(2), 302–315. doi:10.1111/aman.12248

Fuhs, M. W., Nesbitt, K. T., Farran, D. C., & Dong, N. B. (2014). Longitudinal associations between executive functioning and academic skills across content areas. *Developmental Psychology, 50*(6), 1698–1709. doi:10.1037/a0036633

Garner, A. S. (2013). Home visiting and the biology of toxic stress: Opportunities to address early childhood adversity. *Pediatrics, 132*, S65–S73. doi:10.1542/peds.2013-1021D

Gee, J. P. (2005). Meaning making, communities of practice, and analytical toolkits. *Journal of Sociolinguistics, 9*(4), 590–594. doi:10.1111/j.1360-6441.2005.00308.x

Gee, J. P. (2008). *Social linguistics and literacies: Ideology in discourses* (3rd ed.). New York, NY: Routledge.

Geertz, C. (1973). *The interpretation of cultures.* New York, NY: Basic Books.

Gershon, N. B., & High, P. C. (2015). Epigenetics and child abuse: Modern-day darwinism: The miraculous ability of the human genome to adapt, and then adapt again. *American Journal of Medical Genetics Part C-Seminars in Medical Genetics, 169*(4), 353–360. doi:10.1002/ajmg.c.31467

Gertler, P., Heckman, J., Pinto, R., Zanolini, A., Vermeersch, C., Walker, S., . . . Grantham-McGregor, S. (2014). Labor market returns to an early childhood stimulation intervention in Jamaica. *Science, 344*(6187), 998–1001. doi:10.1126/science.1251178

Goffman, E. (1971). *Relations in public*. New York, NY: Harper/Colophon Books.

Golinkoff, R. M., Can, D. D., Soderstrom, M., & Hirsh-Pasek, K. (2015). (Baby) talk to me: The social context of infant-directed speech and its effects on early language acquisition. *Current Directions in Psychological Science, 24*(5), 339–344. doi:10.1177/0963721415595345

Golova, N., Alario, A. J., Vivier, P. M., Rodriguez, M., & High, P. C. (1999). Literacy promotion for Hispanic families in a primary care setting: A randomized, controlled trial. *Pediatrics, 103*(5), 993–997. doi:10.1542/peds.103.5.993

Gonzalez, N., Moll, L. C., Tenery, M. F., Rivera, A., Rendon, P., Gonzales, R., & Amanti, C. (1995). Funds of knowledge for teaching in Latino households. *Urban Education, 29*(4), 443–470. doi:10.1177/0042085995029004005

Graf, E., Garofalo, L., Hundertmark, A. C., Montague, A., Montague, G. L., Polash, N., . . . Suskind, D. L. (2017). *Using formative research to develop a hospital-based perinatal public health intervention in the US: The Thirty Million Words Initiative Newborn Parent Education Curriculum. Journal of Early Hearing Detection and Intervention, 2*(1), 2–11.

Grifenhagen, J. F., Barnes, E. M., Collins, M. F., & Dickinson, D. K. (2017). Talking the talk: Translating research to practice. *Early Child Development and Care, 187*(3-4), 509–526. doi:10.1080/03004430.2016.1246444

Groh, A. M., Fearon, R. P., Bakermans-Kranenburg, M. J., Van Ijzendoorn, M. H., Steele, R. D., & Roisman, G. I. (2014). The significance of attachment security for children's social competence with peers: A meta-analytic study. *Attachment and Human Development, 16*(2), 103–136. doi:10.1080/14616734.2014.883636

Groh, A. M., Roisman, G. I., van Ijzendoorn, M. H., Bakermans-Kranenburg, M. J., & Fearon, R. P. (2012). The significance of insecure and disorganized attachment for children's internalizing symptoms: A meta-analytic study. *Child Development, 83*(2), 591–610. doi:10.1111/j.1467-8624.2011.01711.x

Grossmann, T., Johnson, M. H., Lloyd-Fox, S., Blasi, A., Deligianni, F., Elwell, C., & Csibra, G. (2008). Early cortical specialization for face-to-face communication in human infants. *Proceedings of the Royal Society B-Biological Sciences, 275*(1653), 2803–2811. doi:10.1098/rspb.2008.0986

Grusec, J. E., & Maayan, D. (2010). Integrating different perspectives on socialization theory and research: A domain-specific approach. *Child Development, 81*(3), 687–709.

Guttentag, C. L., Pedrosa-Josic, C., Landry, S. H., Smith, K. E., & Swank, P. R. (2006). Individual variability in parenting profiles and predictors of change: Effects of an intervention with disadvantaged mothers. *Journal of Applied Developmental Psychology, 27*(4), 349–369. doi:10.1016/j.appdev.2006.04.005

Haartsen, R., Jones, E. J. H., & Johnson, M. H. (2016). Human brain development over the early years. *Current Opinion in Behavioral Sciences, 10*, 149–154. doi:10.1016/j.cobeha.2016.05.015

Hammer, C. S., Hoff, E., Uchikoshi, Y., Gillanders, C., Castro, D. C., & Sandilos, L. E. (2014). The language and literacy development of young dual language learners: A critical review. *Early Childhood Research Quarterly, 29*(4), 715–733. doi:10.1016/j.ecresq.2014.05.008

Hammer, C. S., Scarpino, S., & Davison, M. D. (2011). Beginning with language: Spanish–English bilingual preschoolers' early literacy development. In S. B. Neuman & D. K. Dickinson (Eds.), *Handbook of early literacy research* (Vol. III, pp. 118–135). New York, NY: Guilford Press.

Hammond, S. I., Muller, U., Carpendale, J. I. M., Bibok, M. B., & Liebermann-Finestone, D. P. (2012). The effects of parental scaffolding on preschoolers' executive function. *Developmental Psychology, 48*(1), 271–281. doi:10.1037/a0025519

Hamre, B. K., & Pianta, R. C. (2001). Early teacher–child relationships and the trajectory of children's school outcomes through eighth grade. *Child Development, 72,* 625–638.

Han, M., Vukelich, C., Buell, M., & Meacham, S. (2014). Beating the odds: A longitudinal investigation of low-income dual-language and monolingual children's English language and literacy performance. *Early Education and Development, 25*(6), 841–858. doi:10.1080/10409289.2014.866920

Harbison, A. L., McDaniel, J., & Yoder, P. J. (2017). The association of imperative and declarative intentional communication with language in young children with autism spectrum disorder: A meta-analysis. *Research in Autism Spectrum Disorders, 36,* 21–34. doi:10.1016/j.rasd.2017.01.003

Harlaar, N., Meaburn, E. L., Hayiou-Thomas, M. E., Wellcome Trust Case Control Consortium, Davis, O. S. P., Docherty, S., . . . Plomin, R. (2014). Genome-wide association study of receptive language ability of 12-year-olds. *Journal of Speech, Language, and Hearing Research, 57*(1), 96–105. doi:10.1044/1092-4388(2013/12-0303)

Harms, T., Clifford, R., & Cryer, D. (1998). *Early Childhood Environment Rating Scale* (Rev ed.). New York, NY: Teacher's College Press.

Harste, J. C., Woodward, V. A., & Burke, C. L. (1984). *Language stories and literacy lessons.* Portsmouth, NH: Heinemann.

Hart, B., & Risley, T. R. (1995). *Meaningful differences in the everyday experience of young American children.* Baltimore, MD: Paul H. Brookes Publishing Co.

Hayes, D. P., & Ahrens, M. G. (1988). Vocabulary simplification for children: A special case of motherese. *Journal of Child Language, 15*(2), 395–410.

Heath, S. B. (1982). What no bedtime story means. *Language in Society, 11*(2), 49–76.

Heath, S. B. (1983). *Ways with words: Language, life and work in communities and classrooms.* Cambridge, United Kingdom: Cambridge University Press.

Henderson, L. M., Yoder, P. J., Yale, M. E., & McDuffie, A. (2002). Getting the point: Electrophysiological correlates of protodeclarative pointing. *International Journal of Developmental Neuroscience, 20*(3–5), 449–458. doi:10.1016/s0736-5748(02)00038-2

Hernandez, D. J. (2012). *Double jeopardy: How third-grade reading skills and poverty influence high school graduation.* Baltimore, MD: Annie E. Casey Foundation.

High, P. C., LaGasse, L., Becker, S., Ahlgren, I., & Gardner, A. (2000). Literacy promotion in primary care pediatrics: Can we make a difference? *Pediatrics, 105*(4), 927–934.

Hindman, A. H., & Wasik, B. A. (2015). Building vocabulary in two languages: An examination of Spanish-speaking dual language learners in head start. *Early Childhood Research Quarterly, 31,* 19–33. doi:10.1016/j.ecresq.2014.12.006

Hindman, A. H., Wasik, B. A., & Snell, E. K. (2016). Closing the 30 million word gap: Next steps in designing research to inform practice. *Child Development Perspectives, 10*(2), 134–139. doi:10.1111/cdep.12177

Hirsh-Pasek, K., Adamson, L. B., Bakeman, R., Owen, M. T., Golinkoff, R. M., Pace, A., . . . Suma, K. (2015). The contribution of early communication quality to low-income children's language success. *Psychological Science, 26*(7), 1071–1083. doi:10.1177/0956797615581493

Hirsh-Pasek, K., & Golinkoff, R. (2008). King Solomon's take on word meaning: An integrative account from the radical middle. *Advances in Child Development and Behavior, 36,* 1–29.

Hirsh-Pasek, K., Golinkoff, R. M., Berk, L. E., & Singer, D. S. (2009). *The mandate for playful learning: Presenting the evidence.* New York, NY: Oxford.

Hirsh-Pasek, K., Golinkoff, R., Hennon, E. A., & Maguire, M. J. (2004). Hybrid theories at the frontier of developmental psychology: The emergenist coalition of word learning as a case in point. In D. G. Hall & S. R. Waxman (Eds.), *Weaving a lexicon* (pp. 173–204). Cambridge, MA: The MIT Press.

Hirsh-Pasek, K., Golinkoff, R. M., & Hollich, G. (2000). An emergentist coaltion model for word learning: Mapping words to objects is a product of the interaction of multiple cues. In R. M. Golinkoff, K. Hirsh-Pasek, L. B. Smith, A. L. Woodward, N. Akhtar, M. Tomasello, & G. Hollich (Eds.), *Becoming a word learner: A debate on lexical acquisition* (pp. 136–164). New York, NY: Oxford.

Hoff, E. (2003). The specificity of environmental influence: Socioeconomic status affects early vocabulary development via maternal speech. *Child Development, 74*(5), 1368–1378. doi:10.1111/1467-8624.00612

Hoff, E. (2006a). Environmental supports for language acquisition. In D. K. Dickinson & S. B. Neuman (Eds.), *Handbook of early literacy research* (Vol. II, pp. 163–172). New York, NY: Guilford Press.

Hoff, E. (2006b). How social contexts support and shape language development. *Developmental Review, 26*(1), 55–88. doi:10.1016/j.dr.2005.11.002

Hoff, E. (2015). Language development in bilingual children. In E. L. Bavin & L. R. Naigles (Eds.), *The Cambridge handbook of child language* (2nd ed., pp. 483–503). New York, NY: Cambridge University Press.

Hoff, E., Core, C., Place, S., Rumiche, R., Senor, M., & Parra, M. (2012). Dual language exposure and early bilingual development. *Journal of Child Language, 39*(1), 1–27. doi:10.1017/s0305000910000759

Hoff, E., & Naigles, L. (2002). How children use input to acquire a lexicon. *Child Development, 73*(2), 418–433. doi:10.1111/1467-8624.00415

Hoff, G., Van den Heuvel, M. P., Benders, M., Kersbergen, K. J., & De Vries, L. S. (2013). On development of functional brain connectivity in the young brain. *Frontiers in Human Neuroscience, 7.* doi:10.3389/fnhum.2013.00650

Hoff-Ginsberg, E. (1991). Mother–child conversation in different social classes and communicative settings. *Child Development, 62*(4), 782–796.

Hoffman, P. R. (1997). Phonological intervention within storybook reading. *Topics in Language Disorders, 17*(2), 69–88.

Hooper, S. R., Roberts, J. E., Zeisel, S. A., & Poe, M. (2003). Core language predictors of behavioral functioning in early elementary school children: Concurrent and longitudinal findings. *Behavioral Disorders, 29*(1), 10–24.

Hopkins, E. J., Collins, M., Dore, R. A., Lawson, J., Schatz, J., Scott, M. E., ... Hirsh-Pasek, K. (2019, March). *Playtime is learning time: A play and reading intervention to teach vocabulary.* Paper presented at the Society for Research in Child Development, Baltimore, MD.

Hostinar, C. E., Sullivan, R. M., & Gunnar, M. R. (2014). Psychobiological mechanisms underlying the social buffering of the hypothalamic-pituitary-adrenocortical axis: A review of animal models and human studies across development. *Psychological Bulletin, 140*(1), 256–282. doi:10.1037/a0032671

Howard, K. S., & Brooks-Gunn, J. (2009). The role of home-visiting programs in preventing child abuse and neglect. *Future of Children, 19*(2), 119–146.

Hurtado, N., Marchman, V. A., & Fernald, A. (2007). Spoken word recognition by Latino children learning Spanish as their first language. *Journal of Child Language, 34*(2), 227–249. doi:10.1017/s0305000906007896

Hurtado, N., Marchman, V. A., & Fernald, A. (2008). Does input influence uptake? Links between maternal talk, processing speed and vocabulary size in Spanish-learning children. *Developmental Science, 11*(6), F31–F39. doi:10.1111/j.1467-7687.2008.00768.x

Huttenlocher, J., Haight, W., Bryk, A., Seltzer, M., & Lyons, T. (1991). Early vocabulary growth: Relation to language input and gender. *Developmental Psychology, 27*, 236–248.

Huttenlocher, J., Vasilyeva, M., Cymerman, E., & Levine, S. (2002). Language input and child syntax. *Cognitive Psychology, 45*(3), 337–374.

Huttenlocher, J., Waterfall, H., Vasilyeva, M., Vevea, J., & Hedges, L. V. (2010). Sources of variability in children's language growth. *Cognitive Psychology, 61*(4), 343–365. doi:10.1016/j.cogpsych.2010.08.002

Huttenlocher, P. R. (2002). *Neural plasticity: The effects of environment on the development of the cerebral cortex.* Cambridge, MA: Harvard University Press.

Jackson, A. M., & Deye, K. (2015). Aspects of abuse: Consequences of childhood victimization. *Current Problems in Pediatric and Adolescent Health Care, 45*(3), 86–93. doi:10.1016/j.cppeds.2015.02.004

Jimenez, R. T., David, S., Fagan, K., Risko, V. J., Pacheco, M., Pray, L., & Gonzales, M. (2015). Using translation to drive conceptual development for students becoming literate in English as an additional language. *Research in the Teaching of English, 49*(3), 248–271.

Johnson, M. H. (2011). Interactive specialization: A domain-general framework for human functional brain development? *Developmental Cognitive Neuroscience, 1*(1), 7–21. doi:10.1016/j.dcn.2010.07.003

Johnson, E. K., & Jusczyk, P. W. (2001). Word segmentation by 8-month-olds: When speech cues count more than statistics. *Journal of Memory and Language, 44*(4), 548–567. doi:10.1006/jmla.2000.2755

Johnson, U. Y., Martinez-Cantu, V., Jacobson, A. L., & Weir, C. M. (2012). The home instruction for parents of preschool youngsters program's relationship with mother and school outcomes. *Early Education and Development, 23*(5), 713–727. doi:10.1080/10409289.2011.596002

Jusczyk, P. W., Houston, D. M., & Newsome, M. (1999). The beginnings of word segmentation in English-learning infants. *Cognitive Psychology, 39*(3-4), 159–207. doi:10.1006/cogp.1999.0716

Jutte, D. P., Miller, J. L., & Erickson, D. J. (2015). Neighborhood adversity, child health, and the role for community development. *Pediatrics, 135,* S48–S57. doi:10.1542/peds.2014-3549F

Kaminski, J. W., Valle, L. A., Filene, J. H., & Boyle, C. L. (2008). A meta-analytic review of components associated with parent training program effectiveness. *Journal of Abnormal Child Psychology, 36*(4), 567–589. doi:10.1007/s10802-007-9201-9

Kendeou, P., White, M. J., van den Broek, P., & Lynch, J. S. (2009). Predicting reading comprehension in early elementary school: The independent contributions of oral language and decoding skills. *Journal of Educational Psychology, 101*(4), 765–778. doi:10.1037/a0015956

Kim, Y. S. (2011). Proximal and distal predictors of reading comprehension: Evidence from young Korean readers. *Scientific Studies of Reading, 15*(2), 167–190. doi:10.1080/10888431003653089

Kim, Y. (2015). Language and cognitive predictors of text comprehension: Evidence from multivariate analysis. *Child Development, 86*(1), 128–144.

King, R. R. (1982). In retrospect: A fifteen-year follow-up report of speech-language-disordered children. *Language, Speech, and Hearing Services in Schools, 13*(1), 24–32.

Kirkorian, H. L., Wartella, E. A., & Anderson, D. R. (2008). Media and young children's learning. *Future of Children, 18*(1), 39–61. doi:10.1353/foc.0.0002

Kochanska, G., Murray, K. T., & Harlan, E. T. (2000). Effortful control in early childhood: Continuity and change, antecedents, and implications for social development. *Developmental Psychology, 36*(2), 220–232. doi:10.1037//0012-1649.36.2.220

Kopp, C. B. (1982). Antecedents of self-regulation: A developmental perspective. *Developmental Psychology, 18*(2), 199–214. doi:10.1037//0012-1649.18.2.199

Korucu, I., Selcuk, B., & Harma, M. (2017). Self-regulation: Relations with theory of mind and social behaviour. *Infant and Child Development, 26*(3). doi:10.1002/icd.1988

Kuhn, L. J., Willoughby, M. T., Vernon-Feagans, L., & Blair, C. B. (2016). The contribution of children's time-specific and longitudinal expressive language skills on developmental trajectories of executive function. *Journal of Experimental Child Psychology, 148*, 20–34. doi:10.1016/j.jecp.2016.03.008

Kuhn, L. J., Willoughby, M. T., Wilbourn, M. P., Vernon-Feagans, L., & Blair, C. B. (2014). Early communicative gestures prospectively predict language development and executive function in early childhood. *Child Development, 85*(5), 1898–1914. doi:10.1111/cdev.12249

Labov, W. (1972). *Language in the inner city: Studies in the Black English vernacular.* Philadelphia, PA: University of Pennsylvania Press.

Lakoff, G., (2003). *Metaphors we live by.* Chicago: The University of Chicago Press.

Landry, S. H., Miller-Loncar, C. L., Smith, K. E., & Swank, P. R. (2002). The role of early parenting in children's development of executive processes. *Developmental Neuropsychology, 21*(1), 15–41. doi:10.1207/s15326942dn2101_2

Landry, S. H., & Smith, K. E. (2006). The influence of parenting on emerging literacy skills. In D. K. Dickinson & S. B. Neuman (Eds.), *Handbook of early literacy research* (Vol. II, pp. 135–148). New York, NY: Guilford Press.

Landry, S. H., Smith, K. E., & Swank, P. R. (2006). Responsive parenting: Establishing early foundations for social, communication, and independent problem-solving skills. *Developmental Psychology, 42*(4), 627–642.

Landry, S. H., Smith, K. E., Swank, P. R., & Guttentag, C. (2008). A responsive parenting intervention: The optimal timing across early childhood for impacting maternal behaviors and child outcomes. *Developmental Psychology, 44*(5), 1335–1353. doi:10.1037/a0013030

Landry, S. H., Smith, K. E., Swank, P. R., & Miller-Loncar, C. L. (2000). Early maternal and child influences on children's later independent cognitive and social functioning. *Child Development, 71*(2), 358–375. doi:10.1111/1467-8624.00150

Landry, S. H., Smith, K. E., Swank, P. R., Zucker, T., Crawford, A. D., & Solari, E. F. (2012). The effects of a responsive parenting intervention on parent–child interactions during shared book reading. *Developmental Psychology, 48*(4), 969–986. doi:10.1037/a0026400

Leseman, P. M., & De Jong, P. F. (1998). Home literacy: Opportunity, instruction, cooperation and social-emotional quality predicting early reading achievement. *Reading Research Quarterly, 33*, 294–318.

Leseman, P. M., Scheele, A. F., Mayo, A. Y., & Messer, M. H. (2007). Home literacy as a special language environment to prepare children for school. *Zeitschrift Fur Erziehungswissenschaft, 10*(3), 334–355. doi:10.1007/s11618-007-0040-9

Leseman, P. M., & van Tuijl, C. (2006). Cultural diversity in early literacy: Findings from Dutch studies. In D. K. Dickinson & S. B. Neuman (Eds.), *Handbook of early literacy research* (Vol. II, pp. 211–228). New York, NY: Guilford Press.

Leung, C. Y. Y., Hernandez, M. W., & Suskind, D. L. (under review). Enriching home language environment among families from low-SES backgrounds: A randomized controlled trial of a home visiting curriculum. *Early Childhood Research Quarterly*.

Leung, C., LoRe, D., Hundertmark, A., Leffel, K., & Suskind, D. (2017, September). *Improving education on child language and cognitive development in the primary care settings through a technology-based curriculum: A randomized controlled trial*. Poster presented at the 2017 American Academy of Pediatrics National Conference & Exhibition, Chicago, IL.

Lever, R., & Senechal, M. (2011). Discussing stories on how a dialogic reading intervention improves kindergartners' oral narrative construction. *Journal of Experimental Child Psychology, 108*(1), 1–24. doi:10.1016/j.jecp.2010.07.002

Levin, I., Both-De Vries, A., Aram, D., & Bus, A. (2005). Writing starts with own name writing: From scribbling to conventional spelling in Israeli and Dutch children. *Applied Psycholinguistics, 26*(3), 463–477. doi:10.1017/s0142716405050253

Levine, R. A., Levine, S., Schnell-Anzola, B., Rowe, M. L., & Dexter, E. (2012). *Literacy and mothering: How women's schooling changes the lives of the world's children*. New York, NY: Oxford.

Lieven, E. (2016). Usage-based approaches to language development: Where do we go from here? *Language and Cognition, 8*(3), 346–368. doi:10.1017/langcog.2016.16

Linebarger, D. L., Kosanic, A. Z., Greenwood, C. R., & Doku, N. S. (2004). Effects of viewing the television program "Between the Lions" on the emergent literacy skills of young children. *Journal of Educational Psychology, 96*(2), 297–308.

Lohmann, H., & Tomasello, M. (2003). The role of language in the development of false belief understanding: A training study. *Child Development, 74*(4), 1130–1144. doi:10.1111/1467-8624.00597

Lonigan, C. J., Allan, D. M., Goodrich, J. M., Farrington, A. L., & Phillips, B. M. (2017). Inhibitory control of Spanish-speaking language-minority preschool children: Measurement and association with language, literacy, and math skills. *Journal of Learning Disabilities, 50*(4), 373–385. doi:10.1177/0022219415618498

Lonigan, C. J., Burgess, S. R., & Anthony, J. L. (2000). Development of emergent literacy and early reading skills in preschool children: Evidence from a latent-variable longitudinal study. *Developmental Psychology, 36*, 596–613. doi:10.1037/0012-1649.36.5.596

Lonigan, C. J., Burgess, S. R., Anthony, J. L., & Barker, T. A. (1998). Development of phonological sensitivity in two- to five-year-old children. *Journal of Educational Psychology, 90*, 294–311.

MacWhinney, B. (2004). A multiple process solution to the logical problem of language acquisition. *Journal of Child Language, 31*(4), 883–914. doi:10.1017/s0305000904006336

Mancilla-Martinez, J., & Lesaux, N. K. (2011a). Early home language use and later vocabulary development. *Journal of Educational Psychology, 103*(3), 535–546. doi:10.1037/a0023655

Mancilla-Martinez, J., & Lesaux, N. K. (2011b). The gap between Spanish speakers' word reading and word knowledge: A longitudinal study. *Child Development, 82*(5), 1544–1560. doi:10.1111/j.1467-8624.2011.01633.x

Mancilla-Martinez, J., & Lesaux, N. K. (2017). Early indicators of later English reading comprehension outcomes among children from Spanish-speaking homes. *Scientific Studies of Reading, 21*(5), 428–448. doi:10.1080/10888438.201 7.1320402

Manz, P. H., Hughes, C., Barnabas, E., Bracaliello, C., & Ginsburg-Block, M. (2010). A descriptive review and meta-analysis of family-based emergent literacy interventions: To what extent is the research applicable to low-income, ethnic-minority or linguistically-diverse young children? *Early Childhood Research Quarterly, 25*(4), 409–431. doi:10.1016/j.ecresq.2010.03.002

Marchman, V. A., Martinez, L. Z., Hurtado, N., Gruter, T., & Fernald, A. (2017). Caregiver talk to young Spanish-English bilinguals: Comparing direct observation and parent-report measures of dual-language exposure. *Developmental Science, 20*(1). doi:10.1111/desc.12425

Marchman, V. A., & Fernald, A. (2008). Speed of word recognition and vocabulary knowledge in infancy predict cognitive and language outcomes in later childhood. *Developmental Science, 11*(3), F9–F16. doi:10.1111/j.1467-7687.2008.00671.x

Martoccio, T. L., Brophy-Herb, H. E., & Onaga, E. E. (2014). Road to readiness pathways from low-income children's early interactions to school readiness skills. *Infants and Young Children, 27*(3), 193–206. doi:10.1097/iyc .0000000000000014

Marulis, L. M., & Neuman, S. B. (2010). The effects of vocabulary intervention on young children's word learning: A meta-analysis. *Review of Educational Research, 80*(3), 300–335.

Matte-Gagne, C., & Bernier, A. (2011). Prospective relations between maternal autonomy support and child executive functioning: Investigating the mediating role of child language ability. *Journal of Experimental Child Psychology, 110*(4), 611–625. doi:10.1016/j.jecp.2011.06.006

May, L., Byers-Heinlein, K., Gervain, J., & Werker, J. F. (2011). Language and the newborn brain: Does prenatal language experience shape the neonate neural response to speech? *Frontiers in Psychology, 2.* doi:10.3389/fpsyg.2011.00222

McCabe, A., & Bliss, L. S. (2003). *Patterns of narrative discourse: A multicultural lifespan approach.* Boston, MA: Allyn & Bacon.

McCormick, M. P., O'Connor, E. E., & Barnes, S. P. (2016). Mother–child attachment styles and math and reading skills in middle childhood: The mediating role of children's exploration and engagement. *Early Childhood Research Quarterly, 36*, 295–306. doi:10.1016/j.ecresq.2016.01.011

McEwen, B. S. (2000). Effects of adverse experiences for brain structure and function. *Biological Psychiatry, 48*(8), 721–731. doi:10.1016/s0006-3223(00)00964-1

Meins, E., Fernyhough, C., Wainwright, R., Das Gupta, M., Fradley, E., & Tuckey, M. (2002). Maternal mind-mindedness and attachment security as predictors of theory of mind understanding. *Child Development, 73*(6), 1715–1726. doi:10.1111/1467-8624.00501

Meltzoff, A. N. (2007). Like me: A foundation for social cognition. *Developmental Science, 10*(1), 126–134. doi:10.1111/j.1467-7687.2007.00574.x

Mendelsohn, A., et al. (2017). *Enhancing child behavioral outcomes through Promotion of parent–child interactions in reading aloud and play.* Biennial Conference for the Society of Research in Child Development. Austin, TX.

Mendelsohn, A. L., Cates, C. B., Weisleder, A., Berkule, S. B., Dreyer, B. P. (2013). Promotion of early school readiness using pediatric primary care as an innovative platform. *Zero to Three, 34*(1), 29–40.

Mendelsohn, A. L., Cates, C. B., Weisleder, A., Berkule Johnson, S., Seery, A. M., Canfield, C. F., . . . Dreyer, B. P. (2018). Reading aloud, play, and social-emotional development. *Pediatrics, 41*(5), e20173393

Mendelsohn, A. L., Dreyer, B. P., Brockmeyer, C. A., Berkule-Silberman, S. B., & Morrow, L. M. (2011a). Fostering early development and school readiness in pediatric settings. In S. B. Neuman & D. K. Dickinson (Eds.), *Handbook of early literacy research* (Vol. II, pp. 279–294). New York, NY: Guildford Press.

Mendelsohn, A. L., Dreyer, B. P., Brockmeyer, C. A., Berkule-Silberman, S. B., Huberman, H. S., & Tomopoulos, S. (2011b). An RCT of primary care pediatric parenting programs: Impacts on reduced media exposure in infants, mediated through enhanced parent-child interaction. *Archives of Pediatrics and Adolescent Medicine, 165*(1), 33–41.

Mendelsohn, A. L., Dreyer, B. P., Flynn, V., Tomopoulos, S., Rovira, I., Tineo, W., . . . Nixon, A. F. (2005). Use of videotaped interactions during pediatric well-child care to promote child development: An RCT. *Journal of Developmental and Behavioral Pediatrics, 26*(1), 34–41.

Mendelsohn, A. L., Mogilner, L. N., Dreyer, B. P., Forman, J. A., Weinstein, S. C., Broderick, M., . . . Napier, C. (2001). The impact of a clinic-based literacy intervention on language development in inner-city preschool children. *Pediatrics, 107*(1), 130–134. doi:10.1542/peds.107.1.130

Mendelsohn, A. L., Valdez, P. T., Flynn, V., Foley, G. M., Berkule, S. B., Tomopoulos, S., . . . Dreyer, B. P. (2007). Use of videotaped interactions during pediatric well-child care: Impact at 33 months on parenting and on child development. *Journal of Developmental and Behavioral Pediatrics, 28*(3), 206–212. doi:10.1097/DBP.0b013e3180324d87

Miller, P. J., Cho, G. E., & Bracey, J. R. (2005). Working-class children's experience through the prism of personal storytelling. *Human Development, 48*(3), 115–135.

Minami, M., & McCabe, A. (1995). Rice balls and bear hunts: Japanese and North-American family narrative patterns. *Journal of Child Language, 22*(2), 423–445.

Moje, E. B., Ciechanowski, K. M., Kramer, K., Ellis, L., Carrillo, R., & Collazo, T. (2004). Working toward third space in content area literacy: An examination of everyday funds of knowledge and discourse. *Reading Research Quarterly, 39*(1), 38–70. doi:10.1598/rrq.39.1.4

Mol, S. E., Bus, A. G., & de Jong, M. T. (2009). Interactive book reading in early education: A tool to stimulate print knowledge as well as oral language. *Review of Educational Research, 79*(2), 979–1007.

Mol, S. E., Bus, A. G., de Jong, M. T., & Smeets, D. J. H. (2008). Added value of dialogic parent-child book reading: A meta-analysis. *Early Education and Development, 19*(1), 7–26.

Muller, U., Liebermann-Finestone, D. P., Carpendale, J. I. M., Hammond, S. I., & Bibok, M. B. (2012). Knowing minds, controlling actions: The developmental relations between theory of mind and executive function from 2 to 4 years of age. *Journal of Experimental Child Psychology, 111*(2), 331–348. doi:10.1016/j.jecp.2011.08.014

Mundy, P., Block, J., Delgado, C., Pomares, Y., Van Hecke, A. V., & Parlade, M. V. (2007). Individual differences and the development of joint attention in infancy. *Child Development, 78*(3), 938–954. doi:10.1111/j.1467-8624.2007.01042.x

Mundy, P., Sullivan, L., & Mastergeorge, A. M. (2009). A parallel and distributed-processing model of joint attention, social cognition and autism. *Autism Research, 2*(1), 2–21. doi:10.1002/aur.61

Muter, V., Hulme, C., Snowling, M. J., & Stevenson, J. (2004). Phonemes, rimes, vocabulary, and grammatical skills as foundations of early reading development: Evidence from a longitudinal study. *Developmental Psychology, 40*(5), 665–681. doi:10.1037/0012-1649.40.5.665

Nagy, W., & Townsend, D. (2012). Words as tools: Learning academic vocabulary as language acquisition. *Reading Research Quarterly, 47*(1), 91–108.

Nakamura, Y. U. (2004). Development of early literacy skills of bilingual kindergarteners: An individual growth modeling approach. *Dissertation Abstracts International Section A: Humanities and Social Sciences, 65*(5-A), 1632.

National Academies of Sciences. (2016a). *Parenting matters: Supporting parents of children ages 0–8.* Washington, DC: National Academies Press.

National Academies of Sciences. (2016b). *Speech and language disorders in children: Implications for the Social Security Administration's Supplemental Security Income program.* Washington, DC: National Academies Press.

National Center for Education Statistics. (2013a). *A first look: 2013 Mathematics and reading* (NCES 2014–451). Washington, DC: U.S. Department of Education, Institute for Educational Sciences.

National Center for Education Statistics. (2013b). *The nation's report card: Vocabulary results from the 2009 and 2011 reading assessments* (NCES 2013 452). Washington, DC: U.S. Department of Education, Institute for Educational Sciences.

National Center for Education Statistics (2013c). *The nation's report card: Trends in academic progress, 2012* (NCES 2013 456). Washington DC: U.S. Department of Education, Institute for Educational Sciences.

National Center for Educational Statistics. (2015). *The Nation's Report Card: 2015 mathematics and reading assessments.* Retrieved from http://www.nationsreportcard.gov/reading_math_2015/#reading/groups?grade=4

National Early Literacy Panel. (2009). *Developing early literacy: Report of the National Early Literacy Panel.* Retrieved from http://lincs.ed.gov/publications/pdf/NELPReport09.pdf

National Institute of Child Health and Human Development Early Child Care Research Network. (2000). The relation of child care to cognitive and language development. *Child Development, 71*(4), 960–980.

National Institute of Child Health and Human Development Early Child Care Research Network. (2005a). Early child care and children's development in the primary grades: Follow-up results from the NICHD study of early child care. *American Educational Research Journal, 42*(3), 537–570.

National Institute of Child Health and Human Development Early Child Care Research Network. (2005b). Pathways to reading: The role of oral language in the transition to reading. *Developmental Psychology, 41*(2), 428–442. doi:10.1037/0012-1649.41.2.428

National Reading Panel. (2000). *Report of the National Reading Panel: Teaching children to read reports of the subgroups.* National Institute for Literacy, Washington, DC.

National Scientific Council on the Developing Child. (2005). *Excessive stress disrupts the architecture of the developing brain: Working paper no. 3.* Retrieved from https://developingchild.harvard.edu/resources/wp3/

Needlman, R., Klass, P., & Zuckerman, B. (2006). A pediatric approach to early literacy. In D. K. Dickinson & S. B. Neuman (Eds.), *Handbook of early literacy research* (Vol. II, pp. 333–346). New York, NY: Guilford Press.

Nelson, C. A. (2001). The development and neural bases of face recognition. *Infant and Child Development, 10*(1-2), 3–18. doi:10.1002/icd.239

Nelson, C. A., & Bloom, F. E. (1997). Child development and neuroscience. *Child Development, 68*(5), 970–987. doi:10.2307/1132045

Nelson, K. (1996). *Language in cognitive development: The emergence of the mediated mind.* New York, NY: Cambridge University Press.

Nesbitt, K. T., Farran, D. C., & Fuhs, M. W. (2015). Executive function skills and academic achievement gains in prekindergarten: Contributions of learning-related behaviors. *Developmental Psychology, 51*(7), 865–878. doi:10.1037/dev0000021

Neuman, S. B. (1999). Books make a difference: A study of access to literacy. *Reading Research Quarterly, 34*(3), 286–311.

Neuman, S. B., & Celano, D. (2001). Access to print in low-income and middle-income communities: An ecological study of four neighborhoods. *Reading Research Quarterly, 36*(1), 8–26.

Neuman, S. B., & Celano, D. (2006). The knowledge gap: Implications of leveling the playing field for low-income and middle-income children. *Reading Research Quarterly, 41*(2), 176–201. doi:10.1598/rrq.41.2.2

Nievar, M. A., Jacobson, A., Chen, Q., Johnson, U., & Dier, S. (2011). Impact of HIPPY on home learning environments of Latino families. *Early Childhood Research Quarterly, 26*(3), 268–277. doi:10.1016/j.ecresq.2011.01.002

Noble, K. G., Norman, M. F., & Farah, M. J. (2005). Neurocognitive correlates of socioeconomic status in kindergarten children. *Developmental Science, 8*(1), 74–87. doi:10.1111/j.1467-7687.2005.00394.x

Nolte, J. (2002). *The human brain: An introduction to its functional anatomy* (5th ed.). St. Louis, MO: Mosby.

Oakhill, J. V., & Cain, K. (2012). The precursors of reading ability in young readers: Evidence from a four-year longitudinal study. *Scientific Studies of Reading, 16*(2), 91–121. doi:10.1080/10888438.2010.529219

O'Brien, L. M., Paratore, J. R., Leighton, C. M., Cassano, C. M., Krol-Sinclair, B., & Green, J. G. (2014). Examining differential effects of a family literacy program on language and literacy growth of english language learners with varying vocabularies. *Journal of Literacy Research, 46*(3), 383–415. doi:10.1177/1086296x14552180

O'Hare, L., & Connolly, P. (2010). *A randomised controlled trial evaluation of Bookstart+: A book gifting intervention for two-year-old children.* Belfast, Northern Ireland: Queen's University, School of Education, Centre for Effective Education.

Olson, R. K., Keenan, J. M., Byrne, B., Samuelsson, S., Coventry, W. L., Corley, R., . . . Hulslander, J. (2011). Genetic and environmental influences on vocabulary and reading development. *Scientific Studies of Reading, 15*(1), 26–46. doi:10.1080/10888438.2011.536128

Organization for Economic Cooperation and Development. (2015). *Universal basic skills: What countries stand to gain.* City, State: Publisher.

Organization for Economic Cooperation and Development. (2016a). *Education at a glance 2016: Highlights.* Retrieved from http://gpseducation.oecd.org/Home

Organization for Economic Cooperation and Development. (2016b). *Skills matter: Further results from the Survey of Adult Skills, OECD Skills Studies.* Paris, France: Publisher.

Paez, M., Bock, K. P., & Pizzo, L. (2011). Supporting the language and early literacy skills of English language learners: Effective practices and future directions. In S. B. Neuman & D. K. Dickinson (Eds.), *Handbook of early literacy research* (Vol. II, pp. 136–152). New York, NY: Guilford Press.

Paez, M. M., Tabors, P. O., & Lopez, L. M. (2007). Dual language and literacy development of Spanish-speaking preschool children. *Journal of Applied Developmental Psychology, 2*(2), 85–102.

Pallas, A. M., Entwisle, D. R., & Cadigan, D. (1987). Children who do exceptionally well in first grade. *Sociology of Education, 60,* 256–271.

Parisi, D. (1971). Development of syntactic comprehension in preschool children as a function of socioeconomic level. *Developmental Psychology, 5*(2), 186–189.

Pearson, B. Z., Fernandez, S. C., Lewedeg, V., & Oller, D. K. (1997). The relation of input factors to lexical learning by bilingual infants. *Applied Psycholinguistics, 18*(1), 41–58. doi:10.1017/s0142716400009863

Pellegrini, A. D., & Galda, L. (1982). The effects of thematic fantasy play training on the development of children's story comprehension. *American Educational Research Journal, 19*(3), 443–452. doi:10.3102/00028312019003443

Perfetti, C. (2007). Reading ability: Lexical quality to comprehension. *Scientific Studies of Reading, 11*(4), 357–383.

Perfetti, C., & Stafura, J. (2014). Word knowledge in a theory of reading comprehension. *Scientific Studies of Reading, 18*(1), 22–37. doi:10.1080/10888438.2013.827687

Peskin, J., & Astington, J. W. (2004). The effects of adding metacognitive language to story texts. *Cognitive Development, 19*(2), 253–273. doi:10.1016/j.cogdev.2004.01.003

Peterson, C., Jesso, B., & McCabe, A. (1999). Encouraging narratives in preschoolers: An intervention study. *Journal of Child Language, 26,* 49–67.

Petitto, L. A., & Marentette, P. F. (1991). Babbling in the manual mode: Evidence for the ontogeny of language. *Science, 251*(5000), 1493–1496. doi:10.1126/science.2006424

Pianta, R. C., Hamre, B., & Stuhlman, M. (2002). Relationships between teachers and children. In G. E. Miller (Ed.), *Comprehensive handbook of psychology: Vol. 7.* New York, NY: Wiley.

Piper, W. (1991). *The little engine that could.* New York, NY: Penguin Random House/Grosset & Dunlap.

Pinker, S. (1994). *The language instinct.* New York, NY: HarperCollins

Pinker, S. (2010). The cognitive niche: Coevolution of intelligence, sociality, and language. *Proceedings of the National Academy of Sciences of the United States of America, 107,* 8993–8999. doi:10.1073/pnas.0914630107

Pinquart, M., & Teubert, D. (2010). Effects of parenting education with expectant and new parents: A meta-analysis. *Journal of Family Psychology, 24*(3), 316–327. doi:10.1037/a0019691

Pisani, L., Borisvoa, K., & Dowd, A. J. (2015). *International Development and Early Learning Assessment technical working paper.* Washington, DC: Save the Children.

Place, S., & Hoff, E. (2011). Properties of dual language exposure that influence 2-year-olds' bilingual proficiency. *Child Development, 82*(6), 1834–1849. doi:10.1111/j.1467-8624.2011.01660.x

Preissler, M. A. (2004). Do both pictures and words function as symbols for 18- and 24-month-old children? *Journal of Cognition and Development, 5*(2), 185–212. doi:10.1207/s15327647jcd0502_2

Proctor, C. P., Silverman, R. D., Harring, J. R., & Montecillo, C. (2012). The role of vocabulary depth in predicting reading comprehension among English monolingual and Spanish-English bilingual children in elementary school. *Reading and Writing, 25*(7), 1635–1664. doi:10.1007/s11145-011-9336-5

Pugh, K. R., Sandak, R., Frost, S. J., Moore, D. L., & Mencl, W. E. (2006). Neurobiological investigations of skilled and impaired readers. In D. K. Dickinson & S. B. Neuman (Eds.), *Handbook of early literacy development* (Vol. II, pp. 64–76). New York, NY: Guilford Press.

Pujol, J., Soriano-Mas, C., Ortiz, H., Sebastian-Galles, N., Losilla, J. M., & Deus, J. (2006). Myelination of language-related areas in the developing brain. *Neurology, 66*(3), 339–343. doi:10.1212/01.wnl.0000201049.66073.8d

Quartz, S. R. (1999). The constructivist brain. *Trends in Cognitive Sciences, 3*(2), 48–57. doi:10.1016/s1364-6613(98)01270-4

Quartz, S. R., & Sejnowski, T. J. (1997). The neural basis of cognitive development: A constructivist manifesto. *Behavioral and Brain Sciences, 20*(4), 537–596.

Razza, R. A., & Blair, C. (2009). Associations among false-belief understanding, executive function, and social competence: A longitudinal analysis. *Journal of Applied Developmental Psychology, 30*(3), 332–343. doi:10.1016/j.appdev.2008.12.020

Reardon, S. F. (2011). The widening academic achievement gap between the rich and poor: New evidence and possible explanations. In G. J. Duncan & R. J. Murnane (Eds.), *Whither opportunity? Rising inequality, schools, and children's life chances* (pp. 91–115). New York, NY: Russell Sage.

Reardon, S. F. (2014). Education. *Pathways, Special Issue: State of the States—The Poverty and Inequality Report*, 51–56.

Reardon, S. F., & Portilla. (2016). Recent trends in income, racial, and ethnic school readiness gaps at kindergarten entry. *AERA Open, 2*(3), 1–18. doi:10.1177/2332858416657343

Rees, C. (2016). Children's attachments. *Pediatrics and Child Health, 26*(5), 185–193. doi:10.1016/j.paed.2015.12.007

Rickford, J. R., Duncan, G. J., Gennetian, L. A., Gou, R. Y., Greene, R., Katz, L. F., . . . Ludwig, J. (2015). Neighborhood effects on use of African-American Vernacular English. *Proceedings of the National Academy of Sciences of the United States of America, 112*(38), 11817–11822. doi:10.1073/pnas.1500176112

Ridge, K. E., Weisberg, D. S., Ilgaz, H., Hirsh-Pasek, K., & Golinkoff, R. M. (2015). Supermarket speak: Increasing talk among low-socioeconomic status families. Mind, Brain, and Education, 9(3), 127-135. https://doi.org/10.1111/mbe.12081

Roberts, T. A. (2008). Home storybook reading in primary or second language with preschool children: Evidence of equal effectiveness for second-language vocabulary acquisition. *Reading Research Quarterly, 43*(2), 103–130. doi:10.1598/rrq.43.2.1

Roberts, M. Y., & Kaiser, A. P. (2011). The effectiveness of parent-implemented language interventions: A meta-analysis. *American Journal of Speech-Language Pathology, 20*(3), 180–199. doi:10.1044/1058-0360(2011/10-0055)

Rowe, D. W., & Fain, J. G. (2013). The family backpack project: Responding to dual-language texts through family journals. *Language Arts, 90*(6), 578–592.

Rowe, D. W., & Wilson, S. J. (2015). The development of a descriptive measure of early childhood writing: Results from the write start! Writing assessment. *Journal of Literacy Research, 47*(2), 245–292. doi:10.1177/1086296x15619723

Rowe, M. L. (2008). Child-directed speech: Relation to socioeconomic status, knowledge of child development and child vocabulary skill. *Journal of Child Language, 35*(1), 185–205. doi:10.1017/s0305000907008343

Rowe, M. L. (2012). A longitudinal investigation of the role of quantity and quality of child-directed speech in vocabulary development. *Child Development, 83*(5), 1762–1774. doi:10.1111/j.1467-8624.2012.01805.x

Rowe, M. L., Denmark, N., Harden, B. J., & Stapleton, L. M. (2016). The role of parent education and parenting knowledge in children's language and literacy skills among White, Black, and Latino families. *Infant and Child Development*, 25(2), 198–220. doi:10.1002/icd.1924

Rowe, M. L., & Goldin-Meadow, S. (2009). Differences in early gesture explain SES disparities in child vocabulary size at school entry. *Science*, 323(5916), 951–953. doi:10.1126/science.1167025

Rowe, M. L., Raudenbush, S. W., & Goldin-Meadow, S. (2012). The pace of vocabulary growth helps predict later vocabulary skill. *Child Development*, 83(2), 508–525. doi:10.1111/j.1467-8624.2011.01710.x

Ruffman, T., Slade, L., & Crowe, E. (2002). The relation between children's and mothers' mental state language and theory-of-mind understanding. *Child Development*, 73(3), 734–751. doi:10.1111/1467-8624.00435

Saltz, E., & Johnson, J. (1974). Training for thematic-fantasy play in culturally disadvantaged children: Preliminary results. *Journal of Educational Psychology*, 66(4), 623–630. doi:10.1037/h0036930

Sama-Miller, E., Akers, L., Mraz-Esposito, A., Zukiewicz, M., Avellar, S., Paulsell, D., & Del Grosso, P. (2018). *Home visiting evidence of effectiveness: Effectiveness research*. [Office of Planning, Research and Evaluation: U.S. Department of Health and Human Service] Retrieved from https://homvee.acf.hhs.gov/models.aspx

Samuelsson, S., Byrne, B., Quain, P., Wadsworth, S., Corley, R., DeFries, J. C., . . . Olson, R. (2005). Environmental and genetic influences on prereading skills in Australia, Scandinavia, and the United States. *Journal of Educational Psychology*, 97(4), 705–722. doi:10.1037/0022-0663.97.4.705

Satter, C. (2014). *An analysis of early literacy assessment performance among Knox County Imagination Library participants*. Knox County, TN: Imagination Library Board of Advisors and Knox County Schools Supervisor of Research and Evaluation.

Save the Children. (n.d.). *Save the Children's global strategy: Ambition for children 2030 and 2016-2018 strategic plan*. Retrieved from https://www.savethechildren.net/sites/default/files/Global%20Strategy%20-%20Ambition%20for%20Children%202030.pdf

Save the Children. (2017). *Windows in early learning and development: Cross country IDELA findings fueling progress on ECD access, quality and equity*. London, United Kingdom: Save the Children International.

Scarborough, H. S. (2001). Connecting early language and literacy to later reading (dis)abilities. In S. B. Neuman & D. K. Dickinson (Eds.), *Handbook of early literacy research* (Vol. II, pp. 97–110). New York, NY: Guilford Press.

Scheele, A. F., Leseman, P. P. M., Mayo, A. Y., & Elbers, E. (2012). The relation of home language and literacy to three-year-old children's emergent academic language in narrative and instruction genres. *Elementary School Journal*, 112(3), 419–444.

Schick, B., de Villiers, P., de Villiers, J., & Hoffmeister, R. (2007). Language and theory of mind: A study of deaf children. *Child Development*, 78(2), 376–396. doi:10.1111/j.1467-8624.2007.01004.x

Schleppegrell, M. J. (2001). Linguistic features of the language of schooling. *Linguistics and Education*, 12(4), 431–459. doi:10.1016/s0898-5898(01)00073-0

Seeding Success. (2017). *Correlation between books from birth enrollment and kindergarten through fourth grade academic outcomes*. Unpublished manuscript. Seeding Success, Memphis, TN.

Segers, E., Damhuis, C. M. P., van de Sande, E., & Verhoeven, L. (2016). Role of executive functioning and home environment in early reading development. *Learning and Individual Differences, 49*, 251–259. doi:10.1016/j.lindif.2016.07.004

Sell, M., Imig, D., & Shahin, S. (2014). *Links between Books from Birth participation and second-grade reading performance. Partnership.* Retrieved from http://www.urbanchildinstitute.org/resources/documents/links-between-books-from-birth-participation-and-second-grade-reading

Sharon, T. (2005). Made to symbolize: Intentionality and children's early understanding of symbols. *Journal of Cognition and Development, 6*(2), 163–178. doi:10.1207/s15327647jcd0602_1

Shneidman, L. A., Arroyo, M. E., Levine, S. C., & Goldin-Meadow, S. (2013). What counts as effective input for word learning? *Journal of Child Language, 40*(3), 672–686. doi:10.1017/s0305000912000141

Shneidman, L. A., & Goldin-Meadow, S. (2012). Language input and acquisition in a Mayan village: How important is directed speech? *Developmental Science, 15*(5), 659–673. doi:10.1111/j.1467-7687.2012.01168.x

Shonkoff, J. P. (2016). Capitalizing on advances in science to reduce the health consequences of early childhood adversity. *JAMA Pediatrics, 170*(10), 1003–1007. doi:10.1001/jamapediatrics.2016.1559

Shonkoff, J. P., & Garner, A. S. (2012). The lifelong effects of early childhood adversity and toxic stress. *Pediatrics, 129*(1), E232–E246. doi:10.1542/peds.2011-2663

Shonkoff, J. P., Richter, L., van der Gaag, J., & Bhutta, Z. A. (2012). An integrated scientific framework for child survival and early childhood development. *Pediatrics, 129*(2), E460–E472. doi:10.1542/peds.2011-0366

Siegel, D. J. (2012*). The developing mind: How relationships and the brain interact to shape who we are* (2nd ed.). New York, NY: Guilford Press.

Silvén, M., Poskiparta, E., Niemi, P., & Voeten, M. (2007). Precursors of reading skill from infancy to first grade in Finnish: Continuity and change in a highly inflected language. *Journal of Educational Psychology, 99*(3), 516–531. doi:10.1037/0022-0663.99.3.516

Slaughter, V., Imuta, K., Peterson, C. C., & Henry, J. D. (2015). Meta-analysis of theory of mind and peer popularity in the preschool and early school years. *Child Development, 86*(4), 1159–1174. doi:10.1111/cdev.12372

Smith, L. E., Borkowski, J. G., & Whitman, T. L. (2008). From reading readiness to reading competence: The role of self-regulation in at-risk children. *Scientific Studies of Reading, 12*(2), 131–152. doi:10.1080/10988430801917167

Snow, C. E. (1991). The theoretical basis for relationships between language and literacy in development. *Journal of Research in Childhood Education, 6*(1), 5–10.

Snow, C. E., Barnes, W. S., Chandler, J., Goodman, I. F., & Hemphill, L. (1991). *Unfulfilled expectations: Home and school influences on literacy.* Cambridge, MA: Harvard University Press.

Snow, C. E., Burns, M. S., & Griffin, P. (Eds.). (1998). *Preventing reading difficulties in young children.* Washington, DC: National Academies Press.

Snow, C. E., & Dickinson, D. K. (1991). Skills that aren't basic in a new conception of literacy. In A. C. Purves & E. Jennings (Eds.), *Literate systems and individual lives: Perspectives on literacy and school* (pp. 179-192). Albany, NY: SUNY Press.

Snow, C. E., & Ferguson, C. A. (1977). *Talking to children: Language input and acquisition.* New York, NY: Cambridge University Press.

Snow, C. E., Porche, M. V., Tabors, P. O., & Harris, S. R. (2007). *Is literacy enough: Pathways to academic success for adolescents.* Baltimore, MD: Paul H. Brookes Publishing Co.

Snow, C. E., & Ucelli, P. (2009). The challenge of academic language. In D. R. Olson & N. Torrance (Eds.), *The Cambridge handbook of literacy* (pp. 112–133). New York, NY: Cambridge University Press.

Sperry, D. E., Sperry, L. L., & Miller, P. J. (2018). Reexamining the verbal environments of children from different socioeconomic backgrounds. *Child Development,* 1–16. doi:10.1111/cdev.13072

Spieker, S. J., Nelson, D. C., Petras, A., Jolley, S. N., & Barnard, K. E. (2003). Joint influence of child care and infant attachment security for cognitive and language outcomes of low-income toddlers. *Infant Behavior and Development, 26*(3), 326–344. doi:10.1016/S0163-6383(03)00034-1

Stanovich, K. E. (1986). Matthew effects in reading: Some consequences of individual differences in the acquisition of literacy. *Reading Research Quarterly, 21,* 360–407.

Stephenson, K. A., Parrila, R. K., Georgiou, G. K., & Kirby, J. R. (2008). Effects of home literacy, parents' beliefs, and children's task-focused behavior on emergent literacy and word reading skills. *Scientific Studies of Reading, 12*(1), 24–50. doi:10.1080/10888430701746864

Stevens, R. J., Lu, X. F., Baker, D. P., Ray, M. N., Eckert, S. A., & Gamson, D. A. (2015). Assessing the cognitive demands of a century of reading curricula: An analysis of reading text and comprehension tasks from 1910 to 2000. *American Educational Research Journal, 52*(3), 582–617. doi:10.3102/0002831215573531

Stipek, D., Newton, S., & Chudgar, A. (2010). Learning-related behaviors and literacy achievement in elementary school-aged children. *Early Childhood Research Quarterly, 25*(3), 385–395. doi:10.1016/j.ecresq.2009.12.001

Stoeke, J. M. (1994). *A hat for Minerva Louise.* New York, NY: Puffin Books.

Storch, S. A., & Whitehurst, G. J. (2002). Oral language and code-related precursors to reading: Evidence from a longitudinal structural model. *Developmental Psychology, 38*(6), 934–947. doi:10.1037//0012-1649.38.6.934

Suskind, D. L., Graf, E., Lefel, K. R., Hernandez, M. W., Suskind, E., Webber, R., . . . Nevins, M. E. (2017). Project aspire: Spoken language intervention curriculum for parents of low-socioeconomic status and their deaf and hard-of-hearing children. *Otology and Neurotology, 2016*(37), 110–117.

Suskind, D., Leffel, K. R., Hernandez, M. W., Sapolich, S. G., Suskind, E., Kirkham, E., & Meehan, P. (2013). An exploratory study of "quantitative linguistic feedback": Effect of LENA feedback on adult language production. *Communication Disorders Quarterly, 34*(4), 199–209. doi:10.1177/1525740112473146

Suskind, D. L., Leung, C. Y. Y., Webber, R. J., Hundertmark, A. C., Leffel, K. R., Suskind, E., . . . Graf, E. (2017). Development of the survey of parent/provider expectations and knowledge (speak). *First Language, 38* (3), 1–20. doi:10.1177/0142723717737691

Swanson, H. L., Rosston, K., Gerber, M., & Solari, E. (2008). Influence of oral language and phonological awareness on children's bilingual reading. *Journal of School Psychology, 46*(4), 413–429. doi:10.1016/j.jsp.2007.07.002

Tamis-LeMonda, C. S., Bornstein, M. H., & Baumwell, L. (2001). Maternal responsiveness and children's achievement of language milestones. *Child Development, 72*(3), 748–767. doi:10.1111/1467-8624.00313

Tamis-LeMonda, C. S., Kuchirko, Y., & Song, L. (2014). Why is infant language learning facilitated by parental responsiveness? *Current Directions in Psychological Science, 23*(2), 121–126. doi:10.1177/0963721414522813

Taumoepeau, M., & Ruffman, T. (2008). Stepping stones to others' minds: Maternal talk relates to child mental state language and emotion understanding at 15, 24, and 33 months. *Child Development, 79*(2), 284–302. doi:10.1111/j.1467-8624.2007.01126.x

Taylor, C. L., Zubrick, S. R., & Christensen, D. (2016). Barriers to parent–child book reading in early childhood. *International Journal of Early Childhood, 48)* 3, 1–15. doi:10.1007/s13158-016-0172-2

Teicher, M. H., Samson, J. A., Anderson, C. M., & Ohashi, K. (2016). The effects of childhood maltreatment on brain structure, function and connectivity. *Nature Reviews Neuroscience, 17*(10), 652–656 doi:10.1038/nrn.2016.111

Tennessee Department of Education's Office of Research and Strategy. (2016). *Setting the foundation: A report on the elementary grades reading in tennessee.* Nashville, TN: State Department of Education.

Tomasello, M. (1999). *The cultural origins of human cognition.* Cambridge, MA: Harvard University Press.

Tomasello, M. (2000). Culture and cognitive development. *Current Directions in Psychological Science, 9*(2), 37–40. doi:10.1111/1467-8721.00056

Tomasello, M. (2003). *Constructing a language: A usage-based theory of language acquisition.* Cambridge, MA: Harvard University Press.

Tomasello, M. (2016). Cultural learning redux. *Child Development, 87*(3), 643–653. doi:10.1111/cdev.12499

Tomasello, M., Carpenter, M., Call, J., Behne, T., & Moll, H. (2005). Understanding and sharing intentions: The origins of cultural cognition. *Behavioral and Brain Sciences, 28*(5), 675–735. doi:10.1017/s0140525x05000129

Tomasello, M., & Farrar, M. J. (1986). Joint attention and early language. *Child Development, 57*(6), 1454–1463.

Tomblin, J. B., Barker, B. A., Spencer, L. J., Zhang, X. Y., & Gantz, B. J. (2005). The effect of age at cochlear implant initial stimulation on expressive language growth in infants and toddlers. *Journal of Speech, Language, and Hearing Research, 48*(4), 853–867. doi:10.1044/1092-4388(2005/059)

Tompkins, V. (2015). Improving low-income preschoolers' theory of mind: A training study. *Cognitive Development, 36,* 1–19. doi:10.1016/j.cogdev.2015.07.001

Torgesen, J. K., Wagner, R. K., Rashotte, C. A., Burgess, S. R., & Hecht, S. A. (1997). Contributions of phonological awareness and rapid automatic naming ability to the growth of word-reading skills in second-to-fifth grade children. *Scientific Studies of Reading, 1,* 161–185. doi:10.1207/s1532799xssr0102_4

Tosto, M. G., Hayiou-Thomas, M. E., Harlaar, N., Prom-Wormley, E., Dale, P. S., & Plomin, R. (2017). The genetic architecture of oral language, reading fluency, and reading comprehension: A twin study from 7 to 16 years. *Developmental Psychology, 53*(6), 1115–1129. doi:10.1037/dev0000297

Toub, T. S., Hassinger-Das, B., Nesbitt, K. T., Ilgaz, H., Weisberg, D. S., Collins, M. F., . . . Dickinson, D. K. (2018). The language of play: Developing preschool vocabulary through play following shared book-reading. *Early Childhood Research Quarterly, 45.* doi:10.1016/j.ecresq.2018.01.010

Tsujimoto, S. (2008). The prefrontal cortex: Functional neural development during early childhood. *Neuroscientist, 14*(4), 345–358. doi:10.1177/1073858408316002

Tunmer, W. E., & Chapman, J. W. (2012a). Does set for variability mediate the influence of vocabulary knowledge on the development of word recognition skills? *Scientific Studies of Reading, 16*(2), 122–140. doi:10.1080/10888438.2010.5 42527

Tunmer, W. E., & Chapman, J. W. (2012b). The simple view of reading redux: Vocabulary knowledge and the independent components hypothesis. *Journal of Learning Disabilities, 45*(5), 453–466. doi:10.1177/0022219411432685

Tunmer, W. E., & Hoover, W. A. (1992). Cognitive and linguistic factors in learning to read. In P. B. Gough, L. C. Ehri, & R. Treiman (Eds.), *Reading acquisition* (pp. 175–214). Mahwah, NJ: Lawrence Erlbaum Associates.

Turner, V. (1967). *The forest of symbols: Aspects of Ndembu ritual.* Ithaca, NY: Cornell University Press.

United Nations Educational, Scientific and Cultural Organization. (2014). *Sustainable development begins with education: How education can contribute to the proposed post-2015 goals.* Paris, France: Author.

University of Texas Health Science Center. (2018). *Children's Learning Institute's interventions to support preschool teachers and parents.* Retrieved from https://www.childrenslearninginstitute.org/contact-us

The Urban Child Institute. (2017). *An evaluation of the Shelby County Books from Birth program: Executive summary.* Memphis, TN: Memphis City Schools.

U.S. Department of Education. (1993). *Public school kindergarten teachers' views of children's readiness for school* (NCES 93-410). Washington, DC: Office of Educational Research and Improvement.

U.S. Department of Health and Human Services. (2016). *2013 poverty guidelines.* Retrieved from https://aspe.hhs.gov/2013-poverty-guidelines

U.S. Department of Health and Human Services. (2018). *Home visiting evidence of effectiveness.* Retrieved from https://homvee.acf.hhs.gov/HRSA/11/Evidence-based-Models-Eligible-to-Maternal--Infant--and-Early-Childhood-Home-Visiting--MIECHV--Grantees/69

Van den Berg, H. (2015). *From Bookstart to booksmart: About the importance of an early start to parent-child reading* [Doctoral dissertation]. Leiden, Leiden, The Netherlands.

Van den Berg H., & Bus, A.G. (2014). Beneficial effects of BookStart in temperamentally highly reactive infants. *Learning and Individual Differences, 36,* 69–75.

Van Hecke, A. V., Mundy, P., Block, J. J., Delgado, C. E. F., Parlade, M. V., Pomares, Y. B., & Hobson, J. A. (2012). Infant responding to joint attention, executive processes, and self-regulation in preschool children. *Infant Behavior and Development, 35*(2), 303–311. doi:10.1016/j.infbeh.2011.12.001

Van Ijzendoorn, M. H., Dijkstra, J., & Bus, A. G. (1995). Attachment, intelligence, and language: A meta-analysis. *Social Development, 4*(2), 115–128.

van Kleeck, A. (2006). Cultural issues in promoting interactive book sharing in the families of preschoolers. In A. Van Kleeck (Ed.), *Sharing books and stories to promote language and literacy* (pp. 179–230). San Diego, CA: Plural.

Vasilyeva, M., Huttenlocher, J., & Waterfall, H. (2006). Effects of language intervention on syntactic skill levels in preschoolers. *Developmental Psychology, 42*(1), 164–174.

Vasilyeva, M., Waterfall, H., & Huttenlocher, J. (2008). Emergence of syntax: Commonalities and differences across children. *Developmental Science, 11*(1), 84–97. doi:10.1111/j.1467-7687.2007.00656.x

Vellutino, F. R., Tunmer, W. E., Jaccard, J. J., & Chen, R. S. (2007). Components of reading ability: Multivariate evidence for a convergent skills model of reading development. *Scientific Studies of Reading, 11*(1), 3–32. doi:10.1080/10888430709336632

Verhoeven, L., van Leeuwe, J., & Vermeer, A. (2011). Vocabulary growth and reading development across the elementary school years. *Scientific Studies of Reading, 15*(1), 8–25. doi:10.1080/10888438.2011.536125

Vygotsky, L. (1978). *Mind in society: The formation of higher psychological processes.* Cambridge, MA: Harvard University Press.

Walker, D. & Bigelow, K. (2012). *strategies for promoting communication and language of infants and toddlers.* Retrieved from http://www.talk.ku.edu/wp-content/uploads/2014/09/PC-Manual-web-site-and-distrib-9-26-141.pdf

Walker, D., Bigelow, K. M., Turcotte, A. D., Reynolds, L. H., & Muehe, C. (2015). *Promoting Communication Observation System (PCObs): Measuring frequency of caregiver use of communication promoting strategies and child communicative behaviors.* Kansas City, KS: Juniper Gardens Children's Project.

Walker, D., Greenwood, C., Hart, B., & Carta, J. (1994). Prediction of school outcomes based on early language production and socioeconomic factors. *Child Development, 65,* 606–621. doi:10.2307/1131404

Walker, S. P., Chang, S. M., Vera-Hernandez, M., & Grantham-McGregor, S. (2011). Early childhood stimulation benefits adult competence and reduces violent behavior. *Pediatrics, 127*(5), 849–857. doi:10.1542/peds.2010-2231

Wasik, B. A., Hindman, A. H., & Snell, E. K. (2016). Book reading and vocabulary development: A systematic review. *Early Childhood Research Quarterly, 37,* 39–57. doi:10.1016/j.ecresq.2016.04.003

Waters, E., Merrick, S., Treboux, D., Crowell, J., & Albersheim, L. (2000). Attachment security in infancy and early adulthood: A twenty-year longitudinal study. *Child Development, 71*(3), 684–689. doi:10.1111/1467-8624.00176

Webb, A. R., Heller, H. T., Benson, C. B., & Lahav, A. (2015). Mother's voice and heartbeat sounds elicit auditory plasticity in the human brain before full gestation. *Proceedings of the National Academy of Sciences of the United States of America, 112*(10), 3152–3157. doi:10.1073/pnas.1414924112

Weisleder, A., Cates, C. B., Dreyer, B. P., Berkule Johnson, S., Huberman, H. S., Seery, A. M., . . . Mendelsohn, A. L. (2016). Promotion of positive parenting and prevention of socioemotional disparities. *Pediatrics, 137*(2),. doi:10.1542/peds.2015-3239

Weisleder, A., & Fernald, A. (2013). Talking to children matters: Early language experience strengthens processing and builds vocabulary. *Psychological Science, 24*(11), 2143–2152. doi:10.1177/0956797613488145

Weizman, Z. O., & Snow, C. E. (2001). Lexical output as related to children's vocabulary acquisition: Effects of sophisticated exposure and support for meaning. *Developmental Psychology, 37*(2), 265–279.

Wells, G. (1985). *Learning, language and education.* Philadelphia, PA: NFER-Nelson.

Wertsch, J. (1991). *Voices of the mind: A sociocultural approach to mediated action.* Cambridge, MA: Harvard University Press.

White, L. J., Alexander, A., & Greenfield, D. B. (2017). The relationship between executive functioning and language: Examining vocabulary, syntax, and language learning in preschoolers attending head start. *Journal of Experimental Child Psychology, 164,* 16–31. doi:10.1016/j.jecp.2017.06.010

Whiten, A., & Erdal, D. (2012). The human socio-cognitive niche and its evolutionary origins. *Philosophical Transactions of the Royal Society B-Biological Sciences, 367*(1599), 2119–2129. doi:10.1098/rstb.2012.0114

Wiesmann, C. G., Friederici, A. D., Singer, T., & Steinbeis, N. (2017). Implicit and explicit false belief development in preschool children. *Developmental Science, 20*(5). doi:10.1111/desc.12445

Wiig, E. H., Semel, E. M.., &Secord, W. (2004). *Clinical Evaluation of Language Fundamentals–Preschool 2 (CELF–Preschool-2)*. San Antonio, TX: Psychological Corporation.

Willems, M. (2003). *Don't let the pigeon drive the bus*. New York, NY: Hyperion.

Wilson, S. J., Dickinson, D. K., & Rowe, D. W. (2013). Impact of an early reading first program on the language and literacy achievement of children from diverse language backgrounds. *Early Childhood Research Quarterly, 28,* 578–592.

Winsler, A., Diaz, R. M., Atencio, D. J., McCarthy, E. M., & Chabay, L. A. (2000). Verbal self-regulation over time in preschool children at risk for attention and behavior problems. *Journal of Child Psychology and Psychiatry and Allied Disciplines, 41*(7), 875–886. doi:10.1017/s0021963099006228

Yoon, S. (2008). *Eggs, eggs!* New York, NY: Penguin Books.

Zelazo, P. D. (2015). Executive function: Reflection, iterative reprocessing, complexity, and the developing brain. *Developmental Review, 38,* 55–68. doi:10.1016/j.dr.2015.07.001

Zevenbergen, A. A., Whitehurst, G. J., & Zevenbergen, J. A. (2003). Effects of a shared-reading intervention on the inclusion of evaluative devices in narratives of children from low-income families. *Journal of Applied Developmental Psychology, 24*(1), 1–15. doi:10.1016/s0193-3973(03)00021-2

Zimmerman, I. L., Steiner, V. G., & Pond, R. E. (2011). *Preschool Language Scales, Fifth Edition*. San Antonio, TX: Pearson Education/Psychological Corporation.

Ziv, M., Smadja, M. L., & Aram, D. (2013). Mothers' mental-state discourse with preschoolers during storybook reading and wordless storybook telling. *Early Childhood Research Quarterly, 28*(1), 177–186. doi:10.1016/j.ecresq.2012.05.005

Index

Page numbers followed by *f* and *t* indicate figures and tables, respectively.